The Good Food Guide Second Dinner Party Book

Recipes from restaurants in The Good Food Guide
cooked, written, arranged and introduced by Hilary Fawcett

Published by Consumers' Association and
Hodder & Stoughton

The Good Food Guide Second Dinner Party Book

Published by Consumers' Association, 14 Buckingham Street, London WC2N 6DS
and Hodder & Stoughton, 47 Bedford Square, London WC1B 3DP

© The Good Food Club Limited 1979

ISBN 0 340 24777 0

Design by Theo Hodges/John Meek

Illustrations by permission of Radio Times Hulton Picture Library,
Mary Evans Picture Library, Ikon, Fotomas

Printed and bound in England by
The Pitman Press, Lower Bristol Road, Bath BA2 3BL

Contents

Foreword

by Christopher Driver
Editor, *The Good Food Guide*

The *Good Food Guide*, as is well known, has both admirers and detractors. I am tolerably confident that Hilary Fawcett's book, like its predecessors, will attract admirers only, who will use it, over and over again, for much longer than the single year's currency which is the lot of restaurant guides. True, here and there may be detected that passionate pernicketiness about food and its treatment which set Raymond Postgate's enterprise going thirty years ago, and which still protects talented chefs and caterers from the sea of mediocrity surrounding them. But the context here is different. A recipe book describes the ideal. (This is why so many people buy them for perusal, not trial.) A restaurant guide, if it is any good, describes the experienced reality. A consumer's guide to the domestic parties for which Hilary Fawcett's menus will be faithfully followed *serait à lire*. But however good the cooking, the result on the printed page would give a libel lawyer a seizure, and make the *Good Food Guide* seem a model of courtesy and restraint. You can imagine the kind of thing: 'Marjorie was dressed to look like lamb and her lamb was meant to taste like roebuck (she said). I could not help feeling that her interest in her latest husband exceeded only narrowly her interest in mine: is yet another exchange contemplated?' However, geniality reigns at the stage of eager anticipation to which this book is addressed, and if ideals can be achieved anywhere, the place is surely your own kitchen in your own home. There you are both 'a cook and a captain bold', and have a good chance to beat the professionals who provided these recipes at their own game.

Introduction

by Hilary Fawcett

Like its elder sister, the Good Food Guide's first *Dinner Party Book*, this collection is designed not only to share with home cooks some of the best recipes from the best restaurants Britain possesses, but also to incorporate these recipes into balanced menus for dinner parties and other social occasions. These two aims still conflict sometimes, and many of the menus are richer than dieticians and health-worshippers might approve. However, parties and celebrations—like dinners in restaurants—justify the occasional day on celery and mineral water before or after.

It has been easier to achieve a balance of flavour, texture and colour within each menu: you will not find yourself serving an all-beige, all-liquidised, all-creamy meal. The alternative dishes we have suggested are also carefully balanced, which multiplies the number of possible permutations halfway to infinity. We have also kept in mind the cost and effort involved in entertaining. There are several inexpensive menus as well as others better suited to a resounding splash, and while some demand considerable time or effort, others need little or none, and others again lie between those extremes. The last of our balancing acts has been an attempt to suggest foodstuffs when they are in season and likely to be at their cheapest and best.

Why are you giving a party? Everyone asks the question, with appropriate language or gestures, when the parsley withers on the market stalls, the butcher fails to deliver, the mayonnaise curdles and the opened wine tastes like vinegar. In the menu introductions we have suggested various reasons or excuses, from rejuvenating your spouse to dazzling your employer. But writers of cookery books and other delicate plants like to think you give parties because you love cooking and enjoy seeing your friends. If the first becomes such drudgery that the second becomes an ordeal, you should not be giving that particular party. Better a casual casserole where good talk is heard than a banquet whose cook has shot her bolt by the time the gong goes.

Entertaining of all kinds is one of the performing arts, and as with the others, confidence is half the battle. Even in a meal, good food is only one element of the production, albeit the main one. This notion does *not* derive from those restaurateurs whose dining-room is a stage-set, with lighting, music and costumes to match. But a touch of stage company morale does no home or hostess any harm. This may strike contrary to the prevailing wisdom—even in some of the ensuing pages—about naturalness and relaxation, and with most guests there is no point in pretending that your cooking, your income, or your personality are different from what they are. All the same, few people are entirely themselves in the hours before a party. If you don't scrub the children, throw out the cat and the old newspapers, hide the ironing and lecture someone on what not to say, your private life is far removed from ours. You may even take comfort from the old cliché about the show going on—and from the distinguished restaurateur with every reason to be downhearted who once tried to sell a game bird at half price to a guest who had just seen it hit the carpet. After all, your own guests are being fed on a complimentary basis, and no complaints are admissible, at least until the curtain falls and the carriages are driving away . . .

Materials

We stand by our previously declared loyalty to home-made stock, fresh herbs, real mayonnaise, sea salt, freshly-ground black pepper, first-pressing olive oil, best unsalted butter (especially in sweet dishes), freshly-grated Parmesan, non-packaged breadcrumbs, and everything in season as far as possible. We have used branded products only where they were indicated by the restaurant and where the taste of the finished dish might be perceptibly altered by using something different.

Shopping has become no easier since we last wrote an introduction, except perhaps for those lucky enough to have foreign stores nearby. While testing recipes we covered many foot-miles in search of a modest duck, and almost gave up on monk-fish after literally months of effort. As before, we recommend that you encourage your butcher to practise his craft on your behalf—with due notice, of course, for complicated boning or preparation—and ask in your local shops for fresh herbs or slightly unusual vegetables, so that at least the proprietors cannot for ever claim that there is no demand for them. Growing your own has for many become the obvious alternative to high prices and erratic supplies, to say nothing of bland and watery flavours.

We recommend throughout the book taking thought for the morrow in various ways: making and freezing stock when you have the marrow bones and the time; freezing cheap or surplus soft fruit in season for sorbets and ice-creams later in the year; drying mint or sorrel when they are young and prolific; making pesto (which keeps for months) when basil is in bloom; buying Parmesan whenever you are near an Italian grocer's so that you can grate it when needed—or, at second best, buying the loose, grated kind they stock there rather than expensive and inferior packaged versions. And on holidays in France, for example, choose your souvenirs in supermarkets or the household section of department stores: an electric coffee-grinder for spices, a small electric whisk for ices and sorbets, and a nutmeg-grater, are all cheaper there than here, at least at time of writing; so are Meaux mustard, saffron, calvados, Crème de Cassis, walnut oil, saucissons secs, fresh goat's cheese, Muscat de Beaumes de Venise, cidre fermier and a 'tresse' of garlic.

Elsewhere in the book (page 139) we suggest that two or three cheeses in good condition are preferable to numerous small chunks and rinds showing their age or provenance. (This judgment also applies to restaurants.) If you have the strength to give two parties fairly close to each other, you might offer generous wedges of Stilton and Cheddar, for example, at the first, with Stilton soup (page 110) or a dish with a cheese sauce already planned for the second. Creamy cheeses seem to vanish as fast as they are produced, as long as they actually *are* creamy when you come to serve them.

Recipes

All recipes are in quantities for four unless otherwise stated. They have all been tested, translated into a uniform style, and then approved again by the chefs and restaurateurs who originally provided them. In testing, we used no shortcuts or catering substitutes.

Metric measures

At the time of writing, metrication is incomplete, but there are already young cooks who know no other measures, and the products we buy are increasingly sold in metric packs. We have given the recipes with quantities and measurements in both metric and imperial units. FOLLOW ONE COLUMN OR THE OTHER, BUT DO NOT TRY TO INTERCHANGE THEM. The recipes work whichever column you use, but the quantities are not exact equivalents and things may go wrong if you attempt to switch. Obviously this is hardly a problem at all if you are making a homely soup, but it matters where pastry or other refined baking techniques are involved. ALL SPOONSFUL ARE LEVEL.

Wine notes

We have made only very tentative wine suggestions. People's palates vary almost as much as their purses, and with soaring prices in traditional regions it is wiser to stick to what you like and can afford than to be seduced into expensive mistakes by dogmatic recommendations. It is more than ever worth cultivating a wine merchant who not only keeps a decent range of house wines but will give helpful advice on better ones when you need it. And once again remember to use your duty-free allowance in French or Italian supermarkets. In Normandy or Brittany good young Muscadet, for example, can cost a third of the U.K. price.

Acknowledgements

We should like to thank all the people, many of them necessarily anonymous, who have co-operated in the production of this book. We are particularly grateful for the generous co-operation of busy restaurateurs and the infinite pains taken by the *Guide*'s own staff.

Bon appétit—et faites simple!

Menus

Arranged seasonally

Easy mushroom soup
or
Turnip soup

Chicken breast Yolande, hassleback potatis *or*
duchesse potatoes, carrots in orange and coriander *or*
hot beetroot

Banoffi pie
or
Chocolate gateau

What with children insisting on fish fingers and nothing but fish fingers, and adults genteelly raking over embers better doused, a family party can sometimes seem more of an ordeal than a treat. However, if your family gatherings are not like that—or perhaps even if they are—a colourful and tasty meal, based on relatively simple ingredients, is an excitement at best, a distraction at worst. This menu is fairly easy to put together, and involves little or no last-minute preparation, so that you can be on hand most of the time to referee or appreciate the in-fighting.

First course

Real mushroom soup is a treat for most of us, and this one has the advantage of using very little cream, so that it is light enough to be one of three courses, even for small or elderly stomachs. You will have to take the turnip soup on trust from Tullich Lodge, because the idea may be daunting. It is a lovely pale apricot colour, tastes gently of spring turnips rather than winter swedes, and when tested, pleased even dedicated swede-haters. Rename it golden soup if that will help. Otherwise, consider Caroline's pizza (page 186) instead, but serve very small portions.

Main course

The chicken breasts Yolande have many advantages: they look pretty and interesting and are easily served, there are no bones, and the chicken is familiar—though unusually tender—inside its fancy overcoat. The Swedish roast potatoes (page 193) have a high ratio of crisp outside to soft inside, so choose them if that will please the children. Otherwise, make duchesse potatoes well ahead of time (with or without help from the children), or serve little new ones in their skins. Carrots provide a fine colour and textural contrast here and taste in this version (page 195) as though someone has cared for them. The hot beetroot (page 193) is a novelty, or, if asparagus is in season and you can find some sprue (thin green stalks, half the price of fat white ones), serve it as a continuation of Yolande's theme.

2

With an assortment of ages, tastes and sophistication, a white wine which is not too dry would be the best choice: Riesling from Germany, Alsace or Yugoslavia; Gewürztraminer or Muscat if you are flying high. The children could perhaps be allowed a spritzer—a Byronic mixture of half white wine, half soda water, served with ice cubes—useful in the face of thirst or greed.

Sweet course

So far there has been an admirable air of restraint—no heavy spicing, little cream, garlic, butter or other fat—in preparation for a rich and creamy sweet to satisfy the children of all ages, as they say in the ads. Banoffi pie may sound wholly extraordinary but tastes much more intriguing than the sum of its parts might lead you to expect. Be very careful that the tin of milk is covered completely by water while it boils. Otherwise there are no difficulties and the result is a creamy, butterscotch-flavoured pie with banana and coffee-flavoured whipped cream on a thick layer of soft toffee. The chocolate cake would be more appropriate if the party is a specific celebration, but for those who like chocolate cake, no excuse is necessary. Other possible finales are grapefruit cheesecake (page 182) or chestnut and orange roulade (page 146).

Wine suggestion

It seems pointless to suggest special aperitifs or digestifs for a family party, since this is generally one occasion when 'The usual?' is the question, and the gin-and-tonic or port-and-lemon are produced routinely.

Main course

Medium-dry white wine

Easy mushroom soup

Gibson's, Cardiff,			

250 g	mushrooms	8 oz
one	clove of garlic	one
two	sprigs of parsley	two
50 g	butter	2 oz
1 litre	chicken *or* veal stock (page 207)	2 pints
	nutmeg	
	salt, pepper	
two	thick slices of bread	two
50 ml	double cream	2 fl oz
	chopped parsley	

Gibson's, Cardiff, S. Glamorgan Chef: Irene Canning

Wipe the mushrooms (large black ones are best). Chop the garlic finely. Pull the leaves off the parsley and discard the stalks. In a large saucepan, melt the butter over low heat, and tear the mushrooms into pieces into it. Increase the heat and stir until the juice flows freely from the mushrooms. Add the stock, garlic, parsley, a little grated nutmeg, salt, pepper, and the broken-up bread. Boil for ten minutes.

Liquidise the mixture, without making it completely smooth (there should be visible mushroom flecks). Check the seasoning. If serving the soup immediately, reheat in a clean pan, and add the cream. If preparing it ahead, cool it quickly and refrigerate till needed. Do not boil once the cream has been added. Sprinkle each bowl with chopped parsley before serving.

Turnip soup

Tullich Lodge, Ballater, Aberdeenshire Chef/proprietor: Neil Bannister

750 g–1 kg	swedes	1½–2 lb
	water	
one	small onion	one
	salt, pepper	
200 ml	milk	8 fl oz
four 5 ml spoons	whipped cream	4 teasp
	chopped chives	

Blanch the peeled and diced or sliced swedes for two minutes and drain them. Three-quarters cover them with fresh water, add the sliced onion and cook the vegetables until they are soft. Liquidise the soup, season it and thin it down to the right consistency with the milk. Serve it hot with a teaspoonful of whipped cream in each bowl, sprinkled with chopped chives.

Chicken breast Yolande

French Partridge,
Horton,
Northamptonshire
Chef/proprietor:
David Partridge

four	boned chicken breasts	four
	seasoned flour	
two	small eggs	two
250 g	finely-grated Cheddar (approx)	8 oz
25 g	butter	1 oz
two 15 ml spoons	oil	2 tablesp
one	small tin of asparagus spears	one
	butter	

Lightly flatten the chicken breasts and coat them firmly with seasoned flour.
Combine the beaten eggs and enough cheese to give a stiff paste, and spread it
all over the chicken. Fry the breasts gently in the butter and oil until they are
golden brown. Put a few spears of drained asparagus on each chicken breast,
and sprinkle on a little more grated cheese. Add a further knob of butter to
the pan, cover it securely, and cook over low heat until the cheese has melted
and the chicken is tender (about ten minutes). Be careful not to over-cook
and toughen the chicken.

Editor's note: failing canned asparagus, use fresh. . .

Banoffi pie

Hungry Monk,
Jevington, East Sussex
Chefs: Ian Dowding &
Kent Austin

one	large tin of condensed milk	one
175 g	shortcrust pastry (page 202)	6 oz
one	large banana	one
250 ml	double cream	10 fl oz
one 5 ml spoon	instant coffee powder	1 teasp
25 g	caster sugar	1 oz

Immerse the unopened can of condensed milk in boiling water, cover, and
boil gently for three hours. Remove the can from the water and allow it to
cool completely before opening. You will find the milk transformed to soft
toffee.

Line a greased 20.5-cm (8-inch) flan ring with the shortcrust pastry and bake
blind until it is crisp. Allow it to cool. Empty the toffee filling into the flan
case and spread it evenly. Put the sliced banana on top of the toffee. Whip the
cream, coffee and sugar until the mixture is thick and smooth. Spoon or pipe
it over the banana and toffee and chill the flan until it is ready to serve.

Chocolate gateau

Loaves and Fishes,	100 g	cooking fat (e.g. Trex)	4 oz
Wootton Bassett,	300 g	caster sugar	10 oz
Wiltshire	two	eggs	two
Chef/proprietor:	175 g	plain flour	6 oz
Angela Rawson	$\frac{1}{4}$ of a 5 ml spoon	baking powder	$\frac{1}{4}$ teasp
	one 5 ml spoon	bicarbonate of soda	1 teasp
	one	pinch of salt	one
	50 g	cocoa	2 oz
	190 ml	cold water	$7\frac{1}{2}$ fl oz
For the filling	375 ml	double cream	15 fl oz
		icing sugar to taste	
For decoration	250 g	chocolate caraque	8 oz
	250 g	icing sugar	8 oz
	two 15 ml spoons	cocoa	2 tablesp
		hot water	
		chocolate leaves	

Preheat the oven to 180°C (350°F, mark 4).

Beat the cooking fat and sugar together until the mixture is light and fluffy and then whisk in the beaten eggs, a little at a time. Sift the flour with the baking powder, bicarbonate of soda and salt, and stir it into the fat-and-sugar mixture alternately with the mixed cocoa and water. Beat until all the ingredients are thoroughly incorporated and pour the mixture into a greased 25-cm (10-inch) loose-sided cake tin lined with grease-proof paper. Grease it lightly. Bake it for one hour until the cake begins to come away from the sides of the tin. Allow it to cool on a wire rack; split it in half with a sharp knife.

To make the filling, whip the cream until it just holds its shape, gradually adding icing sugar to taste. Spread some of it on one of the cake rounds and sandwich the two together. Reserving half the remaining cream, spread the rest round the sides of the gateau and roll it in the chocolate caraque.

For the icing, mix the icing sugar with the cocoa and enough hot water to make a firm paste and beat it until it is smooth. Cover the top of the gateau with this icing, spreading it smoothly and evenly. Using a large star nozzle, pipe the remaining cream in whirls round the circumference and decorate the centre with chocolate leaves or fresh rosebuds, if you wish.

Editor's note: if caraque is beyond you—it defeats us—settle for shavings (use a potato peeler) or dust (a grater).

Hot avocado with garlic shrimps
or
Mushrooms in garlic butter

Beef in beer with turnips, sprouts and jacket potatoes

Ginger syllabub
or
Whisky and walnut parfait

If all the adults in a household have full-time jobs, time is likely to be shorter than money. Entertaining can put further strain on an already busy life unless you decide, at least occasionally, that it is worth the seeming extravagance of expensive ingredients to compose an appealing menu that costs less in effort. This meal divides into dishes which can be prepared ahead, either entirely or in part, and others which require very little preparation at the last minute. With such a programme you should be able to sit down at table within two hours of reaching home—and that's allowing time for a bath.

First course

If you choose the avocado and shrimps, they should be prepared the night before (or the morning before, if you are a skylark rather than an owl) and finished just before the meal. The mushrooms in garlic butter take only a few minutes to prepare, immediately before serving. If you prefer something less assertive in flavour, try mushroom soup on page 4, or any of the other easy liquidised soups that appear throughout the book. Garlic and fine wine do not get on together, so keep your aperitif glasses if people are drinking dry sherry; otherwise, serve a fairly forceful white wine: perhaps an Italian Soave or Verdicchio, or a white Rioja. Some people like madeira with soup; we don't, unless it is a classy consommé or bisque.

Main course

The beef in beer, a relative of carbonnade, has all the fiddly processes (and there are few) completed the night before, with only the oven-cooking for the evening of the dinner party. If you have a slow cooker or an oven-timer, you can set things going in the morning, but if the meat is of good quality and the dish ready to cook you could even start it on reaching home. Vegetables which need little preparation are the ones to choose here. The jacket potatoes will absorb the good gravy effectively. If sprouts seem too mundane, even when lightly cooked and well buttered, with a pinch of nutmeg, fly higher with mange-tout peas, cooked for just a minute or two in butter with a little sugar. Other possibilities include hot cucumber and carrots with orange and coriander, both on page 195.

7

This simple, hearty main course demands a wine with some body; you could do worse than stick to Italy for the evening, with a Chianti Classico or Spanna from Piedmont; otherwise, a Rhône or burgundy would provide the necessary weight. There is no need to spend the earth, as this is a simple rather than a gourmet dish, and the garlic from the first course may linger. Since the beef is cooked in beer—and if you know your guests enjoy drinking it—you could have a beer-tasting of as many interesting bottles as you can find. Various off-licences now stock a wide range of regional English beers (Samuel Smith's, Theakston's, and so on) as well as imported lagers such as Belgian Chimay and Australian Foster's.

If you prefer a flurry of last-minute activity to planning ahead, consider the escalope au citron (page 73), or the five-minute meal on page 55.

Sweet course

Something which can be taken straight from refrigerator or freezer to table makes the ideal ending to any meal, especially if you are feeling not just relaxed but limp. The ginger syllabub is richly creamy and alcoholic, the whisky and walnut parfait marginally less so. Other fruity alternatives are blackberry syllabub (page 113) and caramel peaches (page 119).

Wine suggestions

Aperitif

Dry sherry or madeira

First course

Dry sherry, madeira, Italian or Spanish white wine

Main course

Italian red, burgundy or Rhône wine or selection of beers and lagers

Hot avocado with garlic shrimps

White Moss House,
Grasmere, Cumbria
Chef/proprietor:
Jean Butterworth

one	clove of garlic	one
125 g	butter	4 oz
125–150 g	small, brown shrimps, shelled	4–6 oz
	pepper	
two	avocados	two
four	slices of wholemeal bread	four
125 g	grated cheese	4 oz

Skin and crush the garlic and cook it gently for five minutes in the butter. (Watch it carefully or it will burn.) Add the shrimps (or cut-up prawns) and a little pepper, and turn up the heat for a minute. Leave the shrimps overnight in a bowl, to set and to absorb the flavours.

Halve the avocados, and remove the stones. Cut circles of bread to fit individual fire-proof dishes, and set an avocado half, cut side up, on each one. Pack a quarter of the shrimps and butter in each avocado hollow, and top with the grated cheese, taking care to cover the avocado flesh as well as the shrimps.

Put under a hot grill until melted and brown, then leave in a warm oven (160°C, 325°F, mark 3) for 5–10 minutes.

Editor's note: this dish is also successful made with potted shrimps. You must, of course, adjust the quantities of butter and pepper to allow for the flavoured butter used in the potting.

Mushrooms in garlic butter

Old Parsonage,
Farrington Gurney,
Avon
Chef: Ann Oakes

500 g	button mushrooms	1 lb
125 g	butter	4 oz
half	lemon	half
	salt, pepper	
four	cloves of garlic	four
three 15 ml spoons	white breadcrumbs	3 tablesp
	parsley	

Wipe the mushrooms with a damp cloth and trim their stems. Beat the butter in a bowl until it is soft, and add to it the lemon juice, salt, pepper and crushed garlic. Mix them thoroughly. Melt the mixture slowly in a saucepan, add the mushrooms, cover, and cook over high heat for about three minutes, shaking the pan frequently.

When the mushrooms have absorbed the butter, sprinkle them with the breadcrumbs and a little chopped parsley. Shake the pan vigorously to blend them with the mushrooms. Serve very hot with crusty bread to mop up the juices.

Beef in beer

White Moss House,
Grasmere, Cumbria
Chef/proprietor:
Jean Butterworth

750 g	braising steak	1½ lb
four 15 ml spoons	seasoned flour	4 tablesp
one	rasher of bacon	one
one 15 ml spoon	oil	1 tablesp
one	onion	one
one	clove of garlic	one
50 g	mushrooms	2 oz
one	bay leaf	one
440 ml	can of lager	15.5 fl oz
one 10 ml spoon	wine vinegar	1 dessertsp
	chopped parsley or fresh herbs	

Trim the meat of all fat and cut it into generous chunks. Toss them in half the seasoned flour and put them in an oven-proof casserole.

Dice the bacon and fry it in the oil until crisp. Fry the chopped onion and crushed garlic in the oil until golden. Add the sliced mushrooms and lightly fry them. Add the bacon, vegetables and bay leaf to the meat, and sprinkle with the remaining seasoned flour. Pour on the lager, cover the casserole and let it stand overnight.

Next day, stir the casserole and cook it, covered, in a moderate oven (180°C, 350°F, mark 4) for two hours. Just before serving, remove the bay leaf, check the seasoning, and stir in the wine vinegar. Garnish with chopped parsley or fresh mixed herbs.

Chef's note: You could brown the meat by frying it just before putting in the casserole, but leaving out this process saves time and calories and doesn't affect the taste of the finished dish.

Editor's note: Any meat would be suitable, from topside to anonymous 'braising beef'. This dish could cook all day in a slow electric casserole.

Ginger syllabub

**White Moss House,
Grasmere, Cumbria
Chef/proprietor:
Jean Butterworth**

375 ml	double cream	15 fl oz
100 ml	advocaat *or* brandy	4 fl oz
75–100 g	ginger marmalade	3–4 oz
	melon *or* pear *or* ginger biscuits and stem ginger	

Whip the cream and advocaat or brandy together until the mixture just holds its shape. Fold in the ginger marmalade and chill thoroughly to allow the flavours to develop (overnight, if you wish).

Serve the syllabub either on balled or diced fresh melon, or on diced fresh pear or poached pear, or spooned over crushed ginger biscuits moistened with brandy and topped with a few slices of stem ginger.

Editor's note: the syllabub tastes delicious even if you have too little time to chill it for more than an hour, say.

Whisky and walnut parfait

**Hotel Petit Champ,
Sark, Channel Islands
Chef: Brian Rolls**

four	egg yolks	four
75 g	caster sugar	3 oz
125 ml	single cream	5 fl oz
25 ml	whisky	1 fl oz
50 g	walnut pieces	2 oz
	whisky-flavoured whipped cream	
	walnut halves	

Whisk the egg yolks in a double-boiler (or bowl set in a pan of boiling water) until they have doubled in bulk. Remove from the heat and continue whisking, slowly adding the sugar, until the mixture has thickened. Fold in the lightly-whipped cream, the whisky and the chopped nuts. Pour the mixture into ramekins or other individual dishes (make sure the walnuts are evenly distributed) and freeze for at least six hours.

Serve the parfait with a rosette of whisky-flavoured cream and a walnut half on top of each dish.

Chef's note: experiment with other spirits or liqueurs—Tia Maria, perhaps. But allow for sweetness and reduce the sugar.

Eliza Acton's salmon pudding with egg sauce
or
Chilled saffron soup with fresh herbs

Gigot d'agneau à la moutarde, new potatoes, broccoli and carrots

Paskha

It is impossible to live in the British Isles, even as an unbeliever, without becoming caught up, at least in part, in the festival of Easter, and the food associated with it is almost as ritually fixed as the roast turkey and plum pudding of Christmas. Our feast is splendidly eclectic, with an old English fish pudding leading to a very French treatment of lamb, and that in turn to a traditional Russian Easter confection. It captures not only the colours of spring and the post-Lenten richness of celebration, but also the flavours of the season's early salmon and lamb. Serve the feast, perhaps, to a fairly grown-up family or sophisticated friends, since the saffron flavour of the soup and the sauce with the lamb may not appeal to young children. Preparations for both lamb and paskha begin the day before the party, and the soup is also made ahead of time, thus leaving you free for church attendance or daffodil-gazing on Easter Sunday itself.

First course

Kathie Scheiding and Eliza Acton both know how to stretch delicate, delicious and expensive salmon to feed many mouths, and the pudding is a triumph of restraint in terms of seasoning—the anchovy essence enhances the salmon flavour without itself obtruding. If you like the idea of a fish pudding but not the price of salmon, try the smoked fish version. On the other hand, if Easter is late and the weather settled, you may prefer the chilled saffron soup, which looks pretty with its pale yellow creaminess set off by the lemon slice and herbs, and also tastes intriguingly complex. It is hard, for once, to suggest alternatives, since these seem so highly appropriate to Easter, but if neither appeals, try eggs with tapénade (page 95) or whiting in cucumber shells (page 51).

Main course

If you wish to have a large party, buy two small legs of lamb, since the seasoning involved in the recipe for gigot à la moutarde is very exactly geared to the weight, and the recipe is less good with a larger leg. The finished dish will have a crisp brown crust, a pink interior, and a deliciously tasty sauce. If you have served the salmon pudding first and anyone guesses that there is anchovy essence in both dishes, we shall be totally surprised. Obviously the

12

flavour of this sauce is more vigorous than the gentle pudding, and no apparent similarity exists. Plain new potatoes and crisp spring vegetables are the best accompaniment to the roast.

Sweet course   Russian Orthodox emigrants have taken paskha all over the world, and it is the most distinguished member of the cheesecake family. Despite the awe-inspiring ingredients it manages to taste rich but not cloying, and even without the traditional truncated-pyramid mould, it looks endearingly like a child's sand-castle, decorated in colourful and homely style with glacé fruit. In Russia, it would be served with a slice of kulich, a light yeast cake, to counteract the richness. Madeira cake, or crisp biscuits (page 204), would be equally suitable. Since it keeps in the refrigerator for a week, you may be tempted to make double quantities so that you have a truly imposing pyramid to decorate. Once again, it seems unnecessary to offer alternatives, because this is the Easter sweet *par excellence*, but one of the other cheesecakes in the book would at least be in the same genre.

Wine suggestions

If the cost of this meal has not already appalled you, you may well wish to serve with the salmon a good white burgundy (Meursault, Puligny-Montrachet, Auxey-Duresses), a *premier-cru* Chablis, or a fine Rheingau (Johannisberger or Winkeler). With less money to spend, consider an Alsace Riesling or Gewürztraminer or a Sancerre. Since the lamb is so highly seasoned, even the rich should not aim too high with the main course and a Spanish Rioja (Marqués de Riscal, say) or a Beaujolais (Juliénas or Fleurie) might be more appropriate than a fine claret or burgundy. Paskha calls for a glass of something sweet: Sauternes or Barsac if you can afford it, Monbazillac or Muscat de Frontignan (or any other sweet Muscat) if not.

First course   Fine white wine

Main course   Spanish Rioja or Beaujolais

Sweet course   Sauternes, Barsac, Monbazillac or Muscat

Eliza Acton's salmon pudding with egg sauce (6)

Hathaways,
London, S.W.11
Chef/proprietor:
Kathie Scheiding

500 g	cooked, boned and skinned salmon	1 lb
one	small onion	one
half 15 ml spoon	anchovy essence	$\frac{1}{2}$ tablesp
	salt, pepper	
one	dash of Tabasco	one
75 g	fresh white breadcrumbs	3 oz
two	eggs	two
125 ml	single cream	5 fl oz

For the sauce

750 ml	béchamel (page 209)	$1\frac{1}{2}$ pints
3–4	hard-boiled eggs	3–4
four 15 ml spoons	chopped parsley	4 tablesp

Butter a 750-ml ($1\frac{1}{2}$-pint) round oven-proof bowl or soufflé dish. Mince the cooled salmon with the onion, add the anchovy essence, salt, pepper, Tabasco and breadcrumbs, and mix thoroughly. Beat the eggs and cream lightly together and add them to the salmon. Put the pudding in the buttered container, cover the top securely with foil, and stand it in a bain-marie (page 213). Bake it in a moderately hot oven (200°C, 400°F, mark 6) for about 50 minutes. When ready, it should be firm but not dry in the centre, and shrinking away from the edge of the dish.

For the egg sauce, make a béchamel while the pudding is cooking and add to it the chopped hard-boiled eggs and parsley.

Turn out the pudding, and serve it in wedges with the sauce.

Chef's note: the pudding is also successful made with trout, or smoked fish (if the latter, use a little extra liquid to prevent the pudding being too dry).

Editor's note: if you have a liquidiser, use it to speed up three steps, in this order, with a quick rinse under the hot tap after the first two: make the breadcrumbs; chop the parsley by covering the sprigs with cold water and turning the motor on and off quickly several times, draining it in a sieve and drying on paper towel; blend the salmon and onion with the cream instead of mincing them.

Chilled saffron soup with fresh herbs (6)

Hintlesham Hall,
Hintlesham, Suffolk
Chef: Nigel Rolfe

250 g	onions	8 oz
one 15 ml spoon	butter	1 tablesp
250 g	potatoes	8 oz
500 ml	milk	1 pint
one	chicken stock cube	one
$\frac{1}{4}$ of a 5 ml spoon	crumbled saffron strands	$\frac{1}{4}$ teasp
125 ml	dry white wine	5 fl oz
500 ml	single cream	1 pint
	salt, pepper	

For garnishing

six	thin lemon slices	six
two 15 ml spoons	sour cream	2 tablesp
	finely chopped parsley, chives *and/or* tarragon	

In a large, heavy pan, sauté the coarsely-chopped onions in the butter until they are soft and transparent but not brown. Add the peeled and coarsely-chopped potatoes and stir for a few seconds until they are glossy. Add the milk, crumble in the stock cube and bring the mixture to the boil.

In a separate pan, bring the saffron strands and wine to the boil. Allow the mixture to boil for 30 seconds and then stir it into the soup. Simmer it, half covered, for about 30 minutes, until the vegetables are disintegrating. Push it through a sieve and return it to the rinsed-out pan. Dilute it with the cream and season with salt and pepper.

Serve the soup chilled, garnished with a lemon slice topped with sour cream and sprinkled with finely-chopped herbs.

Editor's note: if you dislike using stock cubes, consider instead substituting 125 ml (5 fl oz) concentrated chicken stock for the same quantity of milk.

Gigot d'agneau à la moutarde (5–6)

Clifton Hotel, Nairn,
Nairnshire
Chef/proprietor:
J. Gordon Macintyre

1.75 kg	leg of spring lamb	3¾ lb
	olive oil	
	flour	
two	cloves of garlic	two
two 5 ml spoons	black peppercorns	2 teasp
one 5 ml spoon	salt	1 teasp
	chopped fresh herbs (thyme, marjoram, parsley)	
two 15 ml spoons	anchovy essence	2 tablesp
three 15 ml spoons	olive oil	3 tablesp
four 15 ml spoons	Worcestershire sauce	4 tablesp
	dry mustard	
200 ml	red wine	8 fl oz
200 ml	beef stock (page 207)	8 fl oz

Rub the gigot all over with a little olive oil. Dust it with flour and set it in a roasting-pan. In a mortar or bowl, crush the garlic, peppercorns, salt and herbs. Add the anchovy essence, oil and Worcestershire sauce. Stir in enough dry mustard to make a thin paste, and spread it all over the lamb. Pour in the wine and stock, round the lamb rather than over it, cover it loosely with foil, and leave it to marinate in the refrigerator all day (i.e. at least eight hours) to absorb the flavours.

Roast the lamb, uncovered, for 1½–1¾ hours in a moderate oven (180°C, 350°F, mark 4), basting it occasionally. Uncover it for the last half-hour to brown the crust.

Carve the lamb at table and serve the strained sauce separately.

Paskha (8–10)

Royal Exchange
Theatre Restaurant,
Manchester
Chef: Roy Pegram

350 g	full-fat cream cheese	12 oz
175 g	unsalted butter	6 oz
40 g	sultanas	1½ oz
two 15 ml spoons	vodka	2 tablesp
15 g	crushed, blanched almonds	½ oz
half 5 ml spoon	vanilla essence	½ teasp
75 g	caster sugar	3 oz

For the custard

one	egg yolk	one
two 5 ml spoons	caster sugar	2 teasp
75 ml	double cream	3 fl oz

For decoration

	glacé fruit	

Choose an earthenware plant pot or a plastic container (perforated with a hot skewer for drainage). Line it with butter muslin, allowing enough material to fold over the top.

In a large mixing bowl combine the cream cheese, the softened butter, the sultanas soaked in the vodka, the almonds, the vanilla essence and the 75 g (3 oz) caster sugar. Blend the mixture very thoroughly.

To make the custard, beat the egg yolk and sugar together until thick and pale. Bring 50 ml (2 fl oz) of the cream to the boil over moderate heat, pour it onto the egg, whisking constantly, return it to the heat and bring almost to boiling point, stirring all the time. When the sauce begins to thicken and small bubbles appear round the edge, remove the saucepan from the heat. Allow the custard to cool, but not set, before blending it into the cream cheese. Add the remaining cream.

Spoon the mixture into the container, cover the top, and set a heavy weight on top. Stand the container in a curved-bottomed dish (to allow drainage) and refrigerate the sweet for at least 24 hours to allow all the whey to drain off.

Unwrap the paskha and turn it into a serving dish. Decorate it with pieces of glacé fruit (citron peel, cherries and angelica allow you to make a colourful pattern).

Chef's note: the paskha will keep for a week under refrigeration.

Editor's note: 'A sumptuously rich dessert, traditionally presented in Russia at Eastertime, almost always in the form of a pyramid.'

Soufflés jurassienne
or
Endives flamande

Limande Monte Carlo, new potatoes, green salad

Hungarian apple pie
or
Apple Grasmere

Spring is a byword for variable weather, and often one's own moods are equally unpredictable—bursting with manic anticipation one moment and lingering in depressive hibernation the next. This meal is a wonderfully convenient one for the temperamental since the main course is accomplished in a quick, painless spurt, and the first and last courses each offer the alternatives of something simple and workmanlike or something rather more flamboyant. You only have to decide your current mood when you do your shopping for the party—and of course, decide which of your friends will best appreciate this original meal.

First course

Choose the endives flamande if you prefer to have things organised ahead of time and well under control. (There is infinite confusion over the name, since not only do the English and the French exchange the names of chicory and endive, but *flamande* generally implies braised in butter.) The dish is a classic combination of slightly bitter chicory and gently creamy sauce, with the ham not only enhancing this course but acting as a sop to the dedicated meat-eaters who may look dubiously at the main-course fish. The soufflés also combine ham, cheese and a vegetable, this time leeks, in what is more nearly a hot mousse, since it lacks a béchamel base and is therefore very light. Other possible first courses might be cheese and vegetable chowder (page 145) or chicche del nonno verdi (page 198).

Main course

The lemon sole recipe is the sort all cookery writers—and probably many troubled hostesses—dream of inventing for themselves. It is simple and very tasty, and, as fish goes these days, not too expensive. Add to that the absence of a creamy sauce, and it becomes as irresistible as a little black dress, to be produced whenever you want to seem unobtrusively smart. The restaurant's suggested accompaniments are a wise choice, but hot cucumber (page 195) or mushroom salad (page 199) are also worth considering.

Sweet course

Choose between the two apple sweets: the rather showy Hungarian pie with

18

its rich pastry, ground almonds, apple and egg filling; or the more homely apple Grasmere with a gingerbread-like topping made like a crumble. If you would prefer something lighter, consider one of our ice-creams or sorbets.

Wine suggestions

You may decide to drink white wine throughout the meal. Either arrange a sequence of your favourites among lesser white wines (lesser, because of the anchovies, garlic and salad with the main course) such as French Bergerac or Montravel; German table wine; Yugoslav or Hungarian Riesling or Traminer. Otherwise serve the same wine throughout: you should choose one with some character, the Traminer or Italian Soave for example.

Either   Several minor wines from France, Germany, Hungary or Yugoslavia

or   One characterful white wine

Soufflés jurassienne (8)

Stane Street Hollow, Pulborough, West Sussex
Chef: René Kaiser

75 g	streaky bacon	3 oz
100 g	leeks, trimmed weight	4 oz
two	eggs	two
25 g	butter	1 oz
65 ml	milk	2½ fl oz
150 g	Cheddar	6 oz
	salt, pepper	

Chop the bacon and leeks finely, blanch the pieces in boiling water, and drain thoroughly. Separate the eggs. Melt the butter in a saucepan, add the milk, egg yolks, grated cheese, salt and pepper, and stir the mixture over low heat until it thickens to a creamy consistency. Do not allow it to boil. Add the bacon and leeks and leave the mixture to cool.

Whisk the egg whites until they are very stiff. Gently fold them into the sauce and fill eight greased ramekins about two-thirds full with the mixture. Bake the soufflés in a hot oven (200°C, 400°F, mark 6) for 15–20 minutes, until they are well-risen and brown. Serve immediately.

Editor's note: the sauce can be prepared in advance, kept warm in a bain-marie, and the freshly-beaten egg whites added just before baking.

Endives flamande

La Sorbonne, Oxford,
Oxfordshire
Chef/proprietor:
A. P. Chavagnon

four	medium-sized heads of chicory	four
500 ml	béchamel sauce (page 209)	1 pint
175 g	Gruyère	6 oz
four	slices of lean ham	four

Cook the chicory in boiling water for 10–15 minutes. Make the béchamel sauce and add half the grated Gruyère to it. (Do not allow it to boil.)

Strain the chicory very well and pat the heads dry with kitchen paper. Wrap each one in a slice of ham and place them in an oven-proof dish. Pour the sauce over them and sprinkle the remaining grated cheese on top. Put them in a hot oven or grill under high heat for a few minutes until the cheese is golden and bubbling.

Limande Monte Carlo

La Frégate, St Peter
Port, Guernsey
Chef: Konrad Holleis

four	lemon sole	four
three	cloves of garlic	three
six	anchovy fillets	six
125 g	butter	4 oz
	salt	
two	small lemons	two
four 15 ml spoons	flour	4 tablesp
	chopped parsley	
	watercress	

Choose fish weighing about 500 g (1 lb) each and ask the fishmonger to skin and fillet them, or do it yourself. Gently fry the pressed or finely-chopped garlic and the chopped anchovy fillets in the melted butter for about two minutes until the flavours are well blended. Season the sole fillets with salt and the juice of one lemon and dip them first in the flour, then in the flavoured butter. Arrange them on a grilling tray, skinned side down and grill them under high heat for 3–5 minutes until they are cooked and browned. Serve the fish on very hot plates with parsley, watercress and lemon wedges.

Chef's note: we serve the fish with buttered new potatoes and a mixed green salad: lettuce, watercress, cucumber, dill and fennel, dressed with lemon juice, white wine, vinegar and olive oil.

Hungarian apple pie (6)

Overscaig Hotel,
Overscaig, Highland
Chef/proprietor:
Sheila Hamilton-Hesse

500 g	cooking apples	1 lb
	sugar to taste	
100 g	butter	4 oz
150 g	flour	6 oz
one	egg	one
one-two 15 ml spoons	sour cream	1–2 tablesp
50 g	ground almonds	2 oz
50 g	sugar	2 oz
	strawberry or raspberry jam	
	cinnamon or cloves (optional)	

For the glaze

	egg white	
	sugar	

For decoration

	whipped cream	
	glacé cherries	

Stew the peeled, cored and sliced apples with sugar to taste in the minimum of water until they are tender.

Rub the butter into the sieved flour, and mix to a dough with the egg yolk and sour cream. Knead the dough well and chill it for at least 30 minutes. Line an 18-cm (7-inch) loose-bottomed cake-tin with half the pastry and bake it blind in a hot oven (220°C, 425°F, mark 7) for ten minutes.

To make the filling, mix together the ground almonds and sugar, spread the partly-cooked pastry with jam, and cover it with half the almond-and-sugar mixture. Fold the stiffly-beaten egg white into the stewed apple, adding the ground cinnamon or cloves if you wish, and spread it in an even layer. Cover this with the remaining almond mixture and finally with the rest of the pastry. Glaze the pastry with the egg white and sprinkle it with sugar. Bake the pie in a hot oven (220°C, 425°F, mark 7) for about 30 minutes. Let it cool somewhat before removing it from the tin. Decorate it with whipped cream and glacé cherries and serve warm or cold.

Apple Grasmere (6–8)

**White Moss House,
Grasmere, Cumbria
Chef/proprietor:
Jean Butterworth**

1 kg	cooking apples	2 lb
125 g	sugar	4 oz
165 g	butter	5½ oz
250 g	flour	8 oz
two 5 ml spoons	ground ginger	2 teasp
one	pinch of bicarbonate of soda	one
60 g	light brown sugar	2 oz
60 g	caster sugar	2 oz
two	pieces of crystallised ginger	two
	caster sugar	
	double cream	

Peel, core and slice the apples and cook them with the 125 g (4 oz) of sugar, 15 g (½ oz) of butter and a little water until they form a puree. Put the puree in an oven-proof dish and allow it to cool.

Rub the remaining butter into the sieved flour, ground ginger, and bicarbonate of soda and stir in the brown and caster sugars and finely-chopped ginger. Cover the apples with this mixture and pat it down gently.

Bake the dish in a moderate oven (180°C, 350°F, mark 4) for 30 minutes until the topping is a pale biscuit colour. Sprinkle with caster sugar and serve hot or cold with double cream.

Cobi bhaji with chapatis

Chicken and almond curry, stir-fried vegetables,
runner beans *or* ladies' fingers, pilaff, raita, salads,
poppadums, lemon pickle

Ginger pear sorbet

Britain's relationship with curry—let alone India itself—is too complex for
investigation in a light-hearted cookery book. Sufficient to say that the bad
old days of the yellow-ochre shroud for yesterday's remains have largely
passed away, and that even simple Indian take-aways in this country are
usually more genuine than their Chinese (or American) rivals, so that most of
us have some idea at least of what a 'real' curry tastes like. However, until
you have mixed your own spices you cannot anticipate the pleasures ahead.

If you wish to explore further, read 'Curry and other spiced dishes' in one of
this book's predecessors, *The Good Cook's Guide* (Consumers' Association
and Hodder & Stoughton), or, for a more thorough grounding, *Indian
Cookery* by Dharamjit Singh (Penguin).

This meal is not authentic, in that it adheres to no one regional style, and
none of the recipes come from Indian restaurants, whose resources and
practice may differ too widely from your own. But the present menu is fun
and appetising and can at least start you off on your own experiments: for
example, even without a clay oven it is possible to make an approximation to
tandoori chicken, because at least the yoghourt and spices for effective
marination are freely available all over the country. (Explore Indian grocery
stores—they generally have English-speaking owners and they always have
the widest possible range of herbs and spices at the lowest prices.)

First course   The anglicised bhaji uses native vegetables and the short-cut of curry paste,
but nevertheless it makes an interesting start to the meal, served with
chapatis. It would be wise to have a practice session on these, since the hearty
thumping involved in the instructions is probably not in your repertoire (at
least as applied to inanimate objects), and yet it is essential to the
achievement of the correctly flaky interiors. If all this sounds too much, you
could perfectly well serve the aubergine fritters on page 144, with a mint and
yoghourt dip, but call them bhajia rather than aubergine viennoise.
Otherwise, half a melon, nicely iced, would be as appealing at the beginning
as at the end of this meal.

Main course

The chicken and almond curry should be prepared a day ahead, which is relaxing for the nervous cook. It is bright yellow and slightly sweet, best served with a plain pilaff, a crunchy green vegetable (runner beans or ladies' fingers, for example), lemon pickle (page 200) and some simple salads. Most Indian salads are either a variation on raita (plain yoghourt with, say, grated cucumber, chopped tomato and a little chopped mint or crushed cumin and coriander) or simply sliced raw vegetables with lemon juice and spices. Try the tomato and onion one on page 199, or invent your own. If you have chosen not to serve the cobi bhaji as an appetiser, you could serve the stir-fried vegetables on page 197 with the main course. (Do not serve them in the same meal since they duplicate so many ingredients.) Poppadums are just as crisply delicious grilled as fried, and can be prepared immediately before dinner.

Sweet course

Fresh fruit salad is a soothing end to a spicy meal, and if your shopping is successful you can include mango or guava as well as the more run-of-the-mill oranges, pears, and so on. Our ginger pear sorbet, borrowed from the friend-of-a-friend, is also refreshing, and lacks gingery heat, so that you need not fear a renewed attack on your palate. If neither of those appeals, and you have access to a shop selling good Indian sweetmeats, try barfi, a fudge-like sweet flavoured with coconut and rosewater, or ladu, pastry balls dipped in syrup.

Drinks suggestions

Most people prefer lager to wine as an accompaniment to Indian food, but Gewürztraminer is spicy enough to stand up well to firm flavours.

Main course

Lager or spicy white wine

Cobi bhaji with chapatis

**Annfield House,
Kingskettle, Fife
Chef/proprietor:
Dorothy Kelly**

Unleavened bread with spiced vegetables

For the bhaji

500 g	onions	1 lb
25 g	butter *or* ghee	1 oz
one 15 ml spoon	curry paste	1 tablesp
250 g	tomatoes	8 oz
250 g	carrots	8 oz
250 g	swede	8 oz
250 g	cauliflower	8 oz
175 g	cabbage	6 oz

For the chapatis

100 g	wheatmeal flour	4 oz
one	pinch of salt	one
15 g	white cooking fat	$\frac{1}{2}$ oz
	water to mix	

For garnishing

	lemon wedges	

Fry the coarsely-chopped onions in the butter or ghee until they are glossy. Stir in the curry paste and let it cook for a few minutes before adding the skinned and chopped tomatoes. Cook the mixture slowly for ten minutes. Add the chopped carrots and swede, and simmer gently, covered, for a further twenty minutes. Add the cauliflower in florets and the finely-shredded cabbage and cook until just tender, about three minutes longer.

To make the chapatis, mix the ingredients to a scone-like dough. Pinch off pieces the size of an egg and roll them into circles about 12 cm (5 inches) in diameter. Cook them on a heavy griddle or frying-pan (ungreased) over fairly high heat. (They take about as long as pancakes to cook.) Before you turn them, bunch a tea towel into a pad and clap each chapati firmly. Do the same on the other side before removing them from the griddle. (This breaks the layers which enclose the steam.) Serve immediately with the bhaji and a lemon wedge, or keep hot stacked in a warm, covered saucepan.

Chicken and almond curry (6)

**Dunain Park,
Inverness, Highland
Chef/proprietor:
Judith Bulger**

one	cooked chicken	one
900 g	onions	2 lb
four	cloves of garlic	four
100 g	butter	4 oz
one 5 ml spoon	turmeric	1 teasp
one 5 ml spoon	coriander	1 teasp
one 5 ml spoon	cumin	1 teasp
one 5 ml spoon	onion seed	1 teasp
one 5 ml spoon	cloves	1 teasp
one 5 ml spoon	nutmeg	1 teasp
one 5 ml spoon	cinnamon	1 teasp
one 5 ml spoon	fenugreek	1 teasp
one 5 ml spoon	fennel seed	1 teasp
one 5 ml spoon	mace	1 teasp
half 5 ml spoon	vindaloo paste or chilli powder	$\frac{1}{2}$ teasp
three	bay leaves	three
six	pieces of stem ginger	six
25 g	flour	1 oz
125 ml	plain yoghourt	5 fl oz
one 15 ml spoon	honey	1 tablesp
500 ml	chicken stock (page 207)	1 pint
	salt, pepper	
50 g	flaked almonds	2 oz

If you poach the chicken or boiling-fowl with the other ingredients for stock listed on page 207, you will have stock for the sauce. Skin, bone and cube the chicken meat.

Fry the finely-chopped onion and garlic very gently in the butter until they are transparent. (Add a little oil if you are using salted butter, to prevent its burning.) Grind all the spices together, chop the ginger, and add them to the pan. Fry them until the butter begins to separate from the spices. Stir the flour into the yoghourt and add it to the onions off the heat. Then add the honey and about 500 ml (one pint) of stock. Bring it to the boil, and allow it to simmer gently for about an hour. Check the consistency and add a little beurre manié (page 206) or more stock if necessary. Season the sauce with salt and pepper, add the chicken and the almonds, and reheat the curry.

Chef's note: the curry is best made a day ahead so that the meat absorbs all the spices.

Editor's note: a cheap coffee-grinder brought back from a European holiday and kept solely for spices is a boon if you are a regular curry-maker.

Ginger pear sorbet

For the syrup

150 g	caster sugar	6 oz
175 ml	water	7 fl oz
two	lemons	two
25 g	stem ginger	1 oz
two	very ripe, medium-sized pears	two
one	large egg white	one

Pre-set the refrigerator at its coldest setting.

Gently heat the sugar and water together. When the sugar has dissolved, add the thinly-pared lemon rind and bring the mixture to the boil. Simmer it for six minutes and leave it to cool. Add 60 ml (2½ fl oz) of lemon juice to the syrup and strain it into an ice-cream container. Freeze in the coldest part of the freezer or freezing compartment until it is mushy (about two hours).

Finely chop the ginger, and peel, core and mash or liquidise the pears. Beat the part-frozen mixture and carefully fold in the ginger, pears and stiffly-beaten egg white. Freeze the sorbet until it is stiff.

Crème flamande
or
Lettuce cream soup

Lambs' tongues in red wine, lemon-baked cabbage, jacket potatoes

Champagne Charlie
or
Sorbet au cognac

Philosophers, psychologists and comedians spend much of their time—and earn at least a living wage—ruminating on basic human personality differences. Some of us are optimists, some pessimists; some consume what's going while they can, others take thought for the morrow with budgets, insurance policies and other forms of righteous living. Our eating patterns reflect similar variety. There may not be many people left, certainly among readers of this book, who identify with the White Queen: 'The rule is jam tomorrow, jam yesterday—but never jam today.' However, in composing meals some people like to begin lavishly and end conservatively (if you recognise yourself, see page 114). Others proceed on opposite lines, and this spring meal is for those who habitually save the best mouthful till the end: you start quite modestly in terms of cost and calorie-count—though not quality—and work up to a spectacular alcoholic splash. This would be wasted on people who neither drink nor eat puddings, so choose your guests with care.

First course

Crème flamande is comforting on a chilly spring day, a tasty vegetarian soup lifted out of the ordinary by its fried-onion-and-croûton garnish. The lettuce cream soup is a pretty colour, more delicate in flavour, and useful for unpredictable weather since it can be served either hot or chilled. (Remember the recipe later in the year when your garden lettuces have bolted.) Possible alternatives are fennel soup (page 88) or aubergine viennoise (page 144).

Main course

The lambs' tongues make an easy and interesting stew, with the boeuf bourguignonne trimmings of bacon, mushrooms and onions, and a dash of Dubonnet to lift it at the end. (Be sure that the tongues are cooked long enough to be tender—otherwise they can be difficult to skin.) Spring cabbage, lightly dressed with lemon juice (page 194), is a suitable leafy accompaniment. Artichoke and potato puree (page 192) is another possibility. Since the stew uses quite a lot of wine, you may have to abandon the usual precept that one should put the same wine in casserole as in glass.

To drink, you should serve a fairly forceful one, perhaps Côtes du Rhône or Italian red. And for an aperitif, you will already have a bottle of Dubonnet open, but as not everyone likes it, offer alternatives, perhaps other French aperitifs, such as Suze, Lillet, or Chambéry. (The provident will have brought them back from continental holidays as duty-free trophies. . .)

Sweet course

And we now turn to, if not the liquid lunch, at least the frozen dinner finale. Both sweets use brandy, wine, lemons and oranges. And, happily, neither cooks out the alcohol before freezing, so that you can almost feel the champagne bubbles on your tongue or smell the Gewürztraminer as if from a wine glass. However, the results are quite different in each case because of the egg whites in the sorbet and the cream in Champagne Charlie. Choose the latter for the gesture's sake, the sorbet if the occasion calls for just a little more restraint. If such blatant alcoholic intake appals you, consider instead Quark Kuchen mit Himbeeren (page 53) or chocolate and praline cream (page 74). After all, you would not wish to have it said, as a correspondent once reported of a now vanished *Good Food Guide* restaurant, 'Mr Jones was in the bar, and by the end of the evening most of the bar was in Mr Jones.'

Wine suggestion

Aperitif

French vermouth or bitters

Main course

Full red wine

Crème flamande

La Potinière, Gullane,
Lothian
Chef/proprietor:
Hilary Brown

two	onions	two
50 g	butter	2 oz
750 g	potatoes	1½ lb
750 ml	water	1½ pints
one 5 ml spoon	salt	1 teasp
	pepper	
half	small onion	half
15 g	butter	½ oz
four 15 ml spoons	double cream	4 tablesp
	croûtons	

Finely chop the onions and fry them very gently in the butter for about 20–30 minutes until they are starting to turn golden. Add the peeled and sliced potatoes and cover them with cold water. Bring the mixture to the boil and simmer it gently until the vegetables are soft, stirring occasionally to prevent the potatoes from sticking. If the soup becomes too thick, add more water. Liquidise the soup until it is perfectly smooth. Pour it back into the rinsed pan, season well with salt and pepper, and, if necessary, add more water to thin it down. For garnishing, finely slice the half onion and fry it in the butter until it is soft and golden. Serve the soup hot, garnished with the fried onions, a swirl of cream, and croûtons.

Chef's note: the flavour of this soup is dependent on the long, slow cooking of the onions at the beginning of the recipe.

Lettuce cream soup (6)

Rothay Manor,
Ambleside, Cumbria
Chef/proprietor:
Bronwen Nixon

500 ml	béchamel sauce (page 209)	1 pint
one	medium-sized onion	one
25 g	butter	1 oz
two	medium-sized lettuces (or the same quantity of outside leaves)	two
1 litre	chicken stock (page 207)	2 pints
two	egg yolks	two

Make the béchamel sauce, using milk that has been infused with an onion *clouté* (with two cloves stuck into it). Sweat the finely-chopped onion in the butter, add the shredded lettuce leaves (reserving three for the final preparation), and sweat them with the onion until they are soft. Liquidise this mixture with the stock and whisk it into the béchamel sauce. Simmer gently for about half an hour.

To give the soup a boost just before serving, liquidise the three reserved lettuce leaves with a little of the soup and add it to the pot. Whisk in the egg yolks at the last minute and reheat the soup slowly without allowing it to boil.

Lambs' tongues in red wine

**Copper Inn,
Pangbourne, Berkshire
Chef: John Prince**

twelve	lambs' tongues	twelve
25 g	butter	1 oz
25 ml	olive oil	1 fl oz
125 g	unsmoked fat bacon	4 oz
twelve	button onions	twelve
25 g	flour	1 oz
550 ml	red wine	1 pint
twelve	button mushrooms	twelve
one	bay leaf	one
two	cloves	two
one	sprig of thyme	one
	salt, pepper	
65 ml	Dubonnet	$2\frac{1}{2}$ fl oz
	chopped parsley	

It is best to trim and skin the tongues after cooking, rather than beforehand.

Brown the tongues in the butter and oil. Remove them from the pan and add the bacon in small cubes. Brown it along with the onions in the same fat, and remove them from the pan. Stir the flour into the remaining fat, gradually add the wine, and bring the mixture to the boil. Return the tongues, onion and bacon to the pan with the mushrooms and seasonings. Simmer gently for about two hours until the tongues are tender, or cook them in a slow oven.

Strain all the ingredients through a colander and return the cooking liquor to the pan. Remove the onions, bacon and mushrooms from the colander and add them to the pan. Skin the tongues and trim their roots of any fat. (The skin is tough and comes away easily.) Split them lengthwise and add them to the liquor. Check the seasoning and consistency of the sauce, and if it needs to be thicker, add a little beurre manié (page 206). Bring the sauce to the boil.

Add the Dubonnet just before serving, and sprinkle the meat with chopped parsley.

Champagne Charlie (10–14)

Langley Wood,
Redlynch, Wiltshire
Chef/proprietors:
Mr and Mrs F. Pearce

150 g	caster sugar	6 oz
125 ml	water	5 fl oz
two	oranges	two
two	lemons	two
570 ml	chilled champagne	1 pint
570 ml	double cream	1 pint
150 ml	cooking brandy	6 fl oz
20	ratafia biscuits	20

For decoration

	lemon peel	
	grated chocolate	

Pre-set the refrigerator at its coldest setting.

Make a syrup by boiling the sugar and water for six minutes and cooling it rapidly. Add the grated rind of one orange, the juice from all the fruit, and the champagne. Put the mixture, in a half-gallon container, in the coldest part of the freezer or freezing compartment. After 3–4 hours, beat it to remove any ice particles around the edges (if necessary, use an electric food mixer). Whip the cream until thick but not buttery and fold it into the champagne mixture. Stir in 100 ml (4 fl oz) of the brandy. Return the container to the freezer overnight.

To serve, allow the ice to soften if necessary, put two ratafia biscuits, moistened with a little of the remaining brandy, in the bottom of each glass, spoon the mixture over them, and decorate with twists of lemon peel and grated chocolate.

Editor's notes: we liked the ice-cream even better with rather less brandy. In the proportions listed, it is refreshingly sharp. If you prefer ices sweeter, you could perhaps use demi-sec champagne instead of brut. If you have trouble finding ratafia biscuits, crumbled meringue makes an adequate substitute.

Sorbet au cognac (8)

Chez Nico,
London, S.E.22
Chef/proprietor:
Nico Ladenis

125 ml	water	5 fl oz
250 g	sugar	8 oz
one	lemon	one
one	orange	one
150 ml	cognac	6 fl oz
100 ml	Gewürztraminer	4 fl oz
three	egg whites	three
one 15 ml spoon	icing sugar	1 tablesp
two 5 ml spoons	powdered gelatine	2 teasp

Pre-set the refrigerator at its coldest setting.

In a heavy pan, make a thick syrup with the water, the sugar and the rinds of the lemon and orange in strips. Allow it to cool completely and strain it before adding the lemon juice, cognac and wine. Freeze the mixture until it is mushy.

In a bowl set over a pan of simmering water, whip the egg whites, fold in the icing sugar and continue beating the mixture until it is very stiff.

When the first mixture is ready, liquidise it, and add the gelatine dissolved in a little very hot water. Put the sorbet in a large bowl and fold in the meringue. Freeze the sorbet until it is firm.

Watercress soup
or
Nettle soup

Porc sauté comme à Cannes, rice, salad

Citron surprise

After seemingly endless grey winter days of semi-hibernation, most of us seem to feel the urge to show that we have come alive in as many different ways as possible, with new clothes or figures, and new and interesting recipes in our culinary repertoire. This meal takes advantage of seasonal vegetables (and the nettles, at least, are free) and provides the fresh and tangy tastes which seem to promise health and energy. The only piece of tricky timing is the possible overlap of main course and citron surprise in the oven, but there is a solution. Otherwise, it is an undemanding but not unrewarding menu.

First course

Both soups are green and slightly bitter, with potato as the only thickening in the nettle one and a supplement to flour in the watercress. Spinach or sorrel can be treated in the same way. If you prefer a gentler taste, consider the turnip soup (page 4) or spinach flan (page 150) instead.

Main course

The pork casserole is an attractive and unusual dish with overtones of canard aux petits pois. In other words, the peas dominate the pork, rather than vice versa. The dish tastes almost as good made with frozen petits pois, should you wish to make it out of fresh-pea season, but don't be tempted by tinned red peppers, which have a taste quite unlike their fresh relatives. Rice and a simple green salad complement the pork nicely.

Sweet course

If you choose citron surprise, which is charmingly reminiscent of nursery puddings at their best, remember that it requires 40 minutes undisturbed in the oven and must be served as soon as it is ready, like a soufflé. Unless there is a show or a train to catch, you can probably count on that amount of time—at least—for the main course, and you can put the pudding in the oven as you serve the pork. But if that sounds too worrying, and you are not lucky enough to have a double oven, serve a compote of rhubarb, or rhubarb fool, or strawberry shortbread (page 85) instead.

Wine suggestions

Should the party be a celebration, something light and bubbly would make an attractive aperitif: champagne if you like, or sparkling Vouvray or Saumur from the Loire, or a Vinho Verde from Portugal. No one can drink anything with a bitter green soup, so move on to consider the main course. There are enough strong flavours to recommend modest rather than fine wine. Italian red would be suitable because of its body, but a rosé from Portugal (to continue the theme), Provence or Anjou would look pretty and taste quaffable. A little-known rosé from Sancerre is much drier than the Portuguese.

Aperitif   Champagne or sparkling wine

Main course   Italian red or French or Portuguese rosé

Watercress soup

Tarn End Hotel,
Talkin, Cumbria
Chef: Martin Hoefkens

one	large bunch of watercress	one
one	medium-sized onion	one
one 15 ml spoon	butter	1 tablesp
two	medium-sized potatoes (raw or cooked)	two
one 15 ml spoon	flour	1 tablesp
250 ml	milk	10 fl oz
500 ml	chicken stock (page 207)	1 pint
	salt, pepper	

For garnishing

	watercress leaves	
	croûtons	
	cream	

Reserve some watercress leaves for garnishing.

Chop the remaining leaves, stalks and onion and sweat them in the butter in a large saucepan. Add the chopped potatoes and flour and cook for two or three minutes. Add the milk, stock and seasoning. Allow the soup to come to the boil, and simmer it until the vegetables are tender. Liquidise it or push it through a sieve, and reheat it gently.

Serve the soup hot, garnished with blanched watercress leaves, croûtons, and a swirl of cream.

Nettle soup

Arbutus Lodge, Cork,	one	leek	one
Co Cork	100 g	butter	4 oz
Chef/proprietor:	one	bunch of young nettles	one
Declan Ryan	500 g	potatoes	1 lb
	1 litre	chicken stock (page 207)	2 pints
	125 ml	cream	5 fl oz
		salt, pepper	

Sweat the chopped leek in the butter, add the washed and chopped nettles and stir them until they appear glossy. Stir in the peeled and sliced potatoes and add the stock. Simmer the mixture for 30–35 minutes. Liquidise the soup, return to the heat, and add the cream and salt and pepper. Dilute with stock if too thick. Serve hot.

Editor's note: wear gloves, of course, to pick and prepare the nettles.

Porc sauté comme à Cannes

Vineyard,	1–1.25 kg	chump end of pork, boneless and lean	2½ lb
Northampton,		olive oil *or* butter	
Northamptonshire	twelve	button onions	twelve
Chef/proprietor:	3–4	cloves of garlic	3–4
Maggie Angeloglou		flour	
	half-bottle	dry white wine	half-bottle
		salt, pepper	
	two 150 g	red peppers	two 6 oz
	500 g	young peas, shelled weight *or* frozen peas	1 lb
	200 g	pimento-stuffed green olives	7 oz

Cut the pork into 2·5-cm (one-inch) squares and sauté them in butter or oil, or a mixture of both. When the pieces are slightly browned transfer them to an oven-proof casserole. Lightly fry the peeled onions and crushed garlic and add them to the pork. Sprinkle the surface of the meat with flour and pour the wine over it. Season lightly. Cook the casserole in a slow oven (150°C, 300°F, mark 2) for an hour. Slice the peppers into long thin strips, and add to the casserole with the peas and olives. Cook for a further 20–30 minutes.

Citron surprise (6)

La Potinière, Gullane,
Lothian
Chef/proprietor:
Hilary Brown

50 g	butter	2 oz
two	large eggs	two
90 g	caster sugar	3 oz
15 g	flour	$\frac{1}{2}$ oz
one	large lemon	one
200 ml	milk	8 fl oz

Blend the butter, egg yolks, caster sugar, flour, grated rind, lemon juice and half the milk in a liquidiser until smooth. Add the remaining milk (the mixture may look curdled but this will not spoil the finished sweet) and pour the mixture into a bowl. Allow it to stand for at least an hour.

Fold the stiffly-beaten egg whites into the lemon mixture, ladle it into six ramekins, and bake in a bain-marie (page 213) in a slow to moderate oven (150°C, 300°F, mark 2) for about 40 minutes or until it is golden brown.

Sprinkle with caster sugar, and serve immediately.

Editor's note: the same mixture—which separates into a lemon-curd-like base with a spongy top layer—can also be cooked in one large dish for just over an hour.

Tagliatelle alla carbonara
or
Tenerelli

Agnellino in potacchio, chicche del nonno verdi,
noodles *or* risotto

Oranges in brandy and Grand Marnier syrup
or
Granita di fragole

An Italian meal should be exuberant rather than formal—enjoyable to cook, colourful and interesting to eat. This one can be conducted *con brio* or presented in rather lower key, depending on your choice of dishes.

First course

The tenerelli are splendidly light pancakes, with a creamy filling and sauce, easy to prepare ahead of time. If you have children underfoot, determined to help, let them make the pancakes at tea-time, starting with double quantities so that they can eat one out of every two they make. Alternatively, set them to rolling the plasticine-like chicche, which need time to dry off before they are boiled. If you prefer a short sprint at the last moment, the tagliatelle alla carbonara is ideal, since guests have to wait for it, like a soufflé, rather than the other way round. If your mental calorie-counter is totting up already, serve the filetto de sogliola marinato on page 178 instead.

Main course

The stuffed leg of lamb is a tasty but simple dish, and after a pasta course you will probably want to serve the sauce without cream. If the meal is a family one, you may have to cook the lamb just a little longer than recommended. But it seems a pity, and you could always try convincing a dubious youngster that the pinkness of the meat derives from the tomato stuffing. The chicche del nonno verdi (page 198) are fun to prepare, interesting to watch cooking, and splendidly absorbent of a good sauce. They can be kept hot with butter and Parmesan while you eat the first course. Since they echo the spinach filling of the tenerelli, serve plain noodles or risotto (page 201) if that is your first course choice. If you like to offer several vegetables, you could perhaps pick up the celery theme from the lamb dish itself, or have courgettes or a salad instead.

Sweet course

The sweets are no distraction, for both are prepared ahead of time. Choose the oranges for a tangy flavour, the strawberry granita for a gentler taste. A crisp biscuit (page 204) for contrast is a help with either.

Wine suggestions

All this exuberance demands robust wine as accompaniment. Luckily, Italian wines might have been created to go with Italian cooking, so the choice is wide. If you are stressing the Italian theme, serve Punt é Mes or Campari first (remember that the former is lower in alcohol and also cheaper). Decide whether you want to stick to one red wine throughout the meal, or have a white with the first course and a red thereafter. Soave, Frascati or Verdicchio are all possible wines for the first course; for the red, choose Valpolicella if you like a lightish wine, Barolo if you prefer something meaty, and Chianti for all possibilities between those extremes. (Straw-wrapped flasks don't generally contain the very finest wines, but they do look pretty and there *are* some enjoyable Chiantis in flask.) If your guests are hearty drinkers, you could do worse than buy one of the many blended wines which come in litre or even double-litre bottles. If the meal is turning into a celebration by the sweet course, serve a glass of Asti Spumante with it, or Marsala afterwards. Aurum, one of the best of all orange liqueurs, is also worth remembering when strawberries are on the agenda.

Aperitif	Punt é Mes *or* Campari
First course	Soave, Frascati *or* Verdicchio, *or* the same red wine as the main course
Main course	Valpolicella, Chianti *or* Barolo, *or* a blended wine
Sweet course	Asti Spumante

Tagliatelle alla carbonara

La Frégate, St Peter Port, Guernsey
Chef: Konrad Holleis

500 g	tagliatelle	1 lb
250 g	smoked streaky bacon	8 oz
two	egg yolks	two
	black peppercorns	
two 15 ml spoons	double cream	2 tablesp
	mushrooms (optional)	

Cook the tagliatelle in boiling, salted water for about six minutes, until it is *al dente*. Meantime, using scissors, cut the bacon in small strips or dice, and fry it (no additional fat needed).

When the pasta is cooked, strain it well and quickly return it to the saucepan. Add the lightly-beaten egg yolks and a generous amount of coarsely-ground black pepper. Let it rest for a few seconds before stirring the egg in gently with a fork. Add the bacon and cream, stir thoroughly, and serve at once. Garnish, if you wish, with lightly-cooked chopped mushrooms.

Editor's note: do observe the few seconds' pause before stirring the egg into the pasta, since otherwise there is a danger of it scrambling. The Roman version uses whole eggs and no cream, and scrambles very readily.

Tenerelli

Vasco and Piero's Pavilion, London, W.1
Chef: Claudio le Ponte

A dish from Umbria and Tuscany

For the pancakes			
two	eggs	two
	salt, pepper	
three 15 ml spoons	flour	3 tablesp
200 ml	milk	8 fl oz
	oil	

For the filling			
150 g	spinach	6 oz
	salt, pepper	
one	egg	one
25 g	grated Parmesan	1 oz
150 g	Ricotta	6 oz
	fresh basil (optional)	

For the béchamel			
35 g	butter	1½ oz
25 g	flour	1 oz
300 ml	milk	12 fl oz
	nutmeg, salt	

For the topping		
	grated Parmesan	

To make the pancake batter, beat the eggs thoroughly with a pinch of salt and pepper, and add the flour while continuing to beat, followed by the milk. Heat a heavy frying-pan or crêpe pan, oil it lightly, and cook the pancakes, using a small ladleful of batter for each one. Keep them warm, covered.

To make the filling, boil the cleaned spinach in a little salted water. Drain it thoroughly, chop it finely, and mix it with the salt, pepper, egg, Parmesan, Ricotta, and a little chopped basil, if you wish.

40

Make a béchamel sauce (page 209). (If it is very thick, add a little more milk.) Add a little grated nutmeg and salt.

For the final assembly, take each pancake, cut it in quarters, put a little of the filling in the centre of each quarter, and fold it into a neat parcel. Grease an oval oven-proof dish, put a little sauce on the bottom, and arrange the folded pancakes on top. Cover them with the remaining sauce, sprinkle on some Parmesan, and bake the tenerelli in a moderate oven (180°C, 350°F, mark 4) for 15 minutes.

Agnellino in potacchio

Royal Exchange Theatre Restaurant, Manchester Chef: Roy Pegram

one	leg of lamb, boned	one
250 ml	white wine	10 fl oz
375 g	tomatoes	12 oz
2–3	sprigs of fresh rosemary	2–3
2–3	cloves of garlic	2–3
	salt, pepper	
one 15 ml spoon	olive oil	1 tablesp
2–3	sticks of celery	2–3
	cream (optional)	

Ask your butcher to leave the knuckle on the leg of lamb when he bones it. Sprinkle the cavity with a little of the wine, and stuff it with the skinned and de-seeded tomatoes and half the chopped rosemary. Stuff as firmly as possible and sew up the opening with string or close it with skewers. Make some incisions all over the joint and insert small slivers of garlic (one large clove should suffice). Season the joint well with salt and pepper. (Weigh the stuffed joint.)

Cook the remaining finely-chopped garlic and rosemary in the olive oil until the garlic is pale gold. Stir in about half the wine. Cover the bottom of a roasting-pan with a layer of finely-chopped celery, sit the joint on top, and pour the wine and garlic mixture over it. Roast the lamb in a moderately hot oven (190°C, 375°F, mark 5) for about 20 minutes per lb, stuffed weight. Baste it every ten minutes, adding a little more wine each time.

Serve the lamb with the strained and skimmed gravy which can be heated with some double cream if you wish to make a richer sauce.

Chef's note: this dish tastes marvellous with gratin dauphinoise potatoes.

Oranges in brandy and Grand Marnier syrup (6)

Horn of Plenty,
Gulworthy, Devon
Sous-chef: Glyn Green

six	juicy oranges	six
500 g	caster sugar	1 lb
eight	cloves	eight
two	bay leaves	two
one	pinch of mace	one
5 cm	cinnamon stick	2 inches
125 ml	water	5 fl oz
two 15 ml spoons	brandy	2 tablesp
two 15 ml spoons	Grand Marnier	2 tablesp

Remove the zest from three oranges in strips. Peel all the oranges, and remove all the pith. Melt the sugar in a heavy saucepan until it is lightly caramelised (add a spoonful of water if you wish). Add the zest, spices and water, and simmer the syrup for a few minutes, until the sugar is dissolved.

Put the oranges in the syrup and let them simmer for five minutes. Leave them to cool in the syrup, before straining it off. Add to it the brandy and Grand Marnier and pour it back over the oranges.

Serve them either whole, or in slices or segments, with some of the syrup poured over, decorated with a little of the zest and cinnamon stick.

Granita di fragole (6)

Walnut Tree Inn,
Llandewi Skirrid,
Gwent
Chef/proprietor:
Franco Taruschio

250 g	sugar	8 oz
125 ml	water	5 fl oz
1 kg	ripe strawberries	2 lb
half	lemon	half
half	orange	half

Make a syrup by boiling the sugar and water together for five minutes. Allow it to cool.

Pass the strawberries through a sieve, add the lemon and orange juice and the cooled syrup. Freeze in the ice-making compartment or freezer, stirring twice during the freezing process. Serve the granita with a few fresh berries.

Editor's note: superb with very ripe fresh strawberries, successful as a winter treat with good frozen berries (the kind frozen dry, not in a syrup).

Pâté de vendange
or
Salade périgourdine

Salpicon de sole et scampi vermouth, rice,
mange-tout peas *or* hot cucumber

Peaches in red wine
or
Fruit compote

There are as many styles of French cooking as there are styles of dress, but the conventional picture presents either hearty peasant fare, using every last scrap of any beast involved, with plenty of fresh herbs, garlic and goose fat; or 'haute' cuisine involving expensive ingredients and elaborate sauces. While this meal falls somewhere between the two, it is intended for a summer evening, and is therefore concerned with lightness as well as elegance, and ease of preparation as well as sophistication.

First course

The pâté de vendange is a traditional one, made easier if not as tasty by the arrival of frozen boneless rabbit in supermarkets. Make it at least one day ahead to allow the flavours to mature. Serve it, if you like, in French fashion, with a fork and knife, some French bread, and no further garnish than pickled gherkins or olives. The salade périgourdine is not difficult to do just before dinner if you have everything to hand before you start—including the guests, since the omelette will toughen if kept waiting. Other possible first courses are a tomato salad or eggs with tapénade (page 95).

Main course

The salpicon is an elegant—and expensive—dish, with the rich wine-and-cream sauce which embodies the true 'taste of France' for many of us. If you are nervous of actual last-minute work, cook the sole just before your guests arrive and keep it warm in a double-boiler. (In this case, use Dover sole since lemon sole may flake into anonymity.) However, if you make the sauce ahead of time, you have no more to do than cook the scampi and sole, a four-minute job. This hardly seems too long to leave your guests if their conversation is self-generating. If you choose the last-minute option, serve mange-tout peas, which will also cook in under five minutes; otherwise hot cucumber (page 195) is less dependent on split-second timing. If any of your guests need meat before they feel they have been fed, you might consider the rognons à la moutarde (page 129) or porc sauté comme à Cannes (page 36).

43

Sweet course

Apart from dazzling fruit tarts and the occasional *jeu d'esprit* like gâteau de Pithiviers, French housewives and restaurateurs are less enterprising with sweets than we are. Fresh fruit or crème caramel are standard conclusions to a French menu. Follow their example, if you wish, with any fruit which is in season, arranged as attractively as possible. But if you prefer something cooked, this book offers many delicious fruity confections. The compote takes advantage of garden or market, the peach recipe enables you to cope with peaches not quite ripe enough to eat pleasurably raw. Otherwise, serve chestnut and orange roulade (page 146), or an ice or sorbet.

Wine suggestions

The fishy main course calls for as good a white wine as you can afford from Corton Charlemagne downwards. But a decent Meursault or Chablis would be very appropriate, as would an Alsace wine, either fruity Riesling or spicy Gewürztraminer. With the pâté you may consider serving the same wine, or you could open a modest red which can be continued later with some cheese, served in French fashion before the sweet. On the other hand, the decision to stick to Alsace, for instance, might suggest a lesser wine (Edelzwicker or Sylvaner) to serve with the pâté. If red is your choice, a Beaujolais or a Provencal red would be suitable. If this is an occasion for pushing the boat out, a glass of dessert wine would finish the meal in style: Barsac or Sauternes if you can afford them, Monbazillac if not. If you are serving only one wine throughout the meal, choose a contrasting aperitif, Chambéryzette vermouth, Pernod, or Kir (a teaspoonful of Crème de Cassis to a glass of chilled white wine), say.

Aperitif   Chambéryzette, Pernod, Kir or white wine

First course   Minor Alsace wine or light French red

Main course   White burgundy, Chablis or fine Alsace wine

Sweet course   Sauternes, Barsac or Monbazillac

Pâté de vendange (8)

Bistro Byron,
Eastbourne,
East Sussex
Chef/proprietor:
Simon Scrutton

750 g	boned rabbit	1½ lb
500 g	fat belly of pork	1 lb
175 g	lean veal	6 oz
250 g	onions	8 oz
two	large cloves of garlic	two
two	pinches of dried thyme	two
	salt, pepper	
125 ml	dry white wine	5 fl oz
50 ml	brandy	2 fl oz
one	egg	one
one 15 ml spoon	flour	1 tablesp
250 g	streaky bacon (approx)	8 oz

Chop or mince the rabbit, pork and veal. Mix them together in a large bowl, and add the finely-chopped onions and garlic, the seasonings, wine and brandy. Leave the mixture to ripen for 6–8 hours, stirring it occasionally.

Mix the egg and flour to a smooth paste, adding some of the liquid from the bowl if necessary. Combine the paste thoroughly with the meat mixture. Line an oven-proof dish or baking-tin with the bacon (if you wish, use more than is specified here and arrange overhanging strips which can be brought up over the top once the pâté is ready for the oven). Put the mixture into the tin, cover it with foil, stand it in a bain-marie (page 213) with water coming halfway up the sides, and bake it in a slow oven (150°C, 300°F, mark 2) for two hours.

Compress the pâté under weights. Leave it to cool completely, and refrigerate, at least overnight. If it is to be kept for several days, seal the top with clarified butter (page 213). (This is not necessary if you have covered the top with bacon.)

Editor's note: the pâté freezes well, but eat it within the month.

Salade périgourdine

**Lawrence Restaurant,
Brighton, East Sussex
Chef/proprietor:
Gerald Campion**

one	crisp lettuce	one
four	tomatoes	four
125 g	ham *or* bacon	4 oz
three	eggs	three
	salt, pepper	
25 g	unsalted butter	1 oz
	vinaigrette (page 210)	
75 g	walnut halves	3 oz

In a salad bowl, prepare the lettuce and tomato. Use very crisp lettuce (Webb's, density, cos, endive) and peel the tomatoes if you wish. Refrigerate till thoroughly chilled. Cut the ham or bacon in strips and cook it till fairly crisp. Drain, and keep warm.

Beat the eggs (about ten strokes only) with the salt and pepper and a tablespoonful of cold water. Melt the butter in an omelette pan, and when it foams, increase the heat and pour in the mixture. Ease the omelette away from the edges to allow the uncooked egg to run under. When the omelette is cooked, slide it out flat onto a plate, and cut it into strips.

Dress the salad with vinaigrette (made with walnut oil if possible), scatter first the walnuts and then the bacon on top, and finally the omelette strips. Toss it at table so that the lettuce is not wilted by the ham and omelette.

Editor's note: the vinaigrette should not be too oily: try three parts oil to one of vinegar.

Salpicon de sole et scampi vermouth

Limpets, Lymington,
Hampshire
Chef/proprietor:
Douglas Craig

500 g	fillets of sole	1 lb
15 g	butter	$\frac{1}{2}$ oz
four 15 ml spoons	finely-chopped shallots	4 tablesp
eight	medium-sized mushrooms	eight
175 ml	dry vermouth	7 fl oz
	salt, pepper	
500 g	medium-sized scampi	1 lb
250 ml	single cream	10 fl oz
	chopped parsley	

Cut the sole into 2.5-cm (one-inch) chunks.

Melt the butter in a sauté pan, add the shallots and sliced mushrooms, and fry them lightly. Pour in the vermouth, add the salt and pepper, and bring the mixture to the boil. Add the scampi and cream, and simmer gently for a minute. Add the sole fillets and simmer for a further three minutes. By this time the sauce should be fairly thick. If it is not, remove the fish and keep it warm while you reduce the sauce rapidly to a coating consistency. Serve the fish on a bed of plain rice, garnished with chopped parsley.

Chef's notes: Dover sole is best for this dish. You can use lemon sole but it is more likely to fall apart in the cooking. In the restaurant this dish is served with fried courgettes (page 197).

Peaches in red wine (6)

Lanterna Ristorante,
Scarborough,
North Yorkshire
Chef/proprietor:
Gianluigi Arecco

six	peaches	six
half-bottle	red wine	half-bottle
175 g	sugar	6 oz
	orange and lemon rind	

Peel the peaches, halve them and remove the stones. Crush the stones, remove the kernels, and roast or toast them till they are golden brown.

Boil the wine, sugar and a little grated orange and lemon rind. Drop in the peaches and simmer them for about a minute. (If they are less ripe than you expected, simmer them until they are tender.) Allow the peaches to cool in the syrup. Arrange them in a serving dish (or in individual glasses), pour over a little of the syrup, and garnish them with the crushed kernels.

Fruit compote

**Ballymaloe House,
Shanagarry, Co Cork
Chef/proprietor:
Myrtle Allen**

500 g	sugar	1 lb
375 ml	water	15 fl oz
1 kg	mixed soft fruit (see below)	2 lb

To make the stock syrup, boil the sugar and water together for two minutes. Cool the syrup, bottle it, and refrigerate it (it will keep for a week or more).

Choose and prepare the fruit. We use rhubarb, redcurrants, plums, damsons and blackcurrants. Poach the fruit in enough stock syrup to cover, either in a heavy saucepan over very low heat or, better, in a covered oven-proof dish in a slow oven (150°C, 300°F, mark 2) until it is soft. This may take almost an hour. Serve the fruit cold, with cream if you wish.

Editor's note: see also Mrs Allen's compote of pears on page 97.

Whiting in cucumber shells
or
Courgettes with prawns

Chicken cocotte with garlic and fines herbes,
new potatoes, peas

Quark Kuchen mit Himbereen
or
Strawberry Pernod mousse

British summer can mean anything from watching cricket through rain to fetching water from a standpipe during a drought. But even the worst of seasons provide an occasional golden day, and if you pick one of them for entertaining guests, you will want a menu which does not tie you to a hot stove all day and at the same time offers your friends light, seasonal food, kind to both the digestion and the waistline. This menu involves no last-minute flaps, and not even very much hard work ahead of time. Dr Banting himself would approve of the first two courses, and the bikini-conscious can always ask for small helpings of the mousse or cheesecake.

First course   Both first courses have a salady feel to them, and neither will break the bank, even if you are lavish with the prawns. Since courgettes seem to have taken over British gardens as relentlessly as bindweed, it is good to know how pleasant they are served cold. If cold fish does not appeal, consider instead one of the chilled soups (plum on page 71, tomato and mint on page 68, and saffron on page 15) or, if you are a pessimist, use the lettuce and green pea soup (page 62), which can be served either hot or cold. If you are lucky enough to have a productive vegetable garden, you could serve raw and blanched vegetables vinaigrette, with a few olives for contrast.

Main course   The chicken en cocotte is a conversation piece, partly because it is a *cuisine minceur* recipe, and partly because it uses what sounds like an intimidating amount of garlic. Serve it to people who enjoy talking about food. (The old guard who think it ill-bred to notice what is on the plate in front of them should be given something less arresting.) It is a lovely dish for summer, when fresh herbs are easy to find, but even in winter with some of the herbs dried it is very tasty. Besides, permanent slimmers so often complain that diet food is boring or tasteless, or both, that it is rewarding to offer this contrary evidence. New potatoes in their skins and any young garden vegetable are the best accompaniments, but bread and a green salad would be a good choice if you want literally no last-minute preparation at all. If the weather is so hot that you don't want to use the oven, consider serving chicken with tremalki sauce (page 69) or truite aux aromates (page 83).

Sweet course

The relative abstinence of the first two courses has earned you a faintly decadent finale. Both our sweets qualify admirably: the mousse is refreshingly subtle, the cheesecake creamy without being overfacing. Either of them would look even prettier garnished with whole berries, a luxury denied the winter version. Other possibilities are strawberry shortbread (page 85) or fresh peach Melba (page 118).

Wine suggestions

If the evening is really warm your guests may be thirsty and prefer long aperitifs to short ones. Start, perhaps, with a cheap dry white wine, and offer either a small spoonful of cassis (blackcurrant liqueur, *not* syrup) to turn it into a Kir, or some ice and soda water to make a spritzer. Sparkling wines always seem summery, and if champagne is beyond you, turn to some of the *méthode champenoise* alternatives, Saumur or Vouvray from the Loire, for example. In fact, one of those could last you through the meal, and if the bottles held out, you could even add a spoonful of framboise liqueur (not eau-de-vie) to the last glass to sweeten it enough to match the pudding. Otherwise, consider a Riesling, from Mosel, Rhine or Yugoslavia, or a Loire, perhaps Pouilly Fumé, or a Portuguese Vinho Verde, which has an attractive prickle to it.

Aperitif

Kir, spritzer or sparkling Loire

First and main courses

Sparkling Loire, Riesling or Vinho Verde

Whiting in cucumber shells

The Grange, London, W.C.2 Chef: Jurgens Boldt			
	one 25-cm	cucumber	one 10-inch
		salt	
	1 kg	whiting	2 lb
For the court bouillon	150 ml	water	6 fl oz
	100 ml	white wine	4 fl oz
	ten	black peppercorns	ten
	three	parsley stalks	three
	half	carrot	half
	one	sliced onion	one
	half	bay leaf	half
For garnishing	half	lemon	half
	125 ml	mayonnaise (page 211)	5 fl oz
		black pepper	
		parsley	

Peel the cucumber, cut it in half lengthwise, and remove the seeds with a teaspoon. Sprinkle the halves with salt and allow to stand for a least an hour. Rinse the halves, pat them dry, and cut them into 10-cm (4-inch) 'barquettes'.

Meantime, make the court bouillon (page 213) and in it poach the whiting for a few minutes until it is tender. Allow it to cool in the liquid. Flake the fish finely, discarding all bones and skin, and sprinkle it with lemon juice.

Pile the flesh into the cucumber shells, and spoon over them the mayonnaise to which you have added black pepper and enough finely-chopped parsley to make it a pale green.

Courgettes with prawns

Sea Cow Bistro,
Weymouth, Dorset
Chef/proprietor:
Daphne Jonzen

375–500 g	small courgettes	12 oz–1 lb
125 g	shelled prawns	4 oz
half 5 ml spoon	salt	$\frac{1}{2}$ teasp
	pepper	
one 15 ml spoon	fresh, chopped tarragon (or half quantity dried)	1 tablesp
	paprika	
125 ml	whipping or double cream	5 fl oz

Wipe the courgettes and cut them into small dice. Blanch them for a minute in boiling water, then refresh them by rinsing them in cold water. Drain and pat them dry.

Divide out the courgettes among four individual ramekins, or similar oven-proof dishes. Put the prawns on top, and season them with salt and pepper. Sprinkle over the tarragon and a dash of paprika. Beat the cream until it is light and aerated but not thickened, and spread it over the prawns. Brown the tops slowly under the grill, and chill before serving.

Editor's notes: be careful not to leave the prawns under the grill too long, since they might dry out. At a second attempt, you might like to juggle the quantities of prawns and cream.

Chicken cocotte with garlic and fines herbes

Kinchs, Chesterton,
Oxfordshire
Chef/proprietor:
Christopher Greatorex

1½ kg	chicken, dressed weight	$3\frac{1}{4}$ lb
	salt, pepper	
one	lemon	one
two 15 ml spoons	olive oil	2 tablesp
four	whole heads of garlic	four
	fresh herbs (rosemary, thyme, parsley, fennel, marjoram)	

Rub the chicken inside and out, with salt, pepper, lemon juice and olive oil. Separate the heads of garlic into cloves and bruise them lightly. (There is no need to peel them.) Stuff most of them inside the chicken.

In an oven-proof casserole, prepare a bed of herbs. (Use, say, two tablespoonsful of chopped parsley, two branches of thyme and teaspoonsful of any others you fancy. Avoid rosemary in its dried form, as it kills other flavours.) Add the remaining garlic, and put the chicken on top, breast uppermost. Seal the lid, either with a flour and water paste or by using a sheet of foil between the casserole and its lid, and cook the chicken for 1¼ hours in a moderate oven (190°C, 375°F, mark 5).

Open the casserole at table so that your guests can be 'bowled over by the aroma'. The taste is much subtler.

Chef's note: we serve the chicken with French bread or new potatoes in their skins, and broad beans vinaigrette in summer, or artichoke and potato puree (page 192) in winter.

Editor's notes: if carving in public is not your forte, use chicken joints, and cut the cooking time to 50 minutes.

Look for heads of garlic with large, juicy cloves (the fresh, expensive kind that arrives in the late spring is ideal).

Quark Kuchen mit Himbeeren (8)

Stane Street Hollow,	25 g	unsalted butter	1 oz
Pulborough,	150 g	digestive biscuits	6 oz
West Sussex	350 g	full-fat cream cheese	12 oz
Chef: René Kaiser	50 g	caster sugar	2 oz
	one	lemon	one
	200 ml	milk	8 fl oz
	15 g	gelatine	½ oz
For the topping	500 g	raspberries (approx)	1 lb
	two 5 ml spoons	arrowroot	2 teasp
		sugar	
		whipped cream	

Melt the butter in a saucepan, and stir in the finely-crushed biscuits. Tip them into a 23-cm (9-inch) flan dish and press them gently into a layer to cover the bottom.

Beat together thoroughly in a large, deep bowl the cream cheese, sugar, lemon juice and milk. Dissolve the gelatine in a little hot water, allow it to cool, add it to the cream cheese mixture and beat again. Pour the mixture onto the crushed biscuits and refrigerate it until it is set.

Puree and sieve enough raspberries to obtain 300 ml (12 fl oz). Thicken the puree with the arrowroot, heating the mixture gently until it thickens and clears, and adding sugar to taste. Top the cheese mixture with the cooled puree and decorate it with whipped cream just before serving.

Editor's note: this cheesecake can be made with frozen raspberries.

Strawberry Pernod mousse (5–6)

Clifton Hotel, Nairn,
Highland
Chef/proprietor:
J. Gordon Macintyre

250 g	fresh strawberries	8 oz
two 5 ml spoons	gelatine	2 teasp
50 ml	boiling water	2 fl oz
half	lemon	half
50 g	sugar	2 oz
25 ml	Pernod	1 fl oz
150 ml	double cream	6 fl oz
one	egg white	one

Puree and sieve the strawberries.

Dissolve the gelatine in the boiling water and leave it to cool. Blend the strawberry puree, the juice of the lemon and the sugar together. Add the Pernod and cooled gelatine. Beat the cream until it holds its shape and fold it into the strawberry mixture. Fold in the stiffly-beaten egg white.

Pour the mixture into one large dish or several individual ones. Refrigerate until set (about three hours).

Chef's note: the mousse freezes well, so make larger quantities when strawberries are in season.

Editor's note: if you are short of freezing space, you could freeze the sweetened puree more economically than the completed mousse. You may then need one drop of cochineal to restore the colour.

Simple gazpacho
or
Gambas al ajillo

Julienne of veal in paprika and sour cream, noodles, courgettes

Gooseberry ice-cream
or
Fresh fruit and cheese

You will easily be able to invent your own scenario for this meal: weekend guests to feed (yet again), for whom you've done the ritual roast and the hard-working French spectacular, and with whom you'd now like to spend some time before their departure; a spouse or guests due at an uncertain hour from meeting or plane, to be fed quickly before another engagement; post-Christmas tristesse, when you want to lounge and loll and be loved, rather than slave and stir and stew. In other words, if you need to keep at your fingertips a decent meal that can be put on the table in twenty minutes, this is a useful one to consider.

First course   Quick meals do not come cheap, but if you are diet- as well as budget-conscious, the gazpacho will satisfy your conscience as well as pleasing your guests. If, on the other hand, you are comfortably decadent, you may be glad to know that some people lead on from vodka with tomato to vodka with gazpacho, all sipped in the comfort of an easy chair (omit the croûtons in this case). In fact, even if you choose the prawns in garlic to start the meal, it might be wise to serve them in small dishes (on cool under-plates to save burns and spills) to be eaten with the last of the aperitif, so that you can summon people to table when the main course is cooked. Gambas al ajillo achieves a miracle of balance between the prawns and the garlic and chillies, and looks pretty as well. If neither of these appeals, consider Camembert frit (page 101) or devilled kidneys (page 84).

Main course   The julienne of veal is a splendid party dish: it looks colourful and tastes more complex than seems possible with so few ingredients and such hasty preparation. It is tender enough both for easy digestion and also for eating with a fork, should you have invited more guests than your dining-room seats, or should the living-room fire be irresistible. Serve it with buttered noodles and courgettes, haricots verts, or even a green salad. This meal is not as fiercely hot as it might sound: neither recipe raises more than a pleasant glow. With ten more minutes to spare you could serve the sauté de boeuf Mirabelle on page 157.

Sweet course

Assuming that you are, on occasion, a wise virgin, you now produce a refreshingly fruity ice-cream or sorbet. The gooseberry one suggested here provides a contrast in both taste and colour; blackcurrant leaf sorbet (page 65) is another possibility, fresh fruit and cheese yet another.

Wine suggestions

Such highly-seasoned food suggests modest rather than grand wines. Choose a dry white wine to stand up to the prawns: a Muscadet, or a Sauvignon from the Loire or Provence. For the main course, you may wish to try a Hungarian wine: either Bull's Blood or a commercial blend; otherwise, a decent Spanish red would fill the bill, as would a minor Rhône wine. If you prefer white wine with veal, continue with the first-course wine.

First course

Dry white wine, preferably French

Main course

Hungarian, Spanish or Rhône red wine

Simple gazpacho

Rosleague Manor,
Letterfrack,
Co Galway
Chef/proprietor:
Patrick Foyle

500 ml	tomato juice	1 pint
one	cucumber	one
four	spring onions	four
six	small cloves of garlic	six
two	small green peppers	two
two 15 ml spoons	olive oil	2 tablesp
	salt, pepper	
	cold croûtons	
	chopped parsley	

Liquidise the tomato juice with the coarsely-chopped vegetables, the oil, salt and pepper. Do not over-blend, since the vegetables should be slightly chewy. Chill the soup well and serve it in bowls with croûtons and parsley.

Editor's note: Once you have tried the original recipe, experiment with variations: less garlic, perhaps, a strip of fresh green chilli, a spoonful of wine vinegar or lemon juice. . . It is ideal for picnics and diet lunches.

Gambas al ajillo

Andalucia, Rugby,
Warwickshire
Chef: Carlos Garcia

250 g	peeled prawns	8 oz
four 15 ml spoons	olive oil	4 tablesp
one	small, fresh green chilli	one
four	cloves of garlic	four
	salt, pepper	
two 15 ml spoons	white wine	2 tablesp
	parsley	

If you use fresh prawns, you will need almost four pints to get this quantity, peeled weight. If they are small, leave the heads on; otherwise, peel them completely.

Heat the oil over moderate heat in a shallow, heavy pan. Add the finely-chopped chilli and garlic, and fry until the garlic is pale brown. Season lightly with salt and pepper before adding the prawns and wine. Cook only long enough to heat the prawns thoroughly (unless of course they are raw), since prolonged cooking toughens them—the entire cooking process takes about two minutes. Remove the pan from the heat, add the chopped parsley, and serve on heated plates.

Editor's notes: bread or a little rice are needed to mop up the garlicky juices.

Save a whole prawn for each person if you are using fresh ones, cook them along with the others, and garnish each plate with a prawn in armour.

Julienne of veal in paprika and sour cream

The Grange,
London, W.C.2
Chef: Jurgens Boldt

570 g	tender veal	1¼ lb
three 15 ml spoons	flour	3 tablesp
one 15 ml spoon	sweet paprika	1 tablesp
	salt, pepper	
four	shallots	four
25–35 g	butter	1–1½ oz
150 ml	sour cream	6 fl oz

Choose a tender cut of veal, escalopes, for example. Cut the meat into very thin strips (about 1 cm wide, 3.5 cm long). Mix the flour, paprika, salt and pepper together in a flat dish, and toss the strips in the mixture until they are thoroughly coated. In a heavy frying-pan, sauté the finely-chopped shallots in the melted butter till tender and remove them. Then, very rapidly, sauté the veal until it is cooked and tender (this should take no more than two minutes—longer cooking will toughen the meat). Stir in the sour cream and shallots, heat the sauce quickly, let it bubble until it thickens. Serve very hot.

Chef's note: if any butter remains in the pan after the veal is cooked, pour it off before adding the sour cream.

Editor's note: rice or noodles go well with this dish.

Gooseberry ice-cream (12–16)

Old Parsonage,
Farrington Gurney,
Avon
Chef: Ann Oakes

1 kg	gooseberries	2 lb
250–300 g	granulated sugar	8–10 oz
15 g	gelatine	$\frac{1}{2}$ oz
five 15 ml spoons	water	5 tablesp
two	eggs	two
150 g	caster sugar	6 oz
250 ml	double cream	10 fl oz

Heat the gooseberries slowly with the granulated sugar and cook them until the fruit is tender. Puree the mixture through a sieve and leave it to cool.

Put one half of the puree in the deep freeze or in the freezing compartment of the refrigerator at its coldest setting. Melt the gelatine in the water, add it to the remaining puree and leave it to cool. Separate the eggs, and beat the yolks with 50 g (2 oz) of the caster sugar until they are thick. Gradually add the cooled gelatine and fold in the whipped cream. Refrigerate.

When the frozen puree is nearly firm (after about 1½ hours), stir the stiffly-whipped egg whites and remaining caster sugar into it. Fold this mixture into the refrigerated one, and put it in the deep freeze or freezing compartment. The ice-cream requires no further stirring.

Aubergines à la turque
or
Lettuce and green pea soup

Pork chops Debreczin, creamed potatoes,
buttered carrots, cabbage *or* mixed salad

Mince pies
or
Blackcurrant leaf sorbet

Nothing is more frustrating about a British summer than filling your mind
and refrigerator with moulded mousses and ice-cream only to find the night
of a party better suited to thick soup and cassoulet. The reverse situation is
even worse, since at least if both weather and food are cold you can warm up
your guests with double Scotches and whatever forms of central heating are
handy. But when a succession of chilly days have trapped you into preparing
a meal fit for Antarctic explorers, and the climate turns tropical at the last
minute, even the idea of such nourishing food can put people off.

Our menu hedges its bets with first courses which can be served hot or cold, a
main course equally good with standard vegetables or a salad, and a choice
between a delicate sorbet and little hot pies. Consult the barometer and cross
your fingers before going shopping, and all should be well. If you decide on
the hot meal, all three courses are cooked in the oven. Otherwise it has to be
on only long enough to cook the pork chops.

First course   Aubergines à la turque is both exotic and pretty, reminiscent of handsome
displays of stuffed vegetables in Middle-Eastern restaurants. We prefer it
cold, when the olive oil seems to come more into its own, but it is very tasty
hot too. The lettuce and green pea soup, on the other hand, has a delicate
'English garden' taste and appearance, whether served hot or cold. A possible
alternative is chilled saffron soup (page 15).

Main course   The Czechoslovakian pork chops are an interesting variation on the stuffed
cabbage theme, neatly packaged in cabbage leaves and cooked in a spicy
paprika sauce. The restaurant's suggested vegetables are highly appropriate
to a cool evening; on a warmer one, serve a salad instead, using as many
interesting ingredients as possible. If the weather seems too hot even to
consider baked pork chops, try the salmon pudding on page 14.

Sweet course	The sorbet, as well as having, in effect, one 'free' ingredient, has a subtle and unusual flavour which should keep your guests guessing. Mince pies are often short-changed at Christmas time when people are too full of the joys of the season or turkey and bread sauce to appreciate them properly. Apart from having novelty value in midsummer (we hope they don't match the weather too exactly), they offer the incentive to make enough mincemeat to cover your Christmas needs as well. Any of the strawberry or peach sweets in the book would be equally appealing endings to the meal.

Wine suggestions

Assuming summery weather, serve summery wines: rosé comes into its own at this time of year, and would match the aubergines and the pork chops adequately. Try Provencal, Anjou Cabernet or Portuguese. However, if neither the weather nor your guests seem to go with pink wines, serve a flavoury white with the aubergines (Italian whites are especially suited to oily food, so try Verdicchio or Soave), and full-bodied but not expensive red with the pork chops (a bourgeois claret or something from the South-West of France, or whichever branded blend you most enjoy).

First course	Rosé or Italian white
Main course	Rosé or full-bodied red

Aubergines à la turque

Langley Wood,
Redlynch, Hampshire
Chef/proprietors:
Mr & Mrs F. Pearce

two	medium-sized aubergines	two
	salt, pepper	
100 ml	olive oil	4 fl oz
two	medium-sized onions	two
one	clove of garlic	one
two	tomatoes	two
one	small green pepper	one
one 15 ml spoon	tomato puree	1 tablesp
25 g	fresh breadcrumbs	1 oz
half 5 ml spoon	curry powder	$\frac{1}{2}$ teasp
half 5 ml spoon	paprika	$\frac{1}{2}$ teasp
one 15 ml spoon	chopped almonds	1 tablesp
	chopped parsley	

Plunge the aubergines into boiling water and let them simmer for 12–15 minutes. Put them immediately into cold water. When they are cool enough to handle, halve them lengthwise, and scoop out the flesh with a spoon, being careful not to pierce the skins. Put the aubergine shells in an oven-proof dish, season them well, and pour a couple of spoonsful of oil into each. Bake them in a moderate oven (180°C, 350°F, mark 4) for about half an hour.

Meanwhile, soften the finely-chopped onions and garlic in a little water over medium heat. Mash the aubergine pulp separately, and when the onion is soft, add the pulp to it, with the peeled and sliced tomatoes, finely-chopped green pepper, tomato puree, breadcrumbs, spices and almonds. Stir the mixture and cook it very gently for half an hour (it burns easily). Fill the shells with the mixture and garnish the tops with chopped parsley.

The aubergines can be eaten hot or cold.

Editor's note: there are many versions of aubergine à la turque. Some involve salting the halved aubergines to remove the bitter liquid, and combining the flesh with the other raw ingredients before baking the stuffed aubergines slowly in a shallow bath of oil and water for an hour or so.

Lettuce and green pea soup

White Moss House,
Grasmere, Cumbria
Chef/proprietor:
Jean Butterworth

250 g	podded fresh peas	8 oz
500 ml	chicken stock (page 207)	1 pint
one	onion	one
50 g	butter	2 oz
one	medium-sized lettuce	one
one 15 ml spoon	flour	1 tablesp
one	sprig of mint	one
250 ml	milk	10 fl oz
	salt, pepper	

For garnishing

50 ml	double cream	2 fl oz
	chopped mint *or* mint leaves	

Cook the peas gently in a little water or butter till tender. Liquidise half of them with some of the stock, and sieve. Sweat the chopped onion in the butter till soft. Add the torn lettuce, and stir until it is buttery and considerably reduced in bulk. Stir in the flour and cook for a few minutes. Add the remaining stock and the mint and cook until the lettuce is soft. Remove the mint. Add half the milk and liquidise or sieve the mixture. Add the pea puree and the whole peas. Season. Add enough of the remaining milk to obtain a thin, creamy consistency. Reheat gently. Garnish with a swirl of double cream in each bowl, and either chopped mint or a mint leaf.

Chef's note: pineapple mint looks pretty, apple mint gives a delicate flavour.

Editor's notes: frozen peas are successful in this recipe, even minted ones when fresh mint is out of season. Try it also with two leeks instead of the onion. If the peas are old, you may wish to add a small quantity of sugar to the soup when seasoning it. Use the outside leaves of two lettuces if you need the hearts for a salad. If you wish to serve the soup chilled, it will require thinning with stock or milk.

Pork chops Debreczin

Ramblers of		
Corbridge, Corbridge,		
Northumberland		
Chef/proprietor:		
Heinrich Herrmann		

one	onion	one
50 ml	oil	2 fl oz
25 g	flour	1 oz
25 g	sweet paprika	1 oz
500 ml	chicken stock (page 207)	1 pint
	salt, pepper	
	lemon juice	
eight	large cabbage leaves	eight
four 175–225 g	pork chops	four 6–8 oz
	salt, pepper	
	oil	
	marjoram	
50 ml	single cream	2 fl oz

For garnishing	parsley	
	skinned tomatoes *or* red pepper	

To make the sauce, cook the finely-chopped onion in the oil until it is transparent. Add the flour and paprika to make a roux (page 206). Gradually add the stock, stirring the mixture until it is smooth, and bring it to the boil. Season with salt, pepper and a little lemon juice.

Cut out the thick end of the stem of the cabbage leaves and blanch them in boiling water. Season the chops with salt and pepper and fry them gently in oil, turning once, until they are light brown on both sides. Sprinkle the chops with a little marjoram and wrap them in the cabbage leaves, securing them with a toothpick.

Put the chops in a shallow oven-proof casserole and pour over the paprika sauce. Cook them, covered, in a moderate oven (190°C, 375°F, mark 5) for 35–40 minutes. Transfer the chops to a hot serving plate, add the cream to the gravy in the casserole and pour it over the chops.

Garnish with fresh parsley and quartered skinned tomatoes or raw sliced red pepper.

Chef's note: serve the chops with creamed potatoes, buttered carrots and any remaining cabbage.

Editor's note: this recipe is a close relative of the stuffed cabbage rolls found all over Eastern Europe. They generally have a stuffing of minced pork or meat, and are cooked in a tomato or paprika sauce like this one.

Mince pies

Ballymaloe House,
Shanagarry, Co Cork
Chef/proprietor:
Myrtle Allen

one	cooking apple	one
one	lemon	one
250 g	stoned raisins	8 oz
90 g	currants	3½ oz
125 g	sultanas	5 oz
75 g	candied peel	3 oz
450 g	moist brown sugar	15 oz
315 g	shredded suet	10½ oz
50 ml	whiskey	2 fl oz
one 15 ml spoon	orange marmalade	1 tablesp
250 g	puff or flaky pastry (page 203)	8 oz
	beaten egg	

These ingredients will make about 1.5 kg (3 lb) of mincemeat. You will need about 250 g (8 oz) to fill twelve pies.

Bake the apple in a moderate oven (180°C, 350°F, mark 4) for 15 minutes. Meanwhile, mix the grated lemon rind and the juice with the other mincemeat ingredients, added one at a time. When the apple is cooked, skin and core it and mix the flesh thoroughly into the mincemeat. Pot it, cover securely, and allow it to mature for at least two weeks.

Roll out the pastry *very* thinly and cut it into 24 rounds. Line individual 6-cm (2½-inch) pie tins or a one-dozen bun-tin with half the pastry rounds and put a heaped teaspoon of the mincemeat in the centre of each one. Wet the edges and press on the remaining lids. Cut a slit in the middle of the lids and brush them with beaten egg. Bake them in a hot oven (200°C, 400°F, mark 6) for 20 minutes.

Serve hot or cold, with whipped cream if you wish, or whiskey and sugar.

Chef's note: after cutting the slit in the pastry lids, the pies can be left in the refrigerator for a few days if necessary before baking.

Editor's note: if you like mincemeat more than pastry, cut the lids into fancy little shapes (for example, stars).

Blackcurrant leaf sorbet (6)

Parkend Restaurant,
Caldbeck, Cumbria
Chef: Joyce Arnesen

four dozen	young blackcurrant leaves	four dozen
375 g	sugar	12 oz
500 ml	water	1 pint
two	lemons	two
two	egg whites	two

Choose young, perfect leaves as far as possible, and wash them carefully.
Make a sugar syrup by dissolving the sugar in the water and boiling it for four
minutes. Remove it from the heat, add the leaves, cover the pan, and allow
them to infuse for 30 minutes.

Strain the liquid into a freezing container, add the juice of the lemons and a
very little finely-grated rind, and leave the mixture to cool. Freeze it at the
coldest setting, occasionally stirring it by scraping the frozen sides to the
middle. When it is fairly well frozen, but not solid, whisk the egg whites until
they are firm (with an electric whisk if possible) and while continuing to
whisk, add spoonsful of the frozen mixture, until all has been combined into
a frothy white mass. Return it to the freezer for several hours. Serve the
sorbet in pretty glass dishes decorated with blackcurrant leaves.

Chef's note: another delicious sorbet can be made in the same way,
substituting a grapefruit for one lemon, and steeping two fresh heads of
elderflowers in the syrup instead of the blackcurrant leaves.

Fresh tomato and mint soup
or
Baked sardines

Chicken with tremalki sauce, hot cucumber and
cauliflower *or* mushroom salad *or* raw spinach salad

Fresh fruit salad with melon
or
Orange yoghourt jelly

Slimming is hard work. Partly it is the self-discipline needed, with all the joyous overtones of iron tonics, cold baths, early nights and other things declared to be 'good for you'. But mainly it is the boredom inspired by the virtuous recipes designed to make sylphs of slow-coaches. They seem to deal not so much in real food (let alone good food) as in substitute food: stock cubes, skimmed milk powder, dried onions. . . Few books written for dieters are imaginative enough to suggest new eating patterns which even a gourmet with a galloping waistline can follow with enthusiasm. Michel Guérard, who invented (or defined) *cuisine minceur*, is an outstanding cook who is aware that above all a dieter needs to feel satisfied by a meal. If repletion cannot come from sheer bulk and calorific richness, it must come from other kinds of satisfaction, whether physical or purely aesthetic. To say nothing of a little conspicuous self-indulgence: oysters and caviare are ideal slimming foods for some just because they *are* exotic and expensive. And if you open your own oysters you use up almost as many calories as you would chewing a dozen sticks of celery.

When entertaining, you will want to put on the table a meal which will please your guests without throwing your diet to the winds. Our suggested menu is a satisfying one because all the ingredients are real food, and the flavours are strong and clear, with garlic, herbs and fresh fruit shining forth uncluttered by cream, butter and flour.

First course

The chilled tomato and mint soup is gently refreshing and very easy to make. It looks elegant in individual white bowls with the mint (and sour cream if you're slipping) garnish. If you prefer a hot first course, serve the sardines in their foil packages. They taste quite strongly pickled, and for a slightly blander version you might try replacing the vinegar with lemon juice. Wine would not be appropriate with either of these dishes. For a winter menu, turnip soup (page 4) would make a light and tasty alternative.

66

Main course

The spectacular plum-and-garlic sauce transforms even battery chickens into something tasty. For total slimming virtue, bake the breasts in foil and remove the skin before serving them with the sauce. Use fresh plums, if you prefer: about a pound, poached with 100 g (4 oz) sugar. Another version of this Caucasian sauce (sometimes called tkemali) exchanges the plums and parsley for sour prunes and fresh coriander. We suggest cauliflower instead of a starchy vegetable as a mopper-up of the sauce, and hot cucumber (page 195) for some low-calorie prettiness. Otherwise a salad (mushroom on page 199 or a raw spinach one) would be a suitable accompaniment. With such highly-seasoned food, serve a cheap wine, or dry cider, which might stand up to the flavours moderately well and which is relatively low-calorie.

Sweet course

If you decide to serve a fruit salad, think of all the money you are saving on cream and liqueurs and buy some exotic fruits as well as the run-of-the-mill ones. If several soft fruits are in season, you might like to make, say, an all-red salad with raspberries, strawberries, redcurrants and cherries, served in half melons and garnished with passion-fruit seeds. Or a golden one with mango, plums, peaches and apricots. A whole pineapple makes a lovely container for fruit, as does a water-melon, and one thinly-sliced kiwi fruit adds lacy decoration. If you need juice, either make a stock syrup (page 48), or use a few spoonsful of orange juice, or top the fruit with a raspberry puree (page 107). And remember that yoghourt is lower-calorie than double cream. The orange and yoghourt jelly is a light and simple sweet if you prefer something made up. A bowl of perfect fruit is the simplest sweet of all.

Wine suggestion

Main course

Red or white ordinaire or dry cider

Fresh tomato and mint soup

Milton Ernest Hall,
Milton Ernest,
Bedfordshire
Chef: Robert Andrews

1 kg	tomatoes	2 lb
250 ml	water	10 fl oz
	salt, pepper	
4–5	sprigs of mint	4–5
one 5 ml spoon	sugar	1 teasp
two 15 ml spoons	boiling water	2 tablesp

Wash and chop the tomatoes and simmer them in the water, with a little salt and pepper, until they are soft. Liquidise and sieve the mixture, and allow it to cool. Chop the mint leaves with the sugar, pour on the boiling water, add this to the tomato puree, and check the seasoning. Serve the soup chilled, in chilled bowls.

Editor's note: for dieters, a mint-leaf garnish is called for. For others, a blob of sour cream under the mint leaf looks pretty and tastes nice.

Baked sardines

Don Pasquale,
Gloucester,
Gloucestershire
Chef: Philip Schettini

750 g–1 kg	fresh sardines	1½–2 lb
250 ml	wine vinegar	10 fl oz
half	lemon	half
one 5 ml spoon	ground ginger	1 teasp
two	cloves of garlic, finely-chopped two	
one 5 ml spoon	Angostura bitters	1 teasp
	salt, pepper	

You should have 2–5 sardines per person, depending on their size. Cut off the heads, gut, clean and scale them. Combine the remaining ingredients, and marinate the fish overnight, turning them once.

Divide the sardines among four pieces of foil, and top with a tablespoonful of the marinade. Seal the foil and bake the packages in a moderate oven (180°C, 350°F, mark 4) for 20–30 minutes.

Chicken with tremalki sauce

Royal Exchange
Theatre Restaurant,
Manchester
Chef: Roy Pegram

four	chicken breasts	four
	flour	
	salt, pepper	
	oil, butter	

For the sauce

one 567 g tin	red plums	one 1 lb 4 oz tin
six	large cloves of garlic	six
one	handful of parsley	one

Prepare the chicken breasts, removing bones and skin if you wish. Flour them lightly and season with salt and pepper.

Drain the fruit and remove the stones. Liquidise the plums along with the coarsely-chopped garlic and the parsley heads removed from the stems. Blend until the parsley is quite fine. Warm the sauce very gently, and do not boil it, or the bright pink colour will darken.

Fry the chicken in oil and butter until cooked, and serve with a little of the sauce poured over and the rest in a sauce-boat.

Orange yoghourt jelly

300 ml	fresh orange juice	12 fl oz
15 g	gelatine	$\frac{1}{2}$ oz
two 15 ml spoons	hot water	2 tablesp
125 ml	plain yoghourt	5 fl oz

For decoration

	orange slices	

You will need three or four large, juicy oranges to give the required amount of juice. Dissolve the gelatine in the hot water, heating it further if necessary. Liquidise the orange juice, yoghourt and gelatine. Pour the mixture into a 500-ml (one-pint) mould or individual dishes, and refrigerate it until set. Turn out the mould and decorate it with orange slices.

Editor's note: unless the oranges are very sweet, you may wish to add a little sugar or sweetener. Finely-grated rind would sharpen the orange flavour.

Iced plum soup
or
Creamy baked tomatoes

Escalope de veau au citron, broad beans *or*
steamed courgettes, salad

Frozen praline soufflé
or
Chocolate and praline cream

Summer entertaining can be a joy, with relaxed, balmy evenings and burgeoning gardens. On the other hand, it is all too easy to find the day of the party invaded by the need to take children swimming, or show visitors the local sights, or even lie in the sun and compose yourself. And of course working cooks face the perennial problem of putting a good meal on the table without slipping under it themselves through sheer exhaustion. This dinner menu is flexible enough to take account of a turn for the worse in the weather. The soup and the sweets can be prepared ahead; the tomatoes and the veal both take only a few minutes to prepare and cook.

First course

If plums are in season, the iced plum soup makes an unusual and colourful start to the meal. It is refreshing, not over-sweet, and nicely peppery. The tomatoes baked in cream are gentler and more conventional and would be comforting on a cool or wet night. If you prefer to husband your cream allowance till later in the meal, consider instead the aubergines à la turque (page 61) or whiting in cucumber shells (page 51).

Main course

The veal escalopes are very simply prepared, so good veal is essential. Since both first and last courses are creamy, it seems wise to serve only a green vegetable and salad with the main course. If you dislike last-minute frying, you may prefer a casserole (jugged beef with orange on page 107, for example).

Sweet course

The summer fruit has appeared at the beginning of the meal, and so at the end there is a choice of rich praline sweets. The frozen soufflé is marginally less calorific and uses unblanched almonds for the praline. The other adds chocolate and orange to the coffee and praline to make a sinful temptation, best dispensed in *very* small dishes. If either sweet sounds too decadent to be contemplated, try one of the peach recipes in the book if you have served tomatoes as a first course, and perhaps blackcurrant leaf sorbet (page 65) if you started with the plum soup.

Wine suggestions

If circumstances encourage drinks in the garden, serve something long and cool as an aperitif so that constant refills are not a problem: a light white wine, gin and tonic, or any appropriate cocktail. Plum soup and wine do nothing for each other, and you may well decide to serve a white wine throughout—nothing too ambitious since the lemon with the veal will not flatter a good wine either. Mosel wines make appealing summer drinking and, as they are relatively low in alcohol, they can be swigged with greater freedom than is possible with stronger wines. The cost may well inhibit your thirst, but at the cheaper end of the scale there are many enjoyable wines from, for example, Bernkastel and Piesport. Further up market there are fine wines from those same areas and many others too: Graacher Himmelreich or Wehlener Sonnenuhr, say. White burgundy or Alsace wines would be just as enjoyable. Creamy chocolate and coffee puddings need no wine, but a *digestif* may be welcome afterwards. If your duty-free souvenirs have included an eau-de-vie, serve it now, and the heavy fragrance of framboise or poire Williams will help to bring summer indoors.

Main course	Mosel or other light white wine
Digestif	Eau-de-vie

Iced plum soup (6)

Kinchs, Chesterton, Oxfordshire Chef/proprietor: Christopher Greatorex			
	500 g	dark sour plums (not Victoria)	1 lb
	75 g	sugar	3 oz
	one 5 ml spoon	cinnamon	1 teasp
	one 5 ml spoon	salt	1 teasp
	$\frac{1}{4}$ of a 5 ml spoon	white pepper	$\frac{1}{4}$ teasp
	375 ml	red wine	15 fl oz
	125 ml	double cream	5 fl oz
	one	lemon	one
For garnishing	250 ml	sour cream	10 fl oz
	one 5 ml spoon	brandy (optional)	1 teasp

Set aside three plums for garnishing. Simmer the remaining plums with the sugar, cinnamon, salt, pepper and half the wine, until the liquor has reduced by a quarter. Remove the stones and puree the plums in the liquidiser or through a sieve.

71

Mix the remaining wine with the double cream, the lemon zest and the juice of half the lemon, and heat it gently.

Add it to the plum puree, allow the mixture to cool, and chill it for at least one hour.

Whisk the sour cream (saving a few spoonsful for garnishing, if you wish) and stir it thoroughly into the soup. If you are adding brandy, stir it in now.

Serve the soup in individual bowls, topped with sour cream, a pinch of cinnamon and a slice of fresh plum.

Chef's note: if commercial sour cream is not available, make your own by adding lemon juice to double or whipping cream and allowing it to stand overnight in a cool (but not chilled) place.

Creamy baked tomatoes

Lower Brook House,
Blockley,
Gloucestershire
Chef/proprietors:
Robert & Gill
Greenstock

For garnishing

eight	firm tomatoes	eight
50 g	grated Parmesan	2 oz
two 5 ml spoons	fresh basil (or half quantity dried)	2 teasp
	salt, pepper	
65 ml	double cream	$2\frac{1}{2}$ fl oz
65 ml	single cream	$2\frac{1}{2}$ fl oz
	chopped parsley	

Blanch and peel the tomatoes and slice them thickly. Put them in an oven-proof dish, or four individual dishes, and sprinkle each layer with the cheese, basil and seasonings. Spoon the combined double and single cream over the tomatoes. Put the dish(es) on a baking tray and bake in a moderately hot oven (190°C, 375°F, mark 5) for 15–20 minutes. Serve hot, sprinkled with chopped parsley and accompanied by hot, crusty rolls.

Editor's note: The Greenstocks serve this dish as a starter, but it could be served as an accompaniment to cold meats or plain roasts if you reduced the cream content.

Escalope de veau au citron

Bistro Byron,
Eastbourne,
East Sussex
Chef/proprietor:
Simon Scrutton

four	large veal escalopes	four
	salt, pepper	
50 g	butter	2 oz
one	sprig of fresh rosemary	one
one	lemon	one

Beat the escalopes until they are very thin. Season them with salt and pepper. Melt half the butter over low heat in a large frying-pan, put in the veal, sprinkle it with the rosemary spikes and the juice from the ends of the lemon (keep the middle slices to decorate the finished dish). As soon as the veal becomes white (after about two minutes) turn it and cook it for a further two minutes on the other side, still over moderately low heat so that it does not become crisp. Remove the meat to a heated serving dish and keep it hot in a slow oven (150°C, 300°F, mark 2).

Add the remaining butter to the frying-pan and scrape up the residue from the bottom of the pan to form a brown sauce. Pour this over the veal and serve it at once, decorated with the reserved lemon slices.

Chef's note: if you do not like rosemary very much, strain it off at the last minute. Use four small pinches of dried if fresh is not available.

Frozen praline soufflé

Lawrence Restaurant,
Brighton, East Sussex
Chef/proprietor:
Susan Campion

75 g	unblanched almonds	3 oz
75 g	granulated sugar	3 oz
250 ml	double or whipping cream	10 fl oz
two 15 ml spoons	Tia Maria	2 tablesp
two	egg whites	two

For decoration

	whipped cream	
	toasted split almonds	

Put the almonds and sugar in a small heavy saucepan and melt the sugar over moderate heat. When the sugar begins to caramelise, stir it with a wooden spoon until all the almonds are coated with the golden brown mixture. Turn the mixture onto a lightly-oiled tin and allow it to cool. When it is cold, grind it to a powder in a liquidiser or coffee mill, or under plastic wrap with a rolling-pin.

Whip the cream with the liqueur until it holds its shape and fold in the praline powder and the stiffly-beaten egg whites. Pour the mixture into individual ramekins and freeze it for at least four hours. Just before serving, cover each soufflé with whipped cream and toasted split almonds.

Chocolate and praline cream (6)

Count House, St Just
in Penwith, Cornwall
Chef/proprietor:
Ann Long

75 g	caster sugar	3 oz
75 g	blanched almonds	3 oz
	freshly-made coffee	
one	orange	one
350 g	Bournville chocolate	12 oz
75 g	butter	3 oz
250 ml	double cream	10 fl oz

To make the praline, melt the sugar over a low heat until it is amber-coloured, and add the almonds, stirring until the mixture is nut brown. Pour the mixture onto an oiled slab and when it is hard crush it with a rolling-pin.

Add enough freshly-made coffee to the juice and grated orange rind to make up 125 ml (5 fl oz) of liquid, and heat this with the melted chocolate, in a double-boiler (page 213), until the mixture has the consistency of thick cream. Remove the pan from the heat and beat in the butter a little at a time. Allow it to cool, then stir in the crushed praline, and fold in the lightly-beaten cream. Pour the mixture into one large or six individual pots or glasses, and leave it to set. Decorate with cream, orange or chocolate, if you wish.

Buttered crab
or
Stilton and spring onion wholemeal flan

Vineyard quail, broad beans *or* haricots verts,
new *or* duchesse potatoes

Stilton mousse *or* cheese

Peach and hazelnut galette

Contrary to widely-held belief, fine wine and good food are not soul mates. While there is no denying that a glass of almost any drinkable wine will enhance a lowly snack, and a glass of something special will transform even an already exquisite dish, it is equally true that if you start by thinking of the wine as of prime importance, it is very difficult to find dishes which will do it justice. If you are a dedicated wine-lover rather than a keen cook-hostess-with-vinous-aspirations, your instinct will be to serve the simplest possible food: lightly-seasoned roasts and grills, plainly-poached fish, good but not exuberant cheeses. . . A glance through the menu introductions in this book will soon convince you of the problem: 'not worth a decent wine because of the vinegar, or garlic, or mustard, or curry. . .' And that leaves out the special-effects department: eggs can infect a white wine with sulphurous overtones, smoked fish can make a good wine taste of bad pennies, and chocolate can kill a dessert wine stone dead. If you were tempted to say, when told that the French now drink Sauternes with smoked fish and with foie gras, 'however did they think of trying it?', the answer is now clear: it was sheer desperation. But it works.

The other hurdle to be crossed, if your guests are serious students or lovers of wine, is the theme. There should be a pattern of sorts to the wine. With a Loire dinner, for example, you could serve Loire wines throughout, in all three colours and a variety of sweetnesses if you wish. If you can lay hands on white and red wines from the same area, Chassagne-Montrachet, say, that would make an interesting pattern. You might offer white and red of the same vintage, for many white burgundies or German wines age almost as well as the reds. On the other hand, the theme may simply be, 'Things I could find at a price I could afford: I pray they are drinkable.' In any event, the rule is to serve young before old, and the less good before the better if you offer more than one red wine. We have assumed that you will serve both cheese and a pudding at this meal, simply because that allows the red wines to be enjoyed at leisure without your being deprived of a dessert wine. If you have one very good bottle of claret, arrange to serve it with the cheese, when it will show to greatest advantage.

Our suggested menu is not ideal, but it is delicious, and none of the food will do less than justice to your wine. (You may wish to skip the cheese course entirely if you serve the flan as first course.)

First course

Crab has a gently buttery taste, subtly laced with seaweed, which suggests a mellow white wine rather than a bone dry one: the finest burgundy you can afford, a *grand-cru* Chablis, or a good German Riesling. With the Stilton quiche, an Alsace wine or good Loire Sauvignon would be appropriate, or even a light red (Bourgeuil or Chinon from the Loire, or a Beaujolais). Other possible first courses to consider are Camembert frit (page 101), bourekakia (page 94), fish pâté (page 134) or tenerelli (page 40).

Main course

Since the Vineyard quail are served with a sauce, albeit a gentle one, a full red wine rather than a 'stalky' one would be the best accompaniment. This turns one towards burgundy—and once again, the best you can afford—or a fine Hermitage. If claret is your tipple, choose a St Emilion rather than a Médoc. Otherwise, an Italian Barolo could fill the bill. The quail can be prepared ahead of time and roasted at the last minute. Serve crisp, lightly-buttered beans with them, and duchesse potatoes or new potatoes in their skins. Alternative main course might be Mr Reynaud's juniper hare (page 89) or breast of veal with apple and walnut stuffing (page 117).

Cheese course

The wisest course is to stick to good cheese, whether farmhouse Cheddar, creamy Brie or perfect Stilton (if you did not choose the quiche as first course), served with French bread and butter, or biscuits. But if you would like something more original, try the Stilton mousse, and on this occasion forget the cucumber garnish. Once again, serve bread or biscuits. Either bring out your finest red wine now, or, if it was already started with the main course, finish it off with the cheese or mousse: a good claret, either a Pomerol or a St Julien (the first softer and fuller than the second), or a better burgundy than your first bottle. Unless you are very knowledgeable, this is the time to consult a good wine-merchant. It would be interesting, for example, to serve two vintages of the same wine but you may need advice to get the order of serving right.

Sweet course

The galette is an elegant, undemanding sweet, but in the context of a wine-lovers' banquet, the peaches must be very ripe and sweet. If you have any doubts, poach them briefly in stock syrup (page 48)—or use strawberries instead, as the restaurant suggests. Bring out your favourite dessert wine now: Sauternes or Barsac, Monbazillac, a sweet Vouvray or Quarts de Chaume (appropriate if you have served other Loire wines previously) or a sweet Muscat. A compote of fruit (page 48) or strawberry shortbread (page 85) are other possible sweets.

Note

This meal is truly a banquet, to be planned—and saved for—long ahead, to be savoured in leisurely fashion in the company of like-minded friends. If it strikes you as gross, cut out one course, and restrict the wines to what you think appropriate. If you discard the sweet course, it would be pleasant to end the evening with a glass of port, either as well as, or instead of, the wine with the cheese. A good tawny is delicious, and easy to handle. If you opt for vintage and have to buy it rather than take it out of your own cellar, you could ask your wine merchant to decant it at the appropriate time.

Wine suggestions

Aperitif

Dry white wine, or the same as with the first course

First course

With the crab, fine French or German white
With the quiche, Alsace or Loire white or light red

Main course

Burgundy, St Emilion, Hermitage or Barolo

Cheese course

Claret or better version of main-course wine

Sweet course

Any good dessert wine

Buttered crab

Tate Gallery,
London, S.W.1
Chef: Michael Driver

one	medium-sized cooked crab *or*	one
250 g	frozen crab meat	8 oz
one	anchovy fillet	one
one	pinch of nutmeg	one
	salt, pepper	
two 15 ml spoons	melted butter	2 tablesp
	clarified butter (page 213)	

If you have to use frozen crab, be sure that you get good-quality meat, rather than a dressed version containing rusk. Flake the crab meat, add the mashed anchovy fillet, the seasonings, and the melted butter, and mix the ingredients thoroughly together. Put the mixture in one or more pots and allow it to cool. Cover the top with clarified butter and store in a cool place.

Editor's note: the restaurant now serves Theodora Fitzgibbon's version of this recipe, which includes white wine and stock.

Stilton and spring onion wholemeal flan (6)

Food for Thought,
Cheltenham,
Gloucestershire
Chef/proprietors:
Joanna Jane Mahon &
Christopher Wickens

175 g	wholemeal flour	6 oz
75 g	butter	3 oz
50–100 ml	water (approx)	2–4 fl oz
two	bunches of spring onions	two
25 g	butter	1 oz
two	eggs	two
125 ml	milk	5 fl oz
	salt, pepper	
125 g	Stilton	4 oz

Make shortcrust pastry (page 202) and line a 20.5–23 cm (8–9 inch) flan ring with it. Chill the pastry. Chop the spring onions, including the tops, leaving six whole for decoration, and sauté them all in the butter for 3–4 minutes. Beat the eggs with the milk and seasoning. Add the crumbled Stilton and the chopped spring onions. Pour this mixture into the flan case and arrange the remaining whole spring onions like the spokes of a wheel on top. Bake in a hot oven (200°C, 400°F, mark 6) for 25 minutes. Serve the flan hot or cold.

Vineyard quail

Vineyard,
Northampton,
Northamptonshire
Chef/proprietor:
Maggie Angeloglou

four 200–250 g	quail or	four 6–8 oz
eight 125 g	quail	eight 4 oz
500 g	green grapes (seedless)	1 lb
125 g	hazelnuts	4 oz
four	slices of white bread	four
375 ml	chicken stock	15 fl oz
one	large onion	one
	butter	
half	lemon	half
	salt, pepper	
4–8	vine-leaves	4–8
4–8	rashers of streaky bacon	4–8
25 g	butter	1 oz
25 g	flour	1 oz
125 ml	medium-sweet sherry	5 fl oz

Allow one quail per person if you find the larger size, two if the smaller. Wipe them with a damp cloth. Remove the grape pips if necessary; chop the nuts.

Moisten the bread in a little of the chicken stock. Sauté half the finely-chopped onion in a little butter and combine it with half the grapes, the nuts and the bread. Add the grated rind from the half lemon, and season with salt and pepper. Stuff the mixture into the cavities of the quail and skewer or sew up the opening.

If the vine-leaves are in brine, rinse them to remove excess salt. Cover each quail breast with a vine-leaf and a rasher of bacon, skewered in place with a toothpick. Roast them, uncovered, in a hot oven (220°C, 425°F, mark 7) for about 25–30 minutes until cooked, basting frequently with the cooking juices to prevent the birds drying out.

To make the sauce, sauté the remaining finely-chopped onion in the butter, gradually add the flour, and stir for a minute or two. Add the chicken stock, the sherry and the remaining grapes, and stir until the sauce thickens.

Serve the quail with a little of the sauce poured over them, and the remainder in a sauce-boat, unless your guests are Henry VIIIs at heart, in which case serve finger-bowls, and all the sauce separately.

Stilton mousse (8)

Clifton Hotel, Nairn, Highland
Chef/proprietor:
J. Gordon Macintyre

25 g	butter	1 oz
25 g	flour	1 oz
250 ml	milk	10 fl oz
175 g	Stilton	6 oz
one 15 ml spoon	aspic powder	1 tablesp
200 ml	boiling water	8 fl oz
two	eggs	two
	black pepper	
100 ml	double cream	4 fl oz
For garnishing	cucumber slices	
	whipped cream	
	chopped parsley	

Make a thick béchamel sauce (page 209), using the quantities of butter, flour and milk given, and allow it to cool. Crumble the Stilton. Dissolve the aspic powder in the boiling water. Liquidise the aspic and crumbled cheese. Add the sauce to the Stilton and aspic in the liquidiser.

Separate the eggs. Add the egg yolks and pepper to the cheese mixture, liquidise it, and allow it to cool completely.

Beat the cream and the egg whites in separate bowls until they are stiff, and fold them into the mixture. Pour it into a medium-sized dish or eight individual ramekins and refrigerate till set. Garnish with cucumber slices, whipped cream, and chopped parsley.

Chef's notes: we use Roquefort, Cheshire Blue, and Brie in the same way—'runaway' Brie is remarkably good. The mousse freezes well.

Peach and hazelnut galette (6)

Limpets Restaurant,
Lymington,
Hampshire
Chef/proprietor:
Anthea Craig

90 g	flour	3½ oz
65 g	softened butter	2½ oz
25 g	caster sugar	1 oz
50 g	chopped, roasted hazelnuts	2 oz

four	ripe peaches	four
200–250 ml	double cream	8–10 fl oz
50 g	caster sugar	2 oz
	brandy (optional)	

Grease two 18-cm (7-inch) shallow round baking-tins, and pre-heat the oven to 190°C (375°F, mark 5).

Mix the flour, butter, sugar and hazelnuts in a bowl and knead the mixture until it forms a ball. Divide it in two and roll each half out to roughly 7 inches in diameter, using the tins as a guide. Slide them into the tins and bake them for 10–15 minutes. (Check after ten minutes, since they scorch quickly.) Allow them to cool in the tins, but mark one round into six sections while it is still warm, for ease in serving.

Peel and slice the peaches, and reserve a few slices for decoration. Lightly whip the cream and sugar, and add a little brandy if you wish. Fold the peaches into the cream. Put the uncut round on a serving plate, pile on the peaches and cream, top with the sectioned round, decorate it with the reserved peaches, and serve immediately.

Chef's notes: strawberries and Cointreau may be used instead of peaches and brandy. The biscuit rounds will keep for a day or two in an airtight tin.

Truite aux aromates
or
Devilled kidneys

Loin of pork in yoghourt with ginger and lime, carrots with orange and coriander, stir-fried mushrooms and rice *or* French beans and new potatoes

Strawberry shortbread
or
Grapefruit and elderflower sorbet

For many people still, a real meal involves a roast joint; for others, the very idea speaks of grey meat and grandmothers. The centre-piece of this meal, as well suited to a festive Sunday lunch as to evening entertaining, should keep everyone happy, since it is a loin of pork made tender and fragrant by imaginative treatment. To depart even further from weekend routine we suggest herbed trout or spiced kidneys as first courses, and to finish, a novel treatment of the strawberry shortcake theme. This is by no means an inexpensive meal, but it is certainly an interesting one, worthy of your more sophisticated friends, especially those who love to cook. Since the pork loin is marinated for a day at least, and the first courses are quick and easy to prepare, you are left with undivided attention for the shortbread, which should not be assembled too far ahead of time in case it loses its crispness.

First course

Now that trout are as often bought from farms as fished from rivers, it is useful to have a recipe like this one which enhances their flavour with fresh herbs, butter and wine, yet takes very little effort to prepare. The kidneys are more highly-seasoned, but still undemanding. If you know your guests' tastes well, serve them grilled for a rather shorter time, so that they are still pink in the middle: all 'raw meat' flavour vanishes under the tangy coating. For a cooler start to the meal, in all senses, serve one of the chilled soups described elsewhere in the book.

Main course

The pork is as good cold as hot, which makes it tempting to keep some back for salads and sandwiches. The texture is very tender and moist, the flavour extremely subtle, with the lime and ginger complementing the flavour of the pork most refreshingly. Since the effect is faintly oriental, echo the theme in the vegetables: carrots with coriander and orange (page 195), stir-fried mushrooms (page 192) and rice, perhaps. For a more traditional meal, choose the French beans and potatoes.

Sweet course

Strawberry shortbread is a well-known sweet, but the Pool Court version adds ground almonds to the shortbread and orange to the cream, and makes an elegantly-layered tower of the result. For a lighter sweet, try the grapefruit and elderflower sorbet (see the footnote to blackcurrant leaf sorbet on page 65). And if neither appeals, consult the index under 'strawberry' or 'peach'.

Wine suggestions

You may wish to serve the same wine throughout the meal, and pork accommodates either red or white. With the trout as first course, you might consider Gewürztraminer, which is spicy enough to stand up to oriental food, and delicious enough to drink through two courses without boredom. Otherwise, something from the Loire would suit, perhaps a Pouilly Fumé or Sancerre. If the devilled kidneys are your choice for first course, then red wine would carry you through two courses. It should not be a weighty wine, nor yet a very expensive one, so choose a Beaujolais or Provence red (Bandol, say) or an Italian Bardolino which is light and faintly almondy. If you prefer to serve two different wines, a light white, rather dry, would be best with the trout (Muscadet, perhaps) with a Sauvignon or Sancerre afterwards. For the kidneys, carry over the Fino from the aperitif stage, or a glass of the favourite family plonk, followed by one of the better reds suggested above with the pork. The strawberry shortcake would flatter a good sweet wine (Sauternes, Monbazillac, or sweet Vouvray, or a German Beerenauslese).

First course

With the trout, a light dry white wine
With the kidneys, Fino or ordinaire

Main course

Gewürztraminer or Loire white or Beaujolais, Provencal or light Italian red

Sweet course

Dessert wine (French or German)

Truite aux aromates

Singing Chef,	**50 g**	**butter**	**2 oz**
Badwell Ash, Suffolk		**thyme**	
Chef/proprietor:	**one**	**bay leaf**	**one**
Kenneth Toyé		**chopped fresh parsley**	
	four 250 g	**fresh trout**	**four 8 oz**
	four 15 ml spoons	**flour**	**4 tablesp**
		salt, pepper	
	four	**bunches of fresh herbs (thyme, bay leaf, parsley)**	**four**
		oil	
		butter	
For the sauce	**four 15 ml spoons**	**dry white wine**	**4 tablesp**
	50 g	**butter**	**2 oz**
		chopped parsley	
For garnishing	**four**	**sprigs of fresh parsley**	**four**

Mix the butter with the finely-chopped thyme, bay leaf and parsley, roll it up in plastic wrap, and refrigerate until firm.

Clean the trout and roll them in the flour, seasoned with salt and pepper. Put the fresh herbs inside the fish. Heat the oil and butter in a large heavy pan and when it sizzles, lightly fry the trout for about four minutes on each side. Place the fish on a serving dish and keep them warm.

Moisten the pan with the wine. Add the butter and sprinkle the chopped parsley onto the juices. Pour this light herby sauce over the trout. Slice the herb butter into pats and put one on each fish with a sprig of parsley.

Chef's note: to appreciate the herbs do not serve the trout with lemon.

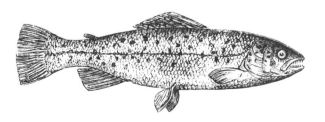

Devilled kidneys

Food for Thought,
Cheltenham,
Gloucestershire
Chef/proprietors:
Joanna Jane Mahon &
Christopher Wickens

six	lambs' kidneys	six
one 15 ml spoon	tomato sauce	1 tablesp
one 5 ml spoon	Worcestershire sauce	1 teasp
half 5 ml spoon	dry mustard	$\frac{1}{2}$ teasp
25 g	soft butter	1 oz
one 5 ml spoon	chutney	1 teasp
two 5 ml spoons	lemon juice	2 teasp
half 5 ml spoon	salt	$\frac{1}{2}$ teasp
	pepper	

Skin the kidneys, cut each in half, and remove the core. Put them in a greased baking-dish or the bottom half of a grill-pan. Mix together all the other ingredients, spread the resultant sauce over the kidneys, and grill them under moderate heat for 8–10 minutes.

Editor's note: we suggest serving the devilled kidneys on toast or a croûte.

Miller Howe,
Windermere, Cumbria
Chef/proprietor:
John Tovey

one	loin of pork, boned	one
175 ml	plain yoghourt	6 fl oz
two	limes (approx)	two
3–4	slices of fresh root ginger	3–4

Ask your butcher to remove the skin and bone the loin. Open it up and spread it generously with yoghourt and then sprinkle it to taste with the juice and grated rind of the limes, and the grated or finely-chopped ginger. Leave it to marinate for 24 hours. Roll it up and tie it tightly. Spread the joint with more yoghourt, lime and ginger and roast it, uncovered, in a moderate oven (180°C, 350°F, mark 4) for about 45 minutes per pound, basting it frequently. (With an electric cooker you may wish to cover the meat loosely with foil halfway through the cooking period.)

Strawberry shortbread (6–8)

Pool Court Restaurant,
Pool-in-Wharfedale,
West Yorkshire
Patisserie chef:
Melvin Barry Jordan

500 g	strawberries	1 lb
360 g	butter	12 oz
155 g	caster sugar	6 oz
400 g	soft flour	14 oz
100 g	ground almonds	$3\frac{1}{2}$ oz

For the orange cream

375 ml	whipping cream	15 fl oz
25 g	caster sugar	1 oz
one	orange	one
one 15 ml spoon	orange curaçao	1 tablesp

For the glaze (optional)

	apricot jam *or* puree	
	kirsch	

Hull and wipe the strawberries.

Cream the butter and sugar until light and fluffy. Add the sieved flour and ground almonds, mix together thoroughly, wrap in grease-proof paper or plastic wrap, and chill for 2–4 hours. After it has rested, knead thoroughly. Roll the shortbread out to about 2.5 mm ($\frac{1}{8}$ inch) thick, and cut it into three rounds. Bake them in a slow oven (150°–160°C, 300°–325°F, mark 2–3) for 8–10 minutes. When pale golden, cut one round into six or eight triangles. Cool the shortbread on racks, dust with caster sugar, and trim the outside edges.

For the orange cream, mix all the ingredients together and whip the mixture to soft-peak consistency.

To assemble the gateau, put one shortbread round on a serving plate. Using about half the orange cream, pipe a large rosette in the centre and small rosettes round the edge. Take half the strawberries, cut them in half, and place them round the cream. Put another shortbread round on top and repeat the process. To finish, put the sectioned round on top and dust it with caster sugar. If you wish, you can glaze the strawberries by brushing them with some warmed, sieved apricot jam blended with a little kirsch or liqueur.

Chef's note: the dish will stand for a few hours without deteriorating.

Editor's note: if you want a smaller cake, use half quantities and make two rounds of shortbread. You will obviously also need to reduce the quantities of cream and strawberries.

Lovage soup
or
Fennel soup

Mr Reynaud's juniper hare, cabbage, artichoke and potato puree *or* barley pilaff

Highland mist
or
Lemon and walnut torte

The fruits of autumn are a great inspiration to the cook, whether from instinctive earth-motherliness, or just plain greed. After thinking of cooling and slimming salads for months, crisp days, falling leaves, and the arrival of winter programmes for concerts and evening classes suggest more sustaining and savoury meals. This is an intriguing menu, with many original tastes, and although suitable for hearty appetites, it is in no way gross.

First course

Lovage and fennel may well be unfamiliar to all your guests. If they like the 'subtly curried celery' taste of lovage as much as we do, a reafforestation scheme may shortly be launched by gardeners and gastronomers, since the bushes grow easily; the fennel soup has a gentler taste. Both are easy to make, and can be prepared ahead. If you prefer a fishy first course, consider mussels and garlic stuffing on page 162.

Main course

Mr Reynaud's juniper hare is visually impressive as well as delicious. It has overtones of caneton rouennaise, with the stewed joints underneath the roasted saddle. Even a 'high' hare will not be alarming to the timid after its days of marinating and its heavy spicing. Serve it with cabbage and artichoke and potato puree (page 192) or barley pilaff. All these vegetables are good-natured and will keep hot during the first course.

Such an impressive dish deserves a good wine, one with some body to stand up to the juniper. A fine burgundy would be appropriate, as would a Barolo or good Rioja (Marqués de Murrieta, say). If you like Rhône wine, try Gigondas, which has a slight pepperiness as well as the weight necessary to match the hare.

Other autumnal choices are pigeon casserole (page 112) and pheasant with pâté and port (page 101).

Sweet course

Highland mist is a dusky pink blackberry fool, lightly flavoured with Drambuie, to be served in small quantities at the end of such a meal. If you have decided to make this dinner your autumn spectacular, you might like the lemon and walnut torte, 'a lighter and more interesting Pavlova', and nicely showy. Either sweet is prepared ahead of time, so that the meal makes no last-minute demands except for the roasting of the saddle of hare. Otherwise, consult the index for the many apple-based sweets in the book.

The sloe gin will not be ready till Christmas, but a glass of Drambuie would slide down pleasantly, or calvados if a dry *digestif* is more to your taste.

Wine suggestions

Main course   Burgundy, Barolo, Rioja or Rhône

Digestif   Drambuie or calvados

Lovage soup

White Moss House,	one	onion	one
Grasmere, Cumbria	50 g	butter	2 oz
Chef/proprietor:	three 15 ml spoons	chopped fresh lovage	3 tablesp
Jean Butterworth	two 15 ml spoons	flour	2 tablesp
	500 ml	chicken stock (page 207)	1 pint
	250 ml	milk	10 fl oz
		salt, pepper	
		lovage leaves	
		double cream	

Sauté the chopped onion in the melted butter until it is soft. Add the chopped lovage and sauté it gently for a minute before stirring in the flour. Cook the mixture for a few minutes, stirring all the time. Add the stock and continue to stir until it comes to the boil and thickens. Cover the pan and simmer the soup until the lovage is tender.

Liquidise the soup, add the milk, bring it back to the boil, and check the seasonings. Serve with a fresh lovage leaf and a swirl of cream in each bowl.

Editor's notes: lovage can be found in nurseries and is easy to grow.
We found it so hard to say goodbye to this soup with the end of the lovage

season, that we stripped our bush at the last possible moment, and sautéed the chopped leaves in butter until they were almost crisp. They were then frozen in small containers, and made a delicious winter soup. (Use the same quantity of 'freeze-dried' leaves as of fresh—and do not be tempted to use more of fresh or dried than is specified, since the flavour is powerful.)

Fennel soup

Pool Court,
Pool in Wharfedale,
West Yorkshire
Chef: Roger Grime

two	carrots	two
two	leeks	two
one	small onion	one
one	stick of celery	one
	chopped parsley	
	peppercorns	
one	bay leaf	one
25 g	butter	1 oz
1 litre	water	2 pints
one	large head of fennel	one
one	large onion	one
one	clove of garlic	one
25 g	butter	1 oz
one	large potato	one
	sea salt, pepper	
four 15 ml spoons	single cream	4 tablesp

To make the stock, soften the sliced carrots, leeks, onion, celery, along with the parsley, peppercorns and bay leaf in the melted butter, add the water, simmer for an hour, and strain. Meanwhile, chop the fennel, reserving the feathery tops. In a large saucepan fry the chopped onion and crushed garlic in the butter until the onion is soft and translucent but not brown. Add the fennel and peeled and chopped potato and stir them gently to coat them with the butter and onion mixture. Cover the pan, and cook the vegetables for 10–15 minutes or until the potato and fennel are tender, shaking the pan occasionally to prevent sticking.

Add the stock, salt and pepper to the fennel mixture and bring the soup to the boil. Simmer it gently for five minutes, then add more salt and pepper if necessary. Puree the soup. Return it to the pan and reheat it.

Serve the soup in a warmed tureen or individual soup bowls with the cream swirled on top, sprinkled with the reserved, roughly-chopped fennel leaves.

Mr Reynaud's juniper hare (4–6)

Leith's, London, W.11
Chef: Jean Reynaud

2 kg	hare (approx)	4½ lb
250 g	carrots	8 oz
one	stick of celery	one
125 g	onions	4 oz
one 5 ml spoon	salt	1 teasp
one 5 ml spoon	crushed black peppercorns	1 teasp
	bouquet garni (page 213)	
75 ml	wine vinegar	3 fl oz
half-bottle	dry white wine	half-bottle
40 g	flour	1½ oz
	oil for frying	
125 ml	stock *or* water	5 fl oz
two 5 ml spoons	tomato puree	2 teasp
one	clove of garlic	one
50 g	juniper berries	2 oz

Ask your butcher to joint the hare, cutting the legs and neck into pieces but keeping the saddle whole. With a small, sharp knife remove the layer of membrane and sinew from the saddle. Put the pieces of hare, saddle included, in a glazed stone crock or plastic bucket with the sliced vegetables, salt, pepper and bouquet garni. Pour in the vinegar and white wine and leave the hare to marinate in a cool place for four days, moving the pieces at least once every 24 hours to ensure even marination.

Remove the hare, strain the vegetables and reserve the marinade. Pat the hare and the vegetables dry with kitchen paper. Set aside the saddle. Dust the other joints with flour and brown them well in a little oil in a frying-pan. Remove them and brown the vegetables. Stir in any remaining flour. Put the joints and the vegetables in a large saucepan, cover them with the marinade, add the stock or water, tomato puree, crushed garlic and juniper berries. Bring the liquid to the boil, skim off any froth and fat, and allow it to simmer until the meat is really tender (about 2½–3 hours). If the sauce seems thin, strain it off into another pan and boil it rapidly until it has reduced to a syrupy consistency, then pour it back over the meat. Check the seasoning.

Seal the saddle by frying it briskly in hot oil until it is brown all over. Roast it in a hot oven (240°C, 475°F, mark 9) for ten minutes only. The flesh should still be pink near the bone. Carefully remove the two large fillets from either side of the backbone, and the two tiny ones from underneath. Cut them into thin slices, arrange them on top of the stewed hare, and serve at once.

Highland mist (6)

Isle of Eriska Hotel,
Eriska, Argyll
Chef/proprietor:
Sheena
Buchanan-Smith

250 g	blackberries	8 oz
250 ml	double cream	10 fl oz
three 15 ml spoons	caster sugar	3 tablesp
one 15 ml spoon	Drambuie	1 tablesp
two	egg whites	two
	a few sugared blackberries	

Liquidise the blackberries. Push them through a sieve to remove the pips. Lightly whip the cream until it just holds its shape, and mix in the blackberry puree, sugar and Drambuie. Beat the egg whites until they are stiff and fold them into the blackberry mixture. Pour into six glasses and refrigerate till chilled. Decorate with a few sugared blackberries.

Editor's note: frozen blackberries work well in this recipe (leave the berries intended for decoration in the freezer until half an hour before serving).

Lemon and walnut torte (8)

David's Place,
Knutsford, Cheshire
Chef: Jennifer Wright

six	egg whites	six
350 g	caster sugar	12 oz
25 g	cornflour	1 oz
half 15 ml spoon	vinegar	$\frac{1}{2}$ tablesp
175 g	chopped walnuts	6 oz

For the filling

175 g	butter	6 oz
three	eggs	three
175 g	caster sugar	6 oz
three	lemons	three
125 ml	double cream	5 fl oz

For decoration

	double cream	
	lemon slices	
	halved walnuts	

Beat the egg whites until they hold peaks and gradually add all but 50 g (2 oz) of the caster sugar, a spoonful at a time, until the mixture is very stiff. Beat in the cornflour and vinegar, and fold in the remaining sugar and chopped walnuts. Divide the mixture between two lightly-oiled sandwich tins and bake them in a slow oven (140°C, 275°F, mark 1) for an hour, or until the meringues are dry. Allow them to cool.

For the filling, melt the butter in the top of a double boiler. Beat the eggs and caster sugar together and add them, along with the lemon juice and grated rind, and cook the mixture until it is thick, stirring it all the time. Allow the lemon curd to cool, fold in the whipped cream, and sandwich the meringues together with the mixture. Decorate the top meringue with whorls of whipped cream, lemon slices and halved walnuts.

Bourekakia
or
Eggs with tapénade

Spiced lamb with aubergines, risotto *or* barley

Ogen melon with raspberry sherbet
or
Compote of pears

To anyone the wrong side of forty, Mediterranean food means *Mediterranean Food* by Elizabeth David, the book which, with its successors, did for the British cooks of the 1950s what Eliza Acton did for those of the 1850s. It was a marvellous solvent of post-war austerity, and a compulsory travelling companion as soon as Sicily and Crete became playgrounds again, rather than theatres of war. Olives, garlic, tomatoes, herbs, anchovies, and melons stretch in a continuous band round the Mediterranean, with variations between two neighbouring villages often as important as those between neighbouring countries. Our menu is neither wholly authentic nor totally consistent, but it captures the strong, exotic tastes of Provence and the Eastern Mediterranean and keeps in tune with a fine summer's evening—or offers a delightful antidote to a grey one. Serve it to friends who cook and travel for pleasure, and sit back and enjoy the tales it is bound to prompt.

First course
The bourekakia are dangerous: once you have tasted utterly fresh filo pastry, you will never be happy with the tired version so often found in restaurant or delicatessen baklavas, usually sandwiching equally *passé* nuts. These are crisp and light, and their only disadvantage is the deep-frying involved. If that is beyond your poise or ventilation system, either compromise by baking them, or choose the tapénade, served with eggs or crudités. It tastes, perhaps, rather as Roman *garum* must have done, and is not recommended for children past the age of indiscretion. If neither of these appeals, you might like Provencal fish soup (page 116) or salade périgourdine (page 46) instead.

Main course
The lamb is a splendidly satisfying dish, colourful and interestingly spiced. The use of tender cuts of meat makes it a very high-class stew indeed, with all the advantages of little last-minute preparation and easy service. The aubergines can be browned ahead of time and added to the casserole when indicated in the recipe. Risotto (page 201) or barley will absorb the sauce effectively, and the yoghourt and mint provide a cooling contrast to all the spices.

Sweet course The melon and raspberry sherbet is a delight to eye and palate, and if you crave greater authenticity, use Charentais instead of Ogen melons. A compote of pears or apricots would make an equally soothing end to the meal. Otherwise serve fresh fruit in generous abundance and a few Italian cheeses.

Wine suggestions

With such highly-seasoned food, it seems sensible to stick to minor French, Greek-Cypriot or Turkish wines. Provencal Sauvignon is often clean and dry, Cassis more lively; Bandol is one of the better reds. Retsina, a taste the Greeks acquired perforce centuries ago, never seems as good in bottle here as it does from the cask there; other wines are mostly branded, with Hymettus, Othello and Kolossi among the best-known names. We have had no luck with Turkish whites, but Buzbag and Trakya reds are interesting. Recreate the holiday feeling with a glass of something sweet and appropriate to end the meal: either a *vin doux naturel* such as Muscat de Frontignan or Muscat de Rivesaltes, or a sweet white Muscat from Samos.

Aperitif Kir (vin blanc cassis—page 44)

First and main courses French, Greek-Cypriot or Turkish white or red wines

Sweet course Vin doux naturel or Greek Muscat

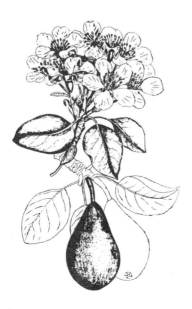

Bourekakia

Blostins, Shepton
Mallet, Somerset
Chef/proprietor:
Bill Austin

125 g	strong cheese	4 oz
one	egg	one
	fresh dill	
	fresh parsley	
	fresh fennel	
	salt, pepper	
2–3	sheets of filo pastry	2–3
	oil for deep-frying	

For garnishing

	salad	
	black olives	

To make the filling, combine the grated cheese (mature Cheddar is ideal), beaten egg, finely-chopped herbs, salt and pepper.

Take a strip of filo pastry about 5 cm by 20 (2 inches by 8). Put two 5-ml (tea)spoonsful of the mixture at one end, leaving a small margin all round. Brush all the edges with water, and fold the short edge over to lie flush with the long one. Continue folding from side to side to make a many-layered triangle. Tuck in the final end securely. Repeat until the filling is used up.

Deep-fry the triangles in very hot oil until they are golden brown, turning them over when the bottom side is cooked. (They take about three minutes in all.) Drain them well on absorbent paper and serve 'in the hand', or garnished with a small salad and black olives. In the restaurant, two bourekakia make one serving. We found we could easily eat more—they are very light, crisp and puffy.

Editor's notes: experiment with different cheeses and herbs: dried oregano and finely-chopped spring onion tops make a good combination. One Greek version involves cream cheese and finely-chopped cooked spinach, nutmeg and an egg.

Frozen filo can be found in most delicatessens, especially those with an Austrian or Middle-Eastern slant. It freezes well. Since it dries out quickly once removed from its packet, keep it under a damp towel while you are preparing the bourekakia.

If deep-frying is not for you, brush each strip with melted butter before you fill and fold it, and bake the triangles in a moderately hot oven for 30–45 minutes.

Eggs with tapénade (6)

Gibson's, Cardiff,
South Glamorgan
Chef/proprietor:
Irene Canning

six	hard-boiled eggs	six
24	black olives	24
24	green olives	24
50 g	tinned anchovies in oil	$1\frac{3}{4}$ oz
90 g	tinned tuna in oil	$3\frac{1}{2}$ oz
one 15 ml spoon	drained capers	1 tablesp
75–100 ml	olive oil	3–4 fl oz

Hard-boil the eggs carefully (use a minimum of cold water, bring quickly to the boil, simmer for eight minutes, cool under running water).

Stone the olives and cut them into pieces. Put the olives, chopped anchovies, tuna and capers in the liquidiser with the oil from both tins, add a spoonful of olive oil, and start liquidising. The mixture is very stiff and difficult and you will frequently have to stop the motor and free the blades with a spatula. Add enough oil, a little at a time, to free it and get the mixture moving, but be careful, since too much oil will encourage it to separate out. The result should be a thinnish paste.

Serve the tapénade in a small pot with the hard-boiled eggs or raw vegetable strips, toast, or biscuits.

Editor's notes: this is one of many versions of Provencal tapenado. Some are made with either black or green olives, rather than a mixture of the two, and the colour is more attractive. In Provence, a little pot of tapénade often appears on the table at the beginning of a meal, with French bread and unsalted butter.

Spiced lamb with aubergines

Crane's, Salisbury,
Wiltshire
Chef/proprietors:
Tim and Sue Cumming

two 15 ml spoons	olive oil	2 tablesp
250 g	onions	8 oz
two	cloves of garlic	two
two 15 ml spoons	cumin seeds	2 tablesp
half 15 ml spoon	fresh coriander seeds	$\frac{1}{2}$ tablesp
500 g	tomatoes	1 lb
one 15 ml spoon	tomato puree	1 tablesp
half 15 ml spoon	basil	$\frac{1}{2}$ tablesp
two 5 ml spoons	chopped parsley	2 teasp
125 ml	white wine	5 fl oz
	salt, pepper	
1 kg	loin of lamb *or* leg fillet	2 lb
	salt, pepper	
	olive oil	
500 g	aubergines	1 lb
	fresh mint	
	yoghourt	

To make the sauce, heat the olive oil in a large oven-proof casserole, and in it fry the finely-sliced onions and finely-chopped garlic. When they have browned, add the cumin and coriander pounded to a powder in a mortar (or with the end of a rolling-pin in a heavy bowl). Stir over the heat for 30 seconds, before adding the peeled tomatoes, tomato puree, basil, parsley, wine, salt and pepper. Stew the sauce for 15–20 minutes, until it thickens.

Cut the lamb into thick chops (if it is loin) or large pieces (if it is leg fillet), trimming off excess fat and discarding bones. Season it with salt and pepper, brown it in the oil, and transfer it to the casserole. Cover, bring to the boil, and cook in a warm oven (160°C, 325°F, mark 3) for about 1–1$\frac{1}{4}$ hours until the lamb is tender.

Cut the aubergines into finger-sized chunks and brown them briefly in the same pan as the lamb, with some additional oil if necessary. Add them to the casserole for the last ten minutes of cooking.

Serve the lamb topped with chopped mint, accompanied by risotto (page 201), and a bowl of yoghourt with more chopped mint in it.

Editor's notes: the restaurant always uses loin of lamb. If you are using powdered cumin and coriander, use a teaspoonful less of each. Italian tinned plum tomatoes are satisfactory if fresh ones are watery and tasteless. Commercial dried mint often tastes like floor sweepings, so take thought for the morrow and dry some while it is in season.

Ogen melon with raspberry sherbet

Rising Sun, St Mawes, Cornwall
Chef: Jeffrey West

two	Ogen melons	two
125 g	sugar	4 oz
250 ml	water	10 fl oz
one	lemon	one
250 g	fresh or dry-frozen raspberries	8 oz

Choose small, perfectly ripe melons.

Mix together the sugar, water and lemon juice and boil for ten minutes. Allow the syrup to cool. Meanwhile, sieve the raspberries to obtain about 175 ml (6 fl oz) of puree. Stir in the cooled syrup and freeze the mixture for about three hours, until it is mushy. Stir it again and re-freeze for at least a further four hours. Cut the melons in half, remove the seeds, and fill the cavities with the sherbet.

Compote of pears

Ballymaloe House, Shanagarry, Co Cork
Chef/proprietor: Myrtle Allen

six	pears	six
125 g	sugar	4 oz
one	lemon	one

Halve the pears, peel thinly, and core them. Put them in an oven-proof dish which will just hold them nicely. Add the sugar, a few thin strips of lemon rind and the juice of the lemon. Cover securely and cook in a slow oven (150°C, 300°F, mark 2) until they are tender (the time will vary with the size and variety of pear). Cool before serving.

Editor's note: fresh apricots can also be cooked in this way. They take an hour to cook.

Crab fritters
or
Camembert frit

Pheasant with pâté, port, mushrooms and cream, rice *or* pommes purées, mange-tout peas *or* salad

Iced chocolate oranges
or
Fresh fruit and cheese

Champagne and oysters in the bath, a ham sandwich on the Langdale Pikes—anniversaries take us all in different ways. But for many, a good dinner is a vital part of the celebration, and if one or both partners enjoy cooking as much as eating, a meal at home can be an extravagant delight, half as extravagant and at least as delightful as a meal in a restaurant. Only you can decide whether it has to be All The Favourite Dishes, an epic struggle in gastronomy, or simply an unusually good meal. The suggested menu is rich, extravagant and intimate. Over to you.

First course

Deep-fried food is a joy, but only when you feel comfortable about preparing it and can serve it virtually straight from the pan. Since this is one occasion on which the 'guest' should feel at home in the kitchen, serve the crab or Camembert fritters there. In both cases the preliminary preparation is done some hours ahead, so you do not have to look like Cinderella before Prince Charming called. Since the crab recipe is marginally simpler, choose that if you tend to feel nervous about new dishes. If champagne is already on the go, it will accompany the fritters admirably, but then so would a dry white wine: choose what you like best, whether it is Muscadet, Chablis, Pouilly Fumé, or some other treasure dear to you both.

If the loved one likes to pretend that kitchen work happens of its own accord, crab soup (page 115) or gambas al ajillo (page 57) are suitably festive alternative first courses which can be delivered to the dining-table as though a butler had been hired for the evening.

Main course

Like bicycles, pheasants tend to be built for two at most, and as few can now afford to buy them by the brace or hecatomb, they are perfect fare for a *dîner intime*. The Cleeveway House pheasant has a richly delicious sauce which is extraordinarily simple to make—once you have paid for the ingredients. Unless fine surgery is a proud accomplishment, carve in the kitchen;

otherwise the performance should take place at table. Since the fritters will tie you to the kitchen in any case, serve mange-tout peas or tiny Kenya haricots verts, which require careful attention and only a couple of minutes' cooking. On the other hand a salad would provide a refreshing contrast to all the richness. Rice, pommes purées or barley pilaff will mop up the sauce efficiently. If pheasants are thin on the poulterer's slab, consider sauté de boeuf Mirabelle (page 157) or duck with garlic and ginger (page 169).

Now is the time to bring on the Serious Wine. It needs weight to match both the occasion and the dish, so dig out the cherished bottle of *cru classé* claret or fine burgundy, or an old Barolo or Rioja. If the cupboard under the stairs fails to rise to such a challenge, buy something decent a month or more ahead so that it has time to collect itself. And if you both prefer white wine, switch to something richer than the first-course wine: a fine white burgundy, perhaps, or a German Auslese. Or the champagne, of course.

Sweet course

Consider the state of your livers when choosing the third course, and if the only wise choice is fruit and cheese, make it very special fruit and very good cheese—a perfect pear bought tissue-wrapped from a wicker hamper at roughly the price of half-a-dozen oysters, with a creamy wedge of Roquefort; or a basket of fresh and exotic fruit (lychees, mangoes, kiwi fruit, fresh dates, a pomegranate . . .) with the creamiest cheese you can find (Petit Suisse, at least, can be found in a good supermarket). But for most of us a party has to end with a party sweet, and the iced chocolate oranges, while delectable, are at least portion-controlled to preserve the decencies.

A glass of port or dessert wine might round off the evening in style (served *after* not *with* the sweet). If you have been drinking German wine, move now to a Beerenauslese; if, on the other hand, the bank manager or common sense looms, a glass of brandy or calvados could provide a pleasant *digestif*.

After all this, best wishes for another happy year—and perhaps a sandwich in the Himalayas on the next anniversary . . .

Wine suggestions

First course   Champagne or dry white wine

Main course   Fine red wine or German Auslese

Digestif   Port, dessert wine, brandy or calvados

Crab fritters (4)

Chef's Kitchen,
Halsetown, Cornwall
Chef/proprietor:
F. N. Tetley

125 g	dark crab meat	4 oz
125 ml	fish stock (page 208)	5 fl oz
25 g	butter	1 oz
	salt, pepper	
50 g	flour	2 oz
two	eggs	two

For the sauce

two 15 ml spoons	plain yoghourt *or* sour cream	2 tablesp
two 15 ml spoons	horseradish	2 tablesp

In a heavy saucepan, bring to the boil the crab, fish stock, butter and seasoning. Add the flour and stir vigorously until it is smoothly amalgamated. Remove the pan from the heat, and allow it to cool a little before stirring in the beaten eggs, one at a time. Spread the paste on a lightly-greased baking sheet, cover, and chill in the refrigerator or freezer till it is firm (about two hours). Cut the paste into fingers, leave them on the baking sheet, and return them to the freezer or refrigerator in a plastic bag until you are ready to cook them.

Deep-fry the fritters in very hot oil (about 190°C, 375°F) for about five minutes, when they should be crisp and golden-brown outside, creamy in the centre. Drain them on absorbent paper.

Serve them with the mixed yoghourt and horseradish, or sour cream and horseradish, or simply lemon wedges. If you serve them with an aperitif, be sure to have paper napkins handy; if as a first course, consider finger-bowls.

Chef's note: since the preparation can be done the day before, the final frying should leave you unruffled.

Camembert frit (4)

Anna's Place,
London, N.1
Chef: Eric Norrgren

six	pre-packed portions of Camembert	six
two	egg whites	two
	white breadcrumbs	
	cooking oil	
	parsley	
	gooseberry jam	

Select Camembert portions which are not too ripe (otherwise they run away while cooking) and leave them in the refrigerator until ready to use them. Beat the egg whites till stiff but not dry. Dip the Camembert wedges first in egg white, then in crumbs, pressing them on firmly.

Have the oil very hot (about 190°C, 375°F). Lower the wedges into it in a basket, and after a minute remove them, and prod with a forefinger. The cheese should be yielding but not too soft. Drain the fritters on absorbent paper. Garnish with parsley and gooseberry jam, serving one fritter to each guest, with the remaining two for seconds.

Editor's notes: in the restaurant, the parsley garnish is deep-fried, and may be prepared ahead of time. If you wish to try, wash the parsley, dry it, and separate it into small sprigs. Lower them into very hot fat for a moment or two, then drain on absorbent paper. (Do not let them brown.) Sprinkle with salt. The taste is delicious. If you wish to serve the fritters as a savoury, omit the jam, so that the main course wine can be finished off with pleasure.

Pheasant with pâté, port, mushrooms and cream (2)

Cleeveway House,
Bishop's Cleeve,
Gloucestershire
Chef/proprietor:
John Marfell

1–1.25 kg	pheasant, dressed weight	2–3 lb
125 g	liver pâté	4 oz
	salt, pepper	
25 g	butter	1 oz
200–250 g	mushrooms	6–8 oz
150 ml	port	6 fl oz
150 ml	double cream	6 fl oz

Wipe the pheasant thoroughly, inside and out, with a damp cloth. Remove any pin feathers. Choose, or make, a well-seasoned liver pâté, and stuff the

101

bird with it. Skewer the vent. Season the bird with salt and pepper before browning it in butter in a flame-proof casserole.

Cook it, covered, in a hot oven (220°C, 425°F, mark 7) for 20–30 minutes (the shorter time for the smaller bird). Remove it and put a layer of mushrooms on the bottom of the casserole (slice them if they are large, leave them whole if they are small buttons), set the bird on top, and pour in enough port to cover the mushrooms. Replace the lid, and cook for a further 20–30 minutes.

Remove the bird, joint or carve it, and keep it hot while you make the sauce. Add the pâté from inside the bird to the mushrooms and juices in the casserole, stir in the cream, heat the sauce, and check the seasoning. Put the bird back in the sauce, bring just to the boil, and serve.

Editor's note: Mr Marfell serves the pheasant with garlic potatoes.

Iced chocolate oranges (4–6)

Ballymaloe House, Shanagarry, Co Cork
Chef/proprietor: Myrtle Allen

four	oranges	four
	stock syrup (page 48)	
two	egg yolks	two
two 15 ml spoons	sugar	2 tablesp
40 g	plain bitter chocolate	1½ oz
250 ml	whipping cream	10 fl oz
one 5 ml spoon	gelatine	1 teasp
one 15 ml spoon	orange juice	1 tablesp

For decoration

	orange-flavoured cream	

Cut the tops off the oranges and scoop out the pulp with a spoon. Liquidise and sieve it. Measure enough juice to quarter-fill the oranges and reserve the rest for drinks. (You will probably need the juice of only two oranges.) Mix the measured juice with an equal quantity of stock syrup.

Beat the egg yolks and sugar together to a thick mousse, and divide the mixture between two bowls. Add the melted chocolate to one half and stir in half the whipped cream. Half-fill the oranges with this mixture and freeze for 2½–3 hours until it is firm.

Dissolve the gelatine in a tablespoonful of heated unsweetened orange juice and combine it with the measured juice and syrup and the remaining egg mixture. Fold in the rest of the whipped cream and fill up the oranges. Freeze for a further three hours.

Half an hour before serving, remove the oranges from the freezer or freezing compartment and place them in the refrigerator to allow them to soften a little.

Cut them in quarters lengthwise and serve them garnished with whipped cream flavoured with orange zest and orange liqueur.

Editor's notes: if the oranges are following a rather rich main course, you may prefer to serve the orange-flavoured cream separately to allow guests to help themselves.

If you are making the oranges some time ahead, wrap them before freezing to protect them from alien tastes.

Shropshire fidget pie
or
Tourtière québecoise

Jugged beef with orange, crusty bread *or* rice, salad

Peaches with raspberry puree
or
Port and claret jelly

Eating 'round' a local theatre, concert, or film can be frustrating. A full dinner before eight is not most people's idea of a good time or a soothing prelude to enjoyment and concentration, and the same meal near midnight guarantees a disturbed night for many of us. It is a better idea to follow the example of a few enlightened London restaurants and split the meal into two parts, with an aperitif and a light and satisfying snack before setting off, and two good-natured courses afterwards. This is particularly convenient if your guests are staying with you.

Before

Unless you hit a perfect summer day, serve something hot for the initial snack—it feels more like real food, less like a hurried sandwich in a bar. The meat pies are useful, since both are eaten with a fork, so that you can enjoy this first course in relaxed fashion rather than at the dining-table. A spoonful of pickles (there is a lemon one on page 200) or olives are all the garnish needed. Serve whatever you like in the way of drink: sherry, Chambéry vermouth, a light and flowery German wine, or even a Beaujolais if you are all dedicated red-wine drinkers. Champagne is always nice. . .

Other ideas to consider are bowls of a fairly hearty soup (cheese and vegetable chowder on page 145, crème flamande on page 30); or potato pancakes with bacon (page 189).

After

After the event, which you and your guests will both want to recollect in tranquillity, rely upon a simple hot dish cooked during your absence, such as the jugged beef with orange given here. If it is summer and you prefer something cold, consider serving the tourtière or savoury braid (page 180) at this stage, and choose another first course from the ones listed above. Anyone with a sensitive digestion will thank you for steering clear of either highly-spiced or fatty foods for this late meal. If you choose the jugged beef, serve it with bread or rice and a simple salad. The savoury smell which greets you is very reassuring and homely on a cold night.

Once again there is a wide range of red wines to choose from, but remember that the orange in the jugged beef is not unduly kind to wine, and avoid the heavyweights. Settle, perhaps, for a lightish Rhône (Côtes du Rhône Villages) or a reliable wine merchant's house claret or burgundy. If you have used cider in the recipe, you could serve a good dry cider instead (some people like Bulmer's No. 7, which we find too acid; others prefer the same maker's Dry Reserve). Holiday souvenirs from the north of France should always include a litre bottle of rough *cidre fermier* for just such an occasion as this.

Sweet course

Finish the meal with something light rather than creamy, which can also be prepared ahead. The port and claret jelly looks very pretty in individual glasses or custard cups and slides down effortlessly. The peaches with raspberry puree capture the essence of summer, and if you like you can transform them into unimpeachable peach Melba with a scoop of home-made vanilla ice-cream (page 118). If your guests are young and strong enough for something more solid, you might offer a cake (there is a showy banana one on page 152, and a grapefruit cheesecake on page 182).

Wine suggestions

Before

Sherry, vermouth, German white wine or Beaujolais

After

Rhône wine, house claret or burgundy, or cider

Shropshire fidget pie (4–6)

Refectory, Richmond, Surrey
Chef/proprietor:
Mary Kingsley

1.75 kg	joint of bacon (corner or similar)	1¾–2 lb
one	onion	one
	butter	
50 g	flour	2 oz
	pepper	
100–150 ml	cider	4–6 fl oz
500 g	cooking apples	1 lb
	brown sugar	
175 g	shortcrust pastry (page 202)	6 oz
	beaten egg	

Cover the bacon with water, bring it slowly to the boil and cook it for about an hour. Allow it to cool; trim off most of the fat, and cut the lean meat into 2.5-cm (one-inch) chunks. Chop the onion and soften it in a little butter.

Preheat the oven to 220°C, 425°F, mark 7.

In a deep pie-dish, put a layer of bacon chunks, sprinkle them with the flour and pepper, add the onion, and pour on enough cider to cover them. Next add a layer of peeled and sliced apple, and sprinkle with a little brown sugar. Cover with the pastry and brush it with beaten egg. Bake for 20 minutes; turn down the oven to 180°C (350°F, mark 4) for a further 20–30 minutes. Serve hot or warm.

Editor's note: like most traditional dishes, this one has infinite variations. Some recipes include sliced or grated potatoes, others use sausage meat instead of bacon.

Tourtière québecoise (4–6)

Hathaways,
London, S.W.11
Chef/proprietor:
Kathie Scheiding

350 g	shortcrust pastry (page 202)	12 oz
500 g	lean, minced pork	1 lb
one	medium-sized onion	one
half 5 ml spoon	salt	$\frac{1}{2}$ teasp
half 5 ml spoon	dried marjoram	$\frac{1}{2}$ teasp
$\frac{1}{4}$ of a 5 ml spoon	ground cloves	$\frac{1}{4}$ teasp
	pepper	
200 ml	light stock (page 207) *or* water	8 fl oz
75 g	fresh, white breadcrumbs	3 oz
	beaten egg	

Line a 23-cm (9-inch) flan case (at least 3.5 cm [1¾ inches] deep) with half of the pastry, and bake it blind for five minutes. Set it aside.

Combine in a saucepan the pork, chopped onion, seasonings and stock. Bring the mixture to the boil and simmer it for ten minutes. Gradually sprinkle in the breadcrumbs, mix thoroughly, and simmer for another five minutes. Allow the mixture to cool slightly.

Put the filling into the baked crust, cover with the remaining pastry, brush the top with beaten egg, cut a hole in the crust, and bake the pie for about 30 minutes in a moderately hot oven (200°C, 400°F, mark 6). Serve it hot with peas and potatoes, or cold with salad and pickles.

Editor's note: most Québecois would add a chopped clove of garlic to the mixture. It is eaten hot on Christmas Eve, cold as a snack when skiing.

Jugged beef with orange

750 g	stewing steak	$1\frac{1}{2}$ lb
three	medium-sized onions	three
25 g	butter	1 oz
one 15 ml spoon	cooking oil	1 tablesp
25 g	flour	1 oz
one	orange	one
	salt, pepper	
several	sprigs of fresh thyme *or*	several
half 5 ml spoon	dried thyme	$\frac{1}{2}$ teasp
two	bay leaves	two
one	clove of garlic	one
250 g	button mushrooms	8 oz
250 ml	white wine or cider	10 fl oz

Refectory, Richmond, Surrey
Chef/proprietor:
Mary Kingsley

Trim the beef and cut it into 3-cm ($1\frac{1}{2}$-inch) cubes. Brown it with the sliced onions in the butter and oil. Sprinkle on the flour and stir thoroughly until it begins to brown. Cut thin strips of peel from the orange and add them with the remaining ingredients, stir well, and bring to boiling point. Transfer the stew to a casserole, cover it securely, and cook it for eight hours at 120°C, 250°F, mark $\frac{1}{2}$, or for a shorter time at a slightly higher temperature.

Fresh peaches with raspberry puree

four	peaches	four
125 ml	white wine	5 fl oz
250 g	raspberries	8 oz
two 15 ml spoons	icing sugar	2 tablesp
	whipped cream (optional)	

White Moss House, Grasmere, Cumbria
Chef/proprietor:
Jean Butterworth

If the peaches are really ripe, simply skin them and remove the stones. Otherwise, poach them gently for a few minutes in two 15 ml (table) spoonsful of sugar dissolved in the wine and 125 ml (5 fl oz) of water. Liquidise the raspberries with the sugar and sieve the puree to remove the seeds. Check the sweetness and add a little more sugar if necessary, though the final taste should be a little tart. Pour the puree over the peaches in one large or four individual dishes, and serve with whipped cream if you wish.

Editor's note: there is no substitute for fresh peaches, but frozen raspberries make a very acceptable sauce.

Port and claret jelly (8)

**Miller Howe,
Windermere, Cumbria
Chef/proprietor:
John Tovey**

250 ml	ruby or tawny port	10 fl oz
375 ml	claret	15 fl oz
25 g	powdered gelatine	1 oz
375 ml	water	15 fl oz
250 g	caster sugar	8 oz
5 cm	cinnamon stick	2 inches
two 15 ml spoons	redcurrant jelly	2 tablesp
two	lemons	two
four	cloves	four

In a saucepan, combine the port and claret, and sprinkle in the gelatine.
Bring the mixture slowly to simmering point and let it simmer very gently for
ten minutes. (This removes any taste of raw alcohol.)

In a second saucepan, mix the water, sugar, cinnamon, redcurrant jelly, the
grated rind and juice of the lemons, and the cloves. Bring the mixture slowly
to simmering point and let it simmer for ten minutes.

Combine the two liquids and pass through a fine strainer into individual glass
or china moulds. Chill till served.

Editor's note: cream and shortbread are both suitable accompaniments.

Stilton soup
or
Cream of artichoke soup

Pigeon casserole, barley pilaff, leeks *or* red cabbage

Blackberry syllabub
or
Apple brûlée

Whether you entertain in an Islington attic or a Home Counties manor it is fun to create a meal whose overtones recall the days when printed or manuscript recipes began, 'First shoot your pigeon . . .' If friends or colleagues from abroad descend on you in autumn, this would help fly the flag as effectively as the 'Winter in England' menu on page 132. The style is rich, the ingredients traditional, the treatment of them original.

First course

Both soups are creamy without being cloying because they have a good strong flavour, so take your choice between Stilton and artichokes. Both could be made ahead of time and reheated carefully. If you prefer a lighter—though equally traditional—start to a meal, try devilled kidneys (page 84) or potted mackerel (page 178). The old habit of serving a dry sherry or madeira with soup is a useful one, since you can, in effect, continue as you have begun. Otherwise, save wine for the main course.

Main course

Pigeons are greedy but—to the cook—ungrateful birds. However, they can be had all the year round at a price that usually seems modest for game, and with the right contacts you may come by them as gifts. The Count House recipe, with its moist stuffing and well-seasoned sauce, turns them out tasting stylishly gamey. Either leeks or red cabbage would be appropriate vegetables, and a barley pilaff a more interesting accompaniment than rice.

A rich, mellow wine would be appropriate here, as a complement to the nuts and port in the recipe. If you have any fine old claret, bring it out now. Otherwise, consider a good Rioja or Barolo—after all, both Spaniards and Italians like shooting anything that moves—or a peppery Rhône wine, such as Gigondas or Hermitage.

Sweet course

If blackberries are in season (or in the freezer), nothing could be nicer than their delicate, scented taste in the syllabub. For a lighter sweet, choose the apple brûlée, which cleverly avoids both cream and eggs, but has a subtle boost from the calvados in the seemingly innocuous apple puree. (Whisky makes a passable substitute for calvados in cooked dishes.) Should neither appeal, consider Victoria plum mousse (page 131) or an autumnal version of summer pudding, perhaps with blackberries, bilberries and cranberries.

A glass of dessert wine would flatter the syllabub or brûlée, but you may prefer to serve tawny port or a *digestif* afterwards instead: calvados, obviously, if you used it with the apples, malt whisky if there are foreigners to convert, cognac or armagnac for general pleasure, framboise or poire Williams if you enjoy the aromatic fragrance of those 'alcools blancs'.

Wine suggestions

First course	Dry sherry or madeira
Main course	Claret, Rioja, Barolo or Rhône wine
Sweet course	Any dessert wine

Stilton soup (6–8)

Leith's, London, W.11
Chef: Max Markarian

one	medium-sized onion *or*	one
four	shallots	four
two	sticks of celery	two
50 g	butter	2 oz
two 10 ml spoons	flour	1½ tablesp
200 ml	dry white wine	8 fl oz
1 litre	chicken *or* veal stock (page 207)	1¾ pints
1 litre	milk	1¾ pints
125 g	Stilton	4 oz
50 g	Cheddar *or* Gruyère	2 oz
three 15 ml spoons	double cream	3 tablesp
	salt, pepper	
For garnishing	croûtons *or* cheese straws	

Soften the finely-chopped onion or shallots and celery in the butter over gentle heat until the onion is translucent. Add the flour and stir for a minute or two. Remove the pan from the heat and stir in the wine and stock. Bring the mixture to the boil, stirring continuously, and simmer for 45 minutes, until the wine has lost its harsh alcoholic flavour. Add the milk and crumbled cheese, and allow the cheese to melt below boiling-point. Add the cream, salt and pepper, and liquidise or sieve the soup. Reheat gently, still without allowing it to boil. Serve hot with croûtons or cheese straws.

Cream of artichoke soup

Loaves and Fishes, Wootton Bassett, Wiltshire Chef/proprietor: Angela Rawson			
	500 g	Jerusalem artichokes	1 lb
	one	large onion	one
	40 g	unsalted butter	1½ oz
	1 litre	chicken or turkey stock (page 207)	2 pints
For the roux	20 g	butter	¾ oz
	20 g	plain flour	¾ oz
		salt, pepper	
	one 5 ml spoon	caster sugar	1 teasp
	125 ml	double cream	5 fl oz
For garnishing		toasted almonds	

Peel and thinly slice the artichokes and onion. Cook them in the melted butter until they are soft, then add a little stock and simmer the vegetables until they start to break up. Add half a pint more of the stock and puree the mixture in a liquidiser. Make a roux (page 206) and gradually add the puree, stirring well after each addition. Add the rest of the stock, the seasoning and the sugar, and cook the soup slowly until the ingredients are well blended. Add the cream, and serve the soup sprinkled with toasted almonds.

Editor's note: some people prefer the soup 'straight', without the toasted almonds. If you are one of them, use croûtons or a little chopped parsley as garnish.

Pigeon casserole

Count House, St Just,
Cornwall
Chef/proprietor:
Ann Long

four	pigeons	four
50 g	bacon	2 oz
125 g	brown breadcrumbs	4 oz
50 g	shredded suet	2 oz
two 15 ml spoons	chopped parsley	2 tablesp
50 g	walnuts	2 oz
half	orange or lemon	half
one	egg	one
	salt, pepper	
25 g	butter	1 oz
one 15 ml spoon	flour	1 tablesp
125 ml	port	5 fl oz
375 ml	brown jellied stock (page 207)	15 fl oz
one	bouquet garni (page 213)	one
	salt, pepper	
175 g	button onions	6 oz
175 g	button mushrooms	6 oz
	arrowroot	
	cream	

Cut down the centre of the breasts and remove the breast bone from the pigeons.

To make the forcemeat, first fry the finely-diced bacon. Then thoroughly combine the breadcrumbs, suet, parsley, bacon, finely-chopped walnuts and grated orange or lemon rind with the beaten egg and seasonings. If you are stuffing the birds, fill them with the forcemeat; otherwise, form it into balls about 2.5 cm (one inch) in diameter and set them aside.

Sew up the pigeons with fine string or heavy cotton and brown them slowly in the butter in a flame-proof casserole. Remove them from the casserole, blend the flour, port, stock, bouquet garni, salt and pepper into the butter and return the birds to the casserole. Cook them, covered, in a moderate oven (180°C, 350°F, mark 4) for one hour. Meantime, blanch the peeled onions in boiling water for five minutes and drain them. Add them with the trimmed mushrooms to the casserole at the end of the hour's cooking. If using forcemeat balls, gently fry them in a little butter and add them at the same time. Cook the casserole for a further 15 minutes.

Remove the pigeons, reduce the cooking liquor slightly over high heat, remove the bouquet garni and thicken the juices with a little arrowroot and cream. Do not allow the sauce to boil once it has thickened. Serve the pigeons with some of the sauce poured over them and the rest separately.

112

Blackberry syllabub (5)

Crane's, Salisbury, Wiltshire
Chef/proprietors: Tim and Sue Cumming

375 g	blackberries	12 oz
75 g	caster sugar	3 oz
250 ml	double cream	10 fl oz
one 15 ml spoon	brandy	1 tablesp
one 15 ml spoon	cassis	1 tablesp
	lemon juice and sugar (to taste)	

For decoration

	blackberries (optional)	
	whipped cream	

Gently simmer the blackberries and sugar together until the fruit is tender. Strain the puree through a fairly fine sieve and allow it to cool. Using a balloon whisk, beat together 125–150 ml (5–6 fl oz) of the puree, the cream, brandy, and cassis, until the mixture thickens. Adjust it with lemon juice and sugar if necessary, and pour the syllabub into individual dishes. Chill until ready to serve.

Editor's notes: garnish the syllabub with whipped cream and a few whole berries, if you wish. Frozen blackberries are quite successful in this recipe. Use the dry-frozen variety or adjust the quantity of sugar.

Apple brûlée

Kinchs, Chesterton, Oxfordshire
Chef/proprietor: Christopher Greatorex

1 kg	cooking apples	2 lb
50–100 g	sugar	2–4 oz
one	clove (optional)	one
50 g	unsalted butter	2 oz
75 ml	calvados (optional)	3 fl oz
three 15 ml spoons	soft brown sugar	3 tablesp

Quarter and core the apples (but do not peel them) and simmer them with the sugar (but no liquid) until cooked. Add the clove, if desired. Puree the apple mixture in a liquidiser, then sieve it. Adjust to taste with sugar and beat in the butter until the puree is smooth. Add the calvados, if you wish.

Pour the mixture into a fire-proof serving dish, or individual ramekins, smooth the surface, and chill for several hours or overnight. Cover the mixture with an even layer of sugar and put under a very hot grill until the top has caramelised. Serve the brûlée immediately, or leave it to cool.

Crab soup
or
Provencal fish soup

Breast of veal with apple and walnut stuffing, spinach
or lemon-baked cabbage, baked potatoes

Fresh peach Melba
or
Caramel peaches

Some people are so addicted to soup that they are quite happy to make it the centre-piece of a meal; others feel the same about sweets (our menu on page 28 panders to the latter). This menu is for those who enjoy distinguished soup enough to contemplate following it with a relatively plain main course and a superior but fairly light sweet. Such a meal allows for the urge which any really delicious soup inspires in even the most restrained guest—the urge to see the bottom of the tureen.

First course

The crab soup is spectacular, expensive and rich. It is well worth both the expense and the effort (and tastes superb even if made with good frozen crab). If you prefer something regional rather than classical, choose the Provencal fish soup with its gentle overtones of garlic, saffron and herbes de Provence. For other unusual soups, consider cheese and vegetable chowder (page 145) or sopa de pescadores, a Spanish fish soup (page 173).

Main course

Stuffed breast of veal is always an appealing dinner-party dish because it looks impressive, carves easily, and is never dry if it is stuffed with care and cooked under cover. The apples and walnuts make a moist and interesting stuffing which matches the veal nicely. Serve plain vegetables—we suggest spinach or lemon-baked cabbage (page 194)—and potatoes baked at the same time as the veal.

Sweet course

Fruit and ice-cream always seem to slip down easily, even after quite a heavy meal, especially if the fruit is peaches and the ice-cream is 'real' vanilla. Mrs Johnson's caramel peaches have a deliciously fudgy sauce, reminiscent of childhood treats, and look attractive on a serving dish. Fresh peach Melba tastes quite unlike the travesties all too often served under that name, with the simplest and freshest of ice-creams and raspberry sauces surrounding the peach halves. Any of the other ice-creams or sorbets in the book would make appropriate alternatives.

114

Wine suggestions

Since cider is an ingredient of the crab soup, and apples are included in the veal stuffing, you might like to serve cider throughout the meal. But British branded ciders are almost all too sweet for the purpose, and you really need to live near a good firm such as Bob Luck's in Kent, or Hills or Inch in Devon. Otherwise, try bringing back *cidre fermier* from holidays in northern France, where it is reasonably priced and devastatingly authentic. White wine is a natural alternative throughout the meal. There is a school of thought which insists that no soup needs a glass of wine, but our rich crab one is an honourable exception. Anything clean and pleasant would be suitable, from a Loire Sauvignon to a more distinguished white burgundy. If you prefer a more assertive taste, choose Italian wine (Frascati or Verdicchio, say) which will stand up to the Provencal soup as well as to the veal. If the occasion demands something fizzy, a bottle of Asti Spumante would slip down as pleasantly as the peaches.

First and main courses   Dry cider or white wine

Sweet course   Asti Spumante

Crab soup

**Lawrence Restaurant,
Brighton, East Sussex
Chef/proprietor:
Susan Campion**

one	medium-sized, cooked crab	one
375 ml	dry cider	15 fl oz
one	bay leaf	one
one 15 ml spoon	olive oil	1 tablesp
one	small onion	one
one	clove of garlic	one
50 g	mushrooms	2 oz
one 15 ml spoon	flour	1 tablesp
	fresh herbs (thyme, fennel)	
125 ml	milk	5 fl oz
75 ml	dry white wine	3 fl oz
50 ml	sherry	2 fl oz
half 15 ml spoon	tomato puree	$\frac{1}{2}$ tablesp
	salt, pepper, Tabasco	
	sour cream, lumpfish roe	

Rinse the crab in cold water and drain it. Pick out all the meat. Pound the shells and put them in a large saucepan with the cider and bay leaf. Simmer for ten minutes, leave the stock to cool, and strain it through a cloth.

Warm the oil in a heavy pan, add the chopped onion and sweat it, covered, till it is transparent. Add the crushed garlic and chopped mushrooms and stew them for a further five minutes. Stir in the flour, gradually add the stock while still stirring, and then the herbs. Simmer the mixture for ten minutes. Add the crab meat and milk, and liquidise the soup.

Return the puree to the pan, bring it slowly to simmering point, add the wine and sherry, and simmer gently for five minutes. Add the tomato puree, salt, pepper and a few drops of Tabasco. Serve the soup in heated bowls with a blob of sour cream and a few grains of lumpfish roe (if you wish). In the restaurant they also serve garlic bread.

Editor's note: garlic croûtons could replace the roe and garlic bread.

Provencal fish soup

Popjoys, Bath, Avon
Chef/proprietor:
Stephen Ross

half	carrot	half
half	onion	half
half	stick of celery	half
one	clove of garlic	one
one 15 ml spoon	olive oil	1 tablesp
one 5 ml spoon	tomato puree	1 teasp
	salt, pepper	
one	pinch of herbes de Provence	one
one	pinch of saffron	one
175 g	tomatoes	6 oz
200 ml	white wine	8 fl oz
800 ml	fish stock (page 208)	1½ pints
250 g	fish (see below)	8 oz

In a large, heavy pan, soften the finely-chopped vegetables and the crushed garlic in the oil. Add the tomato puree, seasonings, skinned and liquidised tomatoes, wine and stock and simmer the mixture for 15 minutes.

Cut the fish (a mixture of whiting—or similar, prawns and a smoked fish is particularly good) into small pieces, add them to the pan and bring back to the boil. Simmer it for a further seven minutes until the fish is cooked.

Chef's note: serve the soup, if you wish, with garlic croûtons, aïoli (page 168), or rouille.

Editor's note: herbes de Provence are a mixture of oregano, thyme, rosemary, lavender and other herbs, available pre-packaged in this country.

Breast of veal with apple and walnut stuffing

**Lower Brook House,
Blockley,
Gloucestershire
Chef/proprietor:
Robert Greenstock**

1–2	breasts of veal	1–2
two	medium-sized onions	two
two 15 ml spoons	chopped walnuts	2 tablesp
two 10 ml spoons	dripping	1½ tablesp
four	cooking apples	four
225 g	fresh breadcrumbs	8 oz
	salt, pepper	
one	egg	one
250 ml	chicken or veal stock (page 207)	10 fl oz

Remove all the bones and any dry skin from the veal, flatten it slightly with a rolling pin, and season it.

Sweat the chopped onions with the walnuts in a half-tablespoonful of the dripping until the onions are transparent, and add the peeled and sliced apple. Cook over low heat for five minutes, and allow the mixture to cool. Add the breadcrumbs, salt, pepper and beaten egg and mix the ingredients well together. Spread this stuffing as evenly as possible over the veal. Roll the meat up firmly, ensuring that you do not lose any of the stuffing in the process. Tie it securely.

Melt the remaining dripping in a roasting-tin on top of the stove, and when it is hot, brown the rolled breast(s) in it. Remove the pan from the heat, add the stock, and loosely cover the pan with foil. Roast the veal in a moderate oven (180°C, 350°F, mark 4) for 1–1½ hours until it is cooked. Remove the meat from the pan, keep it warm, and strain the pan juices for gravy. (Thicken it if you wish.)

Remove the strings, carve the meat into thick slices, and serve it with the gravy.

Fresh peach Melba

Trumps, Lewes,
East Sussex
Chef/proprietor:
Christopher Goff

125 ml	water	5 fl oz
125 g	vanilla sugar (page 213)	4 oz
250 ml	double cream	10 fl oz
two	egg whites	two
four	fresh peaches	four
500 ml	boiling water	1 pint
250 g	granulated sugar	8 oz

For the sauce

125 g	raspberries	4 oz
one-quarter	lemon	one-quarter
two 15 ml spoons	peach syrup	2 tablesp

To make the ice-cream, heat the water and vanilla sugar together until the sugar has dissolved. Allow the syrup to cool. Whisk together the cream and egg whites and, as the mixture begins to thicken, gradually add the cooled vanilla syrup. Continue whisking till firm. Leave the ice-cream in the freezer or freezing compartment for at least 24 hours before serving.

Blanch the peaches, peel and halve them, and remove the stones. Place the peach halves in a saucepan with the sugar, cover them with the boiling water, and poach them for a minute or two until they are tender. Remove them carefully from the pan and reduce the liquor to about 250 ml (8 fl oz) over high heat. Allow the syrup to cool slightly before pouring it over the peaches, reserving two 15 ml (table) spoons for the sauce. Refrigerate the peaches until chilled, and chill the reserved syrup separately.

To make the sauce, combine the sieved raspberries with the lemon juice and the reserved chilled peach syrup.

Assemble the peach Melbas: scoop the ice-cream into individual serving dishes, top with the peach halves and pour over the raspberry sauce.

Caramel peaches

Tullythwaite House,
Underbarrow,
Cumbria
Cook: Barbara
Johnson

four	ripe peaches	four
25 g	freshly-ground almonds	1 oz
125 ml	sweetened whipped cream	5 fl oz
225 g	soft brown sugar	8 oz
two 15 ml spoons	milk	2 tablesp
one 15 ml spoon	butter	1 tablesp
25 g	toasted almonds	1 oz

Choose ripe peaches (freestone not clingstone) for this recipe. Blanch them in boiling water, peel, halve and stone them. Mix the ground almonds with a little of the whipped cream, fill the peach centres with this mixture, and join the halves together. Stand them on a serving dish.

Bring the sugar, milk and butter to the boil, stirring continuously. Simmer the mixture for seven minutes and then beat it until it begins to thicken. Pour the sauce over the peaches and allow them to cool.

Top each peach with a swirl of the remaining cream and sprinkle the tops with the chopped, toasted almonds.

Editor's note: this recipe was originated by the octogenarian owner of Tullythwaite House, Mrs Mary Johnson.

Soufflés aux courgettes
or
Avocado and tomato salad

Garrick steak, duchesse potatoes, salad
or haricots verts

Walnut and honey tart
or
Sussex pond pudding

Somewhere comfortably between hemlock and manna lies the ideal menu for feeding your spouse's boss, or even business clients. Since all entertaining involves rôle-playing, you should analyse the plot and the cast-list with some care before dimming the lights and raising the curtain on your production. If a substantial salary increase is long overdue, turn instead to one of the more economical meals. If cool competence is your line, choose first and last courses which can be prepared ahead. On the other hand, if endearing enthusiasm and involvement are the thing, produce the soufflés and the steamed pudding. Whatever the combination, you will have a tasty and attractive meal, and even dollar- or yen-earning prospects will be impressed by your imaginative handling of the cliché'd avocado-steak-and-sweet menu which is so many restaurateurs' idea of a businessman's lunch.

First course

The individual courgette soufflés look both pretty and impressive. They can be partly prepared ahead of time, and as long as you can summon your guests to table just before the soufflés are removed from the oven, there are no problems. The taste is delicate and relatively kind to wine, so bring on the best white burgundy, or an Alsace Gewürztraminer or Muscat, or a good German Riesling. The avocado and tomato salad is equally pretty, and not as naïve as it might look, since it depends on the careful choice of very good tomatoes and avocados, and an interesting, thick vinaigrette dressing. As the vinegar and garlic don't get on with wine, continue with the aperitif wine or sherry, or open a bottle you don't mind sacrificing in the name of good business relations. Soup is an appropriate alternative here—perhaps tomato (page 155) or mushroom (page 4).

Main course

The Garrick steak is a fine compromise between many people's belief that eating out *means* a good steak and most cooks' desire to serve something rather more creative. The steaks can be stuffed ahead of time and fried at the last minute. Since they are presented in overlapping slices with the filling showing, there is not the anguish of having it all too clearly revealed that you have muddled the orders for 'medium-rare', 'blue', 'medium-to-rare' and so on. Serve duchesse potatoes or French bread to absorb the juices, and a green salad or haricots verts for some textural and colour contrast.

Once again garlic will mask the taste of a fine wine, and it might be best to balance prestige and common sense by serving a decent bourgeois claret rather than a *cru classé*. Alternatively, Italian and Spanish reds accompany highly-seasoned foods in their native lands, and a good Gattinara or Rioja would be a sensibly robust choice here.

Sweet course

If all or most of the guests are schoolboys or clubmen at heart, with tastes and appetites to match, serve the Sussex pond pudding, which is sliced open at table to reveal its liquid golden centre and segmented lemon. The walnut and honey tart will also appeal to the child-at-heart, and is a better choice if you have a poorly ventilated kitchen and would find a steaming pan the last straw on top of frying-pan, oven and grill. You could justify a glass of dessert wine with either, though the tart gets on more easily with wine: try a noble château-bottled Sauternes if expense is no object, Muscat de Beaumes de Venise or a sweet madeira if it is.

Some of us who have put away childish things prefer to end a meal with cheese. A good Stilton and a glass of port (serve tawny if you feel incompetent to deal with the decanting of a vintage) end any good meal in style. If your Stilton is past its best, make the Stilton mousse on page 79 and serve that instead. After a meal like this, the deal should be child's play.

Wine suggestions

First course   White burgundy, Alsace, or German Riesling

Main course   Bourgeois claret, Rioja, or Gattinara

Sweet course   Sauternes, Muscat de Beaumes de Venise or madeira

Savoury   Tawny port

Soufflés aux courgettes (6)

La Potinière, Gullane,
Lothian
Chef/proprietor:
Hilary Brown

625 g	small courgettes	1¼ lb
	salt	
100 ml	flavoured milk (page 209)	4 fl oz
40 g	butter	1½ oz
40 g	flour	1½ oz
50 g	Cheddar *or* Cheddar and Parmesan	2 oz
two	large egg yolks	two
	salt, pepper	
15 g	butter	½ oz
four	large egg whites	four

Wash and finely slice 500 g (1 lb) of the courgettes. In a colander or sieve, sprinkle them with salt and leave them to drain for at least an hour. Dice the remaining courgettes (about 5 mm [¼ inch]), salt and drain them also, and set aside. In a large, heavy pan, cook the sliced courgettes quickly in a very little water, stirring frequently, until just tender. Drain and liquidise till smooth.

Flavour the milk as you would for béchamel sauce. Make a roux (page 206) with the 40 g (1½ oz) butter and the flour. Off the heat, add the milk and courgette puree, whisking well to avoid lumps. Cook the sauce over a moderate heat until it is thick, whisking frequently. Remove it from the heat and beat in first the grated cheese, then the egg yolks, mixing thoroughly. Allow the mixture to cool slightly. Season with salt and pepper. While the sauce is cooling, lightly sauté the diced courgettes in the 15 g (½ oz) butter, until they begin to turn golden.

Grease six ramekins (no. 1 size) and stand them in a roasting- or baking-tin. Whisk the egg whites until they are stiff. Whisk a spoonful of the whites into the sauce to thin it a little, before carefully folding in the remaining egg whites. Ladle the mixture into the ramekins, half filling each one. Put a spoonful of the diced courgettes on top; cover with the remaining mixture.

Fill the roasting-tin with enough boiling water to come halfway up the sides of the ramekins, and bake them in a moderately hot oven (190°C, 375°F, mark 5) for 30 minutes, when the soufflés should be well-risen and slightly brown on top. Serve them immediately.

Editor's notes: this method could be applied to other vegetables (cauliflower, Brussels sprouts, broccoli, leeks, for example). The more 'solid' the vegetable, the less you need. The sauce can be prepared a little time ahead and kept warm in a bain-marie (page 213), so that you have only to add the freshly-beaten egg whites and diced courgettes before putting in the oven.

Avocado and tomato salad (6)

**Highbullen Hotel,
Chittlehamholt, Devon
Chef/proprietor:
Pamela Neil**

six	ripe avocados	six
eight	tomatoes	eight
one	shallot *or* small onion	one
two	cloves of garlic	two
twelve	capers	twelve
one	sprig of parsley	one
two 5 ml spoons	caster sugar	2 teasp
100 ml	wine vinegar	4 fl oz
200 ml	salad oil	8 fl oz
	salt, pepper	

Peel and halve the avocados and place them cut side down on individual serving plates. Slice them finely but leave them in their original shape. Surround them with the quartered, skinned and de-pipped tomatoes.

Liquidise the remaining ingredients and pour the sauce over the avocados.

Garrick steak

**Count House, St Just
in Penwith, Cornwall
Chef/proprietor:
Ann Long**

75–100 g	butter	3–4 oz
two	cloves of garlic	two
	salt	
	lemon juice	
four 250 g	sirloin steaks	four 8 oz

For the stuffing

one	small onion	one
25 g	butter	1 oz
125 g	mushrooms	4 oz
one 5 ml spoon	chopped parsley	1 teasp
one 5 ml spoon	chopped thyme	1 teasp
175 g	cooked ham	6 oz
one 15 ml spoon	white breadcrumbs	1 tablesp
	salt, pepper	
	oil and butter for frying	

Make the garlic butter by creaming the butter and beating in the crushed garlic and a little salt and lemon juice. Form it into a cylinder, wrap in plastic, and chill till firm. Trim the steaks and cut a slit horizontally in each one to form a pocket. Set aside.

To make the stuffing, soften the finely-chopped onion in the butter, add the sliced or chopped mushrooms and the chopped herbs, and cook slowly, covered, for five minutes. Remove the pan from the heat, stir in the ham (minced or in small cubes), the breadcrumbs, salt and pepper, and set aside to cool.

Stuff the steaks and sew up the slit. Ask your guests how they like them, fry them in oil and butter to the desired degree, and remove the thread or string.

To serve, slice each steak vertically in thin slices to reveal the stuffing, and garnish with pats of garlic butter. Use very hot plates.

Walnut and honey tart (6–8)

Hathaways,
London, S.W.11
Chef/proprietor:
Kathie Scheiding

175 g	shortcrust pastry (page 202)	6 oz
75 g	butter	3 oz
125 g	demerara or soft brown sugar	5 oz
three	eggs	three
150 g	clear honey	6 oz
one 5 ml spoon	vanilla essence	1 teasp
100 g	walnut halves	4 oz
	cream (optional)	

Line a greased 20.5-cm (8-inch) shallow pie-dish with the shortcrust pastry and bake it blind in a hot oven (200°C, 400°F, mark 6) for 5–7 minutes. Allow it to cool.

To make the filling, cream the butter in a bowl, gradually add the sugar and beat them together until they are well blended. Add first the beaten eggs, then the honey and vanilla essence. Beat the mixture until it is smooth.

Sprinkle the walnuts in the bottom of the pastry case, pour over the honey mixture (it may seem very runny but it will set), and bake the tart in a hot oven (200°C, 400°F, mark 6) for about 45 minutes, or until it is set. (If, after about 15 minutes, the tart is browning too quickly, reduce the heat.) Serve cold, with or without cream.

Sussex pond pudding (6–8)

**White Moss House,
Grasmere, Cumbria
Chef/proprietor:
Jean Butterworth**

250 g	self-raising flour	8 oz
one	pinch of salt	one
125 g	shredded suet	4 oz
150–175 ml	milk and water (mixed)	6–7 fl oz

For the filling

150 g	butter	6 oz
150 g	demerara sugar	6 oz
one	large, juicy lemon	one

For serving

	double cream	

To make the crust, mix the flour, salt and suet together. Add enough milk and water to form a soft elastic dough. Roll the dough out on a floured board to 5 mm ($\frac{1}{4}$ inch) thickness. Line a greased 750-ml (1½-pint) pudding basin with the dough, reserving a quarter for the lid.

Cut the butter into small pieces and put half of them in the bottom of the basin with half of the sugar. Prick the lemon all over with a fine skewer and put it on top of the butter and sugar. Cover it with the remaining butter and sugar. Damp the edge of the dough and cover with a lid of the remaining dough. Press the edges together and cover with greased foil. Half fill a pan with boiling water. Lower the basin onto a trivet (or a saucer or tin plate) in the pan. Cover it and boil for four hours. (Check the water level, and replenish it when necessary.)

Turn the pudding out into a deep serving plate to catch the buttery 'pond' as you cut it into sections with a piece of the cooked lemon on each portion. Serve with double cream.

Chef's note: use a thin-skinned lemon.

Trippa alla parmigiana
or
Broccoli vinaigrette

Rognons à la moutarde, rice *or* noodles, runner beans
or sprouts

Quark gateau
or
Victoria plum mousse

Offal has had a bad press for a very long time, what with rhyming (nearly) with 'awful' and being called variety meats in North America. But it has always been prized by peasants and would-be peasants who live close to the earth and who have evolved ways of making most parts of a carcase not just edible but delicious. Offal was esteemed in very early times by the aristocracy too, and certainly kidneys and sweetbreads have kept their prestige. Tripe is a different kettle of—well, guts. However, the recent news that there are no likely replacements for the elderly ladies who have earned their living scrubbing tripe will doubtless lead to a shortage, and that in turn to vastly inflated prices, and then tripe—like oysters, another food of the poor only a hundred years ago—will go up in the world. In the meantime, gather round you some like-minded friends and enjoy a balanced and delightful meal. But make sure all your guests *do* enjoy both tripe and kidneys, because one truth about offal is that if you don't like it, you can't swallow it.

First course

We cooked Italian, French, Scottish and Chinese tripe while researching this book, and trippa alla parmigiana was a winner. It has familiar Italian ingredients to modify its own distinctive flavour, and the final result is a comforting, homely and easily-digested stew-in-a-bowl. As an alternative, for those for whom one course of offal is quite enough, we suggest broccoli vinaigrette, tangy and refreshing, and very easy to prepare. Haricots verts and asparagus are equally delicious prepared in this way.

Main course

If you have very little time to prepare this meal on the actual day, the tripe could be cooked ahead and reheated without harm, and the rognons à la moutarde take only half an hour from start to finish. Do not be tempted to over-cook the kidneys, since they toughen very quickly into chunks of radial tyre. But if things go as planned, you will have an elegant dish with very little expenditure of either time or money. The sauce is rich and mustardy, so we suggest rice or noodles to mop it up, with a crisp green vegetable for contrast

Sweet course

Quark gateau is a delightful lemon meringue confection with a name like a rubber duck because of the home-made cheese in the filling. It is equally good in the strawberry-and-orange alternative suggested by the restaurant. The Victoria plum mousse is an attractively simple sweet with the taste of our favourite plums coming through loud and clear. Other possibilities are peaches in red wine (page 47) or Highland mist (page 90).

Wine suggestions

A red wine with plenty of body would go well with both tripe and kidneys: perhaps a Côtes du Rhône or Chianti, or even a good Catalan branded wine (Torres, for example). And if you think your guests deserve a reward for holding out through the offal marathon, serve a glass of something sweet with the gateau or mousse (Monbazillac, Vouvray Moelleux, Muscat de Beaumes de Venise).

Main course   Full red wine

Sweet course   Dessert wine

Trippa alla parmigiana

**Redgauntlet,
Galashiels, Borders
Chef/proprietor:
Carlo Campari**

1 kg	tripe	2 lb
one	onion	one
50 g	butter	2 oz
one	medium-sized carrot	one
	celery leaves	
one	clove of garlic	one
one	pinch of chopped parsley	one
one	bay leaf	one
one	pinch of basil	one
one	pinch of oregano	one
	salt, pepper	
100 ml	dry white wine	4 fl oz
225 g	Italian tinned tomatoes	8 oz
six 15 ml spoons	grated Parmesan	6 tablesp

Wash the tripe very thoroughly in cold water and allow it to drain before cutting it in one-cm (half-inch) slices. Fry the sliced onion in the butter till golden brown. Add the coarsely-grated carrot, the chopped leaves from one

127

stick of celery, the chopped garlic, the herbs, and salt and pepper to taste. Fry the mixture for 3–4 minutes, add the tripe, and cook over high heat for a few minutes to release the juices. Add the wine and the tomatoes, bring the mixture back to the boil, and simmer it for 2–4 hours until the tripe is tender.

Serve the tripe in bowls with a topping of grated Parmesan, and good crusty bread on hand to mop up the juices.

Editor's note: check with your butcher to find out whether the tripe has been cooked for the standard time, or more or less than that. If it has been rather over-cooked originally, it will take no more than two hours—otherwise it loses all texture except sliminess. Cook the tripe uncovered for the last hour for a thicker sauce.

Broccoli vinaigrette

Dixcart Hotel, Sark, Channel Islands Chef: Gary Owston

500–750 g	fresh sprouting broccoli	1–1½ lb
	salt	
250 ml	vinaigrette (page 210)	10 fl oz
one	small onion	one
	parsley	

Cook the washed broccoli in boiling salted water for 8–10 minutes until it is barely tender (it must have a bite to it). Refresh it under cold water and drain it thoroughly. Arrange the broccoli on individual dishes and pour over the vinaigrette. Garnish with thinly-sliced raw onion rings and finely-chopped parsley.

Rognons à la moutarde

Trumps, Lewes,
East Sussex
Chef/proprietor:
Christopher Goff

500 g	lambs' kidneys	1 lb
125 g	button mushrooms	4 oz
25 g	unsalted butter	1 oz
two 15 ml spoons	Dijon mustard	2 tablesp
50 ml	double cream	2 fl oz
	salt, pepper	
one 5 ml spoon	cornflour	1 teasp
one 15 ml spoon	dry white wine	1 tablesp

For garnishing

one 15 ml spoon	chopped parsley	1 tablesp

Skin and quarter the kidneys, removing their cores. Sauté them gently with the sliced mushrooms in the butter until the kidneys are stiff and coloured. Add the mustard and double cream and heat the mixture thoroughly, seasoning it with salt and pepper.

Mix the cornflour with the wine until smooth and stir it into the sauce. Cook the kidneys over low heat for a further minute and serve them garnished with chopped parsley.

Chef's note: if the sauce separates, stir in a little cold cream at the last moment.

Quark gateau (6)

Old Rectory,
Claughton, Lancashire
Chef/proprietor:
Mrs P. Martin

1 litre	plain yoghourt	2 pints
four	egg whites	four
250 g	icing sugar	8 oz
75–100 g	caster sugar	3–4 oz
one	egg	one
two	lemons	two

For decoration

	whipped cream (optional)	

Strain the yoghourt through fine muslin for 48 hours.

To make the meringues, whisk the egg whites until they are very frothy and gradually add the icing sugar. Set the bowl over a saucepan of simmering water and continue whisking until the mixture is very stiff. Pipe the meringue into two large circles on greased baking-sheets lined with grease-proof paper and bake them in a cool oven (120°C, 250°F, mark ½) for about an hour until they are dry. Allow them to cool.

For the filling, beat together the caster sugar, the beaten egg, the grated rind and juice of the lemons. Add this mixture to the strained yoghourt. Spread the filling on one of the cooled meringues and put the other one on top. Decorate with a little whipped cream or some reserved filling.

Chef's note: as an alternative, omit the beaten egg and lemon juice, and add instead two dozen or so halved strawberries mixed with the juice of half an orange.

Editor's notes: do not assemble the gateau too far in advance as the meringue will soften. You may prefer to make individual gateaux: pipe the meringue into twelve circles about 7.5–10 cm (3–4 inches) in diameter and sandwich them with the filling in the same way.

Victoria plum mousse (8)

**Hungry Monk,
Jevington, East Sussex
Chefs: Ian Dowding &
Kent Austin**

1 kg	Victoria plums	2 lb
three 15 ml spoons	granulated sugar	3 tablesp
125 ml	red wine	5 fl oz
125 ml	water	5 fl oz
1.25 cm	cinnamon stick	$\frac{1}{2}$ inch
one	strip of lemon zest	one
15 g	gelatine	$\frac{1}{2}$ oz
three	eggs	three
50 g	caster sugar	2 oz
125 ml	double cream	5 fl oz

Halve and stone the plums. Dissolve the granulated sugar in the wine and water, add the cinnamon stick and the lemon zest, and bring the mixture to the boil. Poach the plums in this syrup until they are soft. Strain and reserve the syrup. Sieve the plums. Sprinkle the gelatine into 250 ml (10 fl oz) fruit syrup and set it aside.

Whisk the eggs and caster sugar until thick (most easily done with an electric mixer or over hot water in a double boiler). Heat the gelatine mixture gently until it has dissolved. Fold it into the egg mixture with the cream and fruit puree, reserving three spoonsful of the puree for decoration.

Pour the mixture into individual dishes and decorate them by marbling the reserved fruit puree into the top surface. Allow the mousse to set in a cool place before serving it with shortbread.

Restaurateur's note: this recipe was originated by Claire Brewster, friend and collaborator on *The Hungry Monk at Home*.

Kipper pâté
or
Fish pâté

Old English brisket with dumplings, cabbage, parsnips
or carrots

Apple and lemon tart
or
Wharfedale orange tart

When the national honour is at stake, as in entertaining foreign visitors, first thoughts might turn to smoked salmon, a good joint of beef, and sherry trifle (known to Italians as zuppa inglese). But just a little more trouble produces a more interesting but no less traditional meal, at considerably lower cost.

First course

Both fish pâtés can be prepared ahead and are easy to serve, important considerations if you like to enjoy relaxed and intelligent conversation before meals. The kipper pâté makes a light yet tasty first course, but since it easily overpowers white wine, consider serving a dry sherry or Manzanilla with it. The mixed fish pâté is gentler and creamier (and more fattening). A bottle of English white wine would be appropriate with it, and there are now many vineyards and several grape varieties to choose from. Only trial and error will tell you which you prefer (Hambledon, Adgestone and Pilton Manor are three of the well-established vineyards), but English wines are dear for what they are (not the growers' fault) and most of them are very dry. If you have a sweetish palate, you may prefer a young moselle or Rhine wine.

Should the weather be arctic rather than temperate, or if you know that one of your guests dislikes fish, try mushroom soup (page 4) or Stilton soup (page 110) instead.

Main course

The preparation of the brisket may daunt you at first reading, but all the steps are manageable, even if you cannot talk your butcher into sharing the task, and the processes require more patience than skill. The suggested size of joint cooks well by this method, and left-overs make tasty sandwiches and salads. The combination of tender beef, genuine gravy and light dumplings should do much to retrieve the national reputation. Choose and cook the accompanying vegetables with care too. Cabbage, finely sliced, lightly cooked, thoroughly drained and well buttered and seasoned, is worlds away from 'school dinner special'. The parsnips may be boiled and pureed, or roasted. You might also consider discarding the carrots in the casserole and serving steamed young ones with chopped parsley instead. The recipes for lemon-baked cabbage (page 194) and carrots in orange and coriander (page 195) are other possibilities, but be careful not to duplicate the fruit flavours in the sweet.

The English love of claret suggests here as good a Médoc as you can afford. A fine wine will show to advantage with this main course, since—for once—there are no strong herbs or spices, sugar, cream, or vinegar to distract the palate. Otherwise, try a 'claretty' Rioja (perhaps Marqués de Riscal) at a much lower price, or desert Europe for the Commonwealth and serve an Australian red from the Hunter or Barrossa Valleys.

Sweet course

Both fruity tarts are tangy and not too heavy, as a counterpoise to the substantial main course. We preferred both served slightly warm, although the apple and lemon one is acceptable cold. In either case, you can do most of the preparation in advance. Cook the lemon and apple tart before the brisket goes in the oven; the orange one can cook at the same time as the meat. If the tart cools completely, reheat it very gently for a short time in the warming oven. The lemon posset on page 159 is another alternative, if you prefer a creamy sweet.

This is a slimmed-down version of the typical 'North Country' meal which Bronwen Nixon puts on her menu at Rothay Manor, Ambleside, quite regularly: 'forced' eggs with salad; lettuce cream soup (page 30); the brisket and dumplings with fried parsnips, cauliflower in batter and jacket potatoes; the lemon and apple tart; and Stilton with wholemeal biscuits. If *your* guests have North-Country appetites, offer them Stilton and a glass of tawny port to round off their fine English meal suitably.

Wine suggestions

First course

With the kipper pâté, dry sherry or Manzanilla. With the fish pâté, English or German white wine.

Main course

Either claret, Rioja, or an Australian wine

Kipper pâté

John Dory, Torquay,
Devon
Chef: Ronald Luggie

four	small kipper fillets	four
50 g	butter	2 oz
50 ml	plain yoghourt	2 fl oz
one 5 ml spoon	lemon juice	1 teasp
	cayenne pepper	
	clarified butter (page 213)	

Poach the kipper fillets gently in a little water until just cooked (about three minutes). Strain thoroughly, and remove any skin or bones. Liquidise the kipper flesh with the 50 g (2 oz) of melted butter, the yoghourt, the lemon juice and a generous dash of cayenne. When you have a smooth paste, pour it into one—or several—earthenware pots, and allow it to cool. When cold, cover the top with clarified butter and refrigerate until needed. Serve with hot French bread or toast.

Editor's notes: if you are using the pâté fairly soon after making it, there is no need to cover it with clarified butter, though since its appearance is not especially attractive, parsley would improve it. If you have difficulty liquidising the mixture, add a little more yoghourt or melted butter, depending on whether you prefer a 'buttery' or lighter pâté. A spoonful of whisky helps the blades go round too, but in that case, let the pâté mature for at least 24 hours.

Fish pâté

Casa Romana,
Weybridge, Surrey
Chef: Corrado di
Michele

250 g	mackerel	8 oz
250 g	whiting	8 oz
one	small clove of garlic	one
	cayenne, salt, pepper	
one 5 ml spoon	brandy	1 teasp
two 15 ml spoons	gelatine	2 tablesp
one 15 ml spoon	mayonnaise (page 211)	1 tablesp
50 ml	double cream	2 fl oz
75 g	butter	3 oz

For garnishing

	parsley, lemon	

Poach the fish gently in about 250 ml (10 fl oz) water till just tender. Fillet the fish carefully, throwing the bones and trimmings back into the pan. Boil the stock vigorously until it is reduced by half. Put the fish, seasonings and about 100 ml (4 fl oz) of the reduced stock in the liquidiser and blend till smooth (add more stock if the blades jam). Add the brandy at the last minute. Leave the mixture to cool.

Dissolve the gelatine in a couple of spoonsful of water. Leave to cool. Fold first the mayonnaise and cream, then the gelatine, into the fish puree. Use about a third of the butter to butter an earthenware dish, put in the pâté, and cover with the remaining butter, melted or clarified (page 213). Refrigerate for at least six hours. Decorate the pâté with parsley and lemon, and serve it in slices with toast or brown bread.

Chef's note: the pâté keeps two or three days in the refrigerator.

Old English brisket with dumplings (6–8)

Rothay Manor, Ambleside, Cumbria Chef/proprietor: Bronwen Nixon

2.75 kg	point end of brisket	6 lb
	salt, pepper	
1 kg	mixed onions, carrots, swedes, celery	2 lb
500 ml–1 litre	brown beef stock (page 207)	1–2 pints

For the dumplings

125 g	self-raising flour	4 oz
40 g	shredded suet	$1\frac{1}{2}$ oz
	salt, pepper	

Carefully prepare the joint by removing all the gristle which is between the layers. In order to do this, you may have to separate pieces of meat from the main joint. Keep the skin and outside layer of fat intact. Season the meat, replace the loose pieces of lean meat, roll the joint tightly, lengthways, in a long narrow roll, and tie it with string in several places.

Prepare the vegetables and cut them into large chunks. Put them with the meat in a large braising-tin, cover the joint with some of the trimmed fat, and pile the remaining fat in a corner of the tin. Add enough stock to come three-quarters up the tin. Cover it with its lid or foil, and cook in a moderate oven (180°C, 350°F, mark 4) for 2–3 hours, or until the meat is tender. Remove the cover to crisp the fat for the last 15 minutes.

To make the dumplings, mix the flour, suet, and seasoning to a stiff dough with cold water. Divide it into twelve pieces and roll them into balls with floured hands. Leave the dumplings for 15 minutes to 'set'.

Put the meat in the warming oven. Simmer the stock and vegetables in a saucepan, and remove excess fat. Drop the dumplings into the simmering liquid. Cover the pan, and allow the dumplings to cook for 15 minutes, over moderate heat. When they bob to the top, they are cooked.

Serve the vegetables and dumplings with the joint, accompanied by the gravy, now slightly thickened by the flour from the dumplings.

Editor's note: a good butcher will prepare the rolled joint for you.

Apple and lemon tart

Rothay Manor,
Ambleside, Cumbria
Chef/proprietor:
Bronwen Nixon

75 g	butter	3 oz
50 g	caster sugar	2 oz
one	egg	one
75 g	plain flour	3 oz
75 g	self-raising flour	3 oz

For the filling

two	medium-sized cooking apples	two
half	large lemon	half
125 g	caster sugar	4 oz
	cream (optional)	

To make the pastry, cream the butter and sugar till white and fluffy, add the beaten egg and then the flour. Mix to form a soft dough, and knead lightly. Cover, and refrigerate for 30 minutes. Roll out the pastry thinly, and line an 18-cm (7-inch) flan case (remembering to leave enough over for the lattice decoration).

Peel and core the apples, quarter and de-pip the lemon, and mince them both finely (including the lemon rind). Add enough sugar to sweeten the mixture adequately without cancelling the tartness. (Apples and lemons vary so greatly in size and sourness that you will have to experiment with quantities.) Put the filling in the prepared case, cover with lattice strips made from the pastry trimmings, and bake in a moderate oven (160°C, 325°F, mark 3) for 30 minutes. Serve warm or cold, with or without cream.

Wharfedale orange tart

Weaver's Shed,
Golcar, West
Yorkshire
Chef: Mrs Margaret
Brook

175 g	shortcrust pastry (page 202)	6 oz
one	large juicy orange	one
100 g	ground almonds	4 oz
125 g	caster sugar	5 oz
	cream (optional)	

Make the shortcrust pastry, line a buttered 18-cm (7-inch) flan case, and chill it for 30 minutes. Mix together the grated orange rind, ground almonds and sugar, and add the strained juice. Put the filling in the pastry case. Bake in a moderate oven (180°C, 350°F, mark 4) for about 30 minutes, until the filling is brown but not quite firm. Serve warm, with cream if you wish.

Fillets of plaice 'Vosgienne'
or
Petite casserole de poisson

Suprême de volaille Quat' Saisons, rice *or* noodles,
haricots verts *or* broccoli

Sorbet au citron
or
Cheese and fruit

There are other menus in the book for soup-lovers and sweet-lovers. This one is for enthusiastic cooks who, like the French, prefer the main course to be the high point of a meal. It is not only classic but classy, and that never comes without effort, but if cooking is a joy and recreation rather than a chore, you will feel the time well spent. As a bonus, you will have mastered the making of a mousseline, a technique useful for fish, veal and liver as well as chicken, and you will have created one of those unctuous butter-and-cream sauces which are the essence of France for many travellers. So turn to this meal when you have time and energy to spare, and serve it, of course, to appreciative guests who will eat it without hankering after a steak or roast as they do so.

First course

The fishy first courses are relatively simple to prepare and not at all rich. The mustard and vinegar juices with the plaice fillets are slightly sharp, but the piquancy enlivens a rather bland fish and awakens the palate for the richness to come. The petite casserole de poisson, unlike the other fish soups in the book, is free of tomato, garlic and saffron, and the fennel and lemon among the ingredients give a pleasant and unusual tang. Neither dish demands a fine white wine, nor a very dry one, so consider a Mâcon Blanc, perhaps, or Mâcon Lugny. Otherwise, serve a glass of your usual 'house' wine. Other suitable first courses are broccoli vinaigrette (page 128) and consommé en gelée au citron (page 156).

Main course

Raymond Blanc's way with chicken breasts is a delight: they are tender and juicy from their short cooking, lightened in texture by the mousseline, and flattered by the creamy sauce. Note that you can do much of the preparation ahead of time, but the dish has to be finished just before the meal. The simplest accompaniments are called for: rice or noodles or even bread for the sauce, and a crisp green vegetable. The ideal wine with such a splendid dish would be fine white burgundy, but that is beyond many people's pockets.

However, if you have a bottle you've been saving for a special occasion, this is it. On the other hand, if you like Alsace wines, a Riesling, Muscat or Gewürztraminer would go well with the chicken, as would a Sancerre or Pouilly Fumé, and of course, any not-too-sweet German wine.

Third course

After this, you may wish to follow the French pattern and serve fruit and cheese, with some carefully-chosen fresh fruit and equally carefully-chosen cheeses. If the party is a large one, offer several cheeses with a contrast in textures and styles, but if there are only four of you, it might be best to serve a generous wedge of Brie or Roquefort, say, rather than small pieces of different cheeses. Epoisses, a delicious cream cheese from Burgundy which comes in 'demi' as well as full size, is a useful one to remember for small parties, as are the various goat cheeses. Your guests may enjoy a glass—it need not be more—of red wine at this stage in the meal, and a good French one, whether claret, burgundy or Rhône, would bring the meal to a triumphant conclusion. Our other suggestion is a palate-cleansing lemon sorbet, rather coarse-textured, but sharply refreshing. A fruit compote (page 48) or port and claret jelly (page 108) would be equally appropriate.

Wine suggestions

First course

Minor white wine, not too dry

Main course

Fine French or German white wine

Cheese

French red wine

Fillets of plaice 'Vosgienne'

Rafters,
Stow-on-the-Wold,
Gloucestershire
Chef/proprietor:
David Price

two	large plaice	two
75 g	button mushrooms	3 oz
150 g	cream cheese	6 oz
one	clove of garlic	one
two 15 ml spoons	fresh chopped parsley	2 tablesp
two 10 ml spoons	French mustard	1½ tablesp
three 15 ml spoons	wine vinegar	3 tablesp
one 5 ml spoon	nutmeg	1 teasp
25 g	butter	1 oz

Ask the fishmonger to fillet each plaice in four and remove the dark skin. Thinly slice the mushrooms and mix 50 g (2 oz) of them with the cheese, garlic, parsley and half the mustard. Spread the filling evenly over one side of each fillet. Fold them in half lengthways and spread the remaining mustard on top. Put the fish in a buttered, oven-proof serving dish, add the remaining sliced mushrooms, vinegar and grated nutmeg. Dot the fish with butter, cover the dish tightly with foil, and bake in a hot oven (200°C, 400°F, mark 6) for 15–20 minutes. Serve hot with some of the juices poured over the fish.

Petite casserole de poisson

M'sieur Frog,
London, N.1
Chef/proprietor:
Howard Rawlinson

500 g	firm white fish (e.g. plaice, cod, monkfish, mackerel, skate, turbot)	1 lb
one	medium-sized head of fennel	one
one	medium-sized onion	one
half 15 ml spoon	oil	½ tablesp
half 15 ml spoon	butter	½ tablesp
half	lemon	half
50 ml	dry white wine	2 fl oz
1.25 litre	fish fumet (page 208)	2 pints
	salt, pepper	
For garnishing	finely-chopped parsley	
	fennel leaves	

Fillet the fish and cut it into 2.5-cm (one-inch) chunks. Finely chop the fennel, reserving the feathery tops for garnishing.

In a heavy gratin dish or flame-proof casserole, fry the finely-chopped onion and fennel together in the oil and butter until they are soft but not coloured. Add the fish, the lemon cut into wedges, the wine and the fish fumet, and season with salt and pepper. Cover the dish with its lid or foil and either simmer it gently or bake it in a moderate oven (180°C, 350°F, mark 4) for about 20 minutes.

Remove the lemon wedges. Serve the soup sprinkled with finely-chopped parsley and the reserved fennel leaves.

Suprême de volaille Quat' Saisons

Les Quat' Saisons, Oxford, Oxfordshire Chef/proprietor: Raymond Blanc			
	four	chicken breasts	four
	30 g	butter	1¼ oz
	one	chicken leg	one
	one	small carrot	one
		parsley stalks *or* an onion and half a leek	
	four	mushrooms	four
	one-quarter	stalk of celery	one-quarter
	one	pinch of chopped French tarragon	one
	175 ml	dry white wine	7 fl oz
	175 ml	water	7 fl oz
	15 g	butter	½ oz
	15 g	flour	½ oz
For the mousseline	150 g	chicken meat (breast)	6 oz
	one	egg white	one
	four 15 ml spoons	whipping cream	4 tablesp
		salt, pepper	
	30 g	foie gras	1¼ oz
For the sauce	15 g	butter	½ oz
	125–200 ml	whipping cream	5–8 fl oz
	one-eighth	lemon	one-eighth
	one	pinch of chopped French tarragon	one
	one	pinch of chopped chives	one

Skin and bone the chicken breasts. To make the velouté, melt the butter and in it gently sauté the bones from the breasts, the chopped chicken leg, carrot, parsley stalks or onion and leek, mushrooms, celery and tarragon. Add the wine and water and simmer the stock for an hour. Make a roux (page 206) with the butter and flour and strain the stock into it. Boil until the quantity is reduced by half.

All ingredients and utensils for the mousseline should be as cold as possible. Remove the nerves and sinews from the chicken meat, and liquidise it. Mix in the beaten egg white and chill the mixture for an hour. Work in the cream with a spatula, add salt and pepper, and combine this mixture with the creamed foie gras. Slit the chicken breasts and, using a piping bag, fill the slits with the mousseline.

Melt 15 g ($\frac{1}{2}$ oz) of the butter in a sauté pan, and start cooking the chicken breasts over gentle heat. Measure the velouté before adding it to the pan, along with an equal quantity of whipping cream, the juice from the lemon wedge, the tarragon and chives. Cover the pan and cook the chicken for 5–10 minutes, till tender and no longer pink.

Chef's note: failing fresh tarragon, use only the best quality of dried.

Editor's note: the ingredients can be prepared up to the last paragraph of the recipe, and chilled, to be finished just before the meal.

Sorbet au citron

one	lemon	one
125 g	sugar	4 oz
375 ml	water	15 fl oz
four 5 ml spoons	powdered gelatine	4 teasp
one	pinch of salt	one

Pre-set the refrigerator at its coldest setting.

In a saucepan, combine the grated lemon rind, sugar and water and bring the mixture to the boil. Simmer it gently for ten minutes. Meanwhile, soak the gelatine in four 5 ml (tea) spoons of cold water. Remove the pan from the heat and add the gelatine and salt, stirring until the gelatine has completely dissolved. Chill the syrup for about 45 minutes. Add the juice of the lemon to the chilled syrup and beat it well for two minutes, or until it is light and frothy. Pour it into a freezing tray and freeze it for at least three hours, until it is firm.

Aubergine viennoise
or
Mushroom and walnut pâté

Cheese and vegetable chowder
Green salad

Chestnut and orange roulade
or
Dried fruit salad with sour cream

Entertaining vegetarians is a daunting prospect to many people. Perhaps the best approach is to discard the three-courses-meat-and-two-veg approach to menu-planning (is this the origin of nut cutlets?) and devise instead an interesting and colourful meal which is appetising and nourishing in its own right, without resorting to the standbys of the beleaguered caterer, an omelette or egg mayonnaise. Not that we would decry either (when well made), but they seem pedestrian solutions to what need not even be a problem.

The rise in the numbers of foreign restaurants in this country, the widening of the scope of foreign travel, and the increase in ethnic and health-food cookery books have all made people much more aware of what can be done with pulses, green vegetables and some fragrant herbs and spices. Whether from religious or climatic necessity, cooks in the Middle and Far East have developed such dishes as samosas, stuffed vine leaves, red-cooked bean-curd, vegetable bhajias, all of which can set you thinking about your own menus if you become addicted to your vegetarian friends or to vegetarianism. Nut cutlets apart, think too of creative substitutes. For example, one of the best moussakas we ever tasted had chopped red kidney beans in place of minced lamb.

First course

The aubergine fritters with tartare sauce are worth the last-minute preparation, but if you prefer to be organised ahead of time, choose the 'trompe l'oeil' mushroom and walnut pâté, with its rich and complex flavour. Other possible first courses are turnip soup (page 4), aubergines à la turque (page 61) and tenerelli (page 40).

Main course

The cheese and vegetable chowder is a creamily satisfying meal-in-a-bowl, ideal either as a hearty snack meal on its own, if you come home from chilly outdoor pursuits with a vast appetite, or as the centre-piece of this more formal menu. Serve it, if you wish, with wholewheat bread (page 205). The suggested green salad can follow as a palate-clearer. Other possibilities are chick peas provençale (page 196), and broccoli vinaigrette (page 128).

Sweet course

We suggest two contrasting puddings: a spectacular 'Swiss roll' made with chestnut puree and flavoured with fresh orange and orange liqueur, or a delicious winter fruit salad, with dried and fresh fruit enlivened by stem ginger and sour cream. Since the meal has been free of cream to this point, you *could* serve any of the most self-indulgent sweets in the book, from Champagne Charlie (page 32) to chocolate and praline cream (page 74).

Wine suggestion

A light red wine would probably be most appropriate with this meal, which poses difficulties with its liquid main course. Choose a Beaujolais Villages, a Provencal red, Valpolicella, or a bourgeois claret, all of which would partner the fritters or pâté and the cheese soup adequately.

First and main course   Light red wine

Aubergine viennoise

Mirabelle, West Runton, Norfolk Chef/proprietor: Manfred Hollwöger

two	medium-sized aubergines	two
	salt	
	flour	
two	eggs	two
	fresh white breadcrumbs	
	oil or butter	

For serving

	tartare sauce (page 212)	

Cut the peeled aubergines into $\frac{1}{2}$-cm ($\frac{1}{4}$-inch) slices, salt them, and dust them with flour. Egg and crumb the aubergine slices, patting the crumbs on firmly. Fry them gently in oil or butter and serve with tartare sauce.

Editor's note: the aubergines will keep fairly well in the warming-oven while you fry successive batches.

144

Mushroom and walnut pâté

Dundas Arms,
Kintbury, Berkshire
Chef/proprietor:
David Dalzell-Piper

one	medium-sized onion	one
	oil	
250 g	mushrooms	8 oz
	marjoram or basil	
half	clove of garlic	half
	salt, pepper	
40 g	walnuts	1½ oz

Chop the onion and fry it in oil until it is translucent. Add the chopped mushrooms and cook for a few minutes. Add the herbs, garlic and seasoning.

Liquidise the walnuts, add the mushroom mixture, and liquidise again. Cool the pâté and serve with brioche or brown bread and butter.

Cheese and vegetable chowder (10–12)

Hathaways,
London, S.W.11
Chef/proprietor:
Kathie Scheiding

two	large leeks	two
six	sticks of celery	six
250 g	carrots	8 oz
one	medium-sized turnip	one
two	medium-sized onions	two
150 g	butter	6 oz
500 ml	water	1 pint
	salt, pepper	
one 15 ml spoon	mixed herbs	1 tablesp
one	bay leaf	one
500 g	potatoes	1 lb
75 g	butter	3 oz
three 15 ml spoons	flour	3 tablesp
1 litre	milk	2 pints
250 g	Cheddar or Edam	8 oz
500 g	frozen peas (or equivalent amount of fresh)	1 lb

For garnishing

	croûtons	

Finely chop and dice the leeks, celery, carrots, turnip and onions and sauté them in the melted butter for a few minutes. Add the water, seasonings and bay leaf, bring the mixture to the boil, and simmer it for 15 minutes.

145

Add the diced potatoes and cook for a further ten minutes or until the potatoes are nearly tender. Set the mixture aside.

In a separate saucepan make a roux (page 206) with the butter and flour, add the milk, and cook it until it is slightly thickened. Add this sauce to the vegetable mixture and stir it well over low heat.

Grate the cheese and reserve a little for garnishing. Gradually add the remaining cheese and peas to the mixture, and cook over low heat for about five minutes, until the cheese has melted and the peas are cooked. Check the seasoning.

Serve the chowder sprinkled with grated cheese and croûtons.

Chef's note: as no stock is used in this recipe, it suits vegetarians.

Chestnut and orange roulade (6)

Isle of Eriska Hotel,
Eriska, Argyll
Chef: Sally Collier

three	eggs	three
125 g	sugar	4 oz
one	orange	one
250 g	unsweetened chestnut puree	8 oz
	orange liqueur	
250 ml	double cream	10 fl oz

For decoration

	whipped cream	
	orange slices	

Separate the eggs, and beat the yolks with the sugar until the mixture is pale and creamy. Beat in the grated orange rind and chestnut puree. Fold in the stiffly-beaten egg whites and pour the mixture into a greased Swiss-roll tin lined with lightly-oiled grease-proof or Bakewell paper. Bake the sponge in a moderate oven (180°C, 350°F, mark 4) for about ten minutes until it is firm and golden. Cover the tin with a damp tea towel and leave it for at least eight hours, taking care not to let the towel dry out.

When ready to serve, turn the sponge onto grease-proof paper and spread it with orange-liqueur-flavoured whipped cream. Roll it up like a Swiss roll, set it seam-side down on a serving plate and decorate it with whipped cream and orange slices.

Editor's note: if the edges of the sponge are at all crisp, cut them off before rolling it up.

146

Dried fruit salad with sour cream

Henderson's Salad Table, Edinburgh Chefs: Catherine M. Henderson & Jim McBain

25 g	dried apricots	1 oz
25 g	dried prunes	1 oz
25 g	dried apples	1 oz
25 g	dried pears	1 oz
25 g	dried peaches	1 oz
25 g	dried figs	1 oz
25 g	raisins	1 oz
one	lemon	one
three	pieces of stem ginger	three
two	bananas	two
two	cooking apples	two
	sour cream	

For decoration

	raisins
	orange segments
	tinned ginger chips

Wash the dried fruit thoroughly, mix it with the zest of the lemon and leave it to soak in enough water to cover for 12 hours. Add the chopped stem ginger and sliced bananas and apples to the mixture. Put the fruit in a serving dish and top it with a layer of sour cream. Decorate the salad with raisins, orange segments and ginger chips.

Editor's note: failing ginger chips for decoration, use chopped stem ginger.

Spinach flan
or
Devilled mackerel

Braised breast of lamb with onion puree and
tomato sauce, boiled potatoes *or* rice, sprouts,
hot cucumber

Banana cake
or
Syrup flan

Some of us feel poverty-stricken all the time, others suffer from attacks at the
end of the month or after Christmas. But no one who entertains at all can be
unfamiliar with the problem of planning a party with more good-will and
time than house-keeping money. One of the most agreeable solutions is to
choose dishes using relatively cheap ingredients, put together in a way which
makes the whole much more than the sum of its parts. French housewives
have the reputation of doing this constantly, and it is a habit worth
cultivating for regular family meals as well as for parties.

First course

If you decide to serve the spinach flan, make it before the lamb goes in the
oven, and warm it gently before serving. It uses 'seasonal' greens, and
yoghourt instead of cream, so that it is healthy and nutritious as well as
economical. The devilled mackerel have, of course, a much stronger taste,
but their piquant sauce makes an appealing contrast to the rich-tasting main
course. The flan could be accompanied by a glass of the main-course wine,
but the mackerel will fight almost anything. So you might decide to miss
wine with this course, or encourage guests to bring their sherries with them
to table. Other reasonably-priced dishes to consider are the turnip soup on
page 4, and the kipper pâté on page 134.

Main course

The lamb recipe is long but not over-demanding, since the initial preparation
takes place the day before the party. A liquidiser also makes quick work of
several otherwise more laborious processes. The dish is probably too fat-rich
for young children, but appeals to many adults, even those who prefer to see
a 'sheet of meat' on their plates. 'You do have to like onions', was one
test-eater's comment. Serve it with plain vegetables which provide a colour
contrast, and avoid spinach, of course, if you have already chosen it for your
first course. (The recipe for hot cucumber is on page 195.) With strong
flavours and a thick sauce, this is the time to serve a simple but forceful red

wine, either a minor French one, perhaps from the South-West (Gaillac or Minervois, for example), an Italian (Chianti or Barbera) or a reliable Spanish (from Panadés, say).

Sweet course   The syrup flan, a good 'nursery sweet', as nostalgic as tea-dipped madeleines, will cook at the same time as the lamb. The banana cake, which is prepared ahead, is lighter than you might expect and makes an impressive finish to a meal. Be sure to choose it if you are serving the spinach flan as a first course, so that pastry does not appear twice on the menu. If you prefer something fruitier to end this rich meal, try, perhaps, the apple brûlée (page 113) or —with the same proviso about pastry—the apple and lemon tart (page 136).

No one is going to leave the table after this meal feeling either under-fed or over-conscious of your bank manager standing behind the chair. And on another occasion, when time rather than money is in short supply, you can dazzle your guests with the menu on page 55. However, if you generally feel hard-up in summer too, turn to the menu on page 66.

Wine suggestions

First course   Dry sherry with either dish, or start the main-course wine with the flan

Main course   Either French regional, Italian or Spanish red wine

Spinach flan (6)

Glaisters Lodge,
Corsock,
Dumfriesshire
Chef/proprietor:
Mrs Judith Edwards

1 kg	spinach	2 lb
175 g	shortcrust pastry (page 202)	6 oz
three	eggs	three
125 ml	plain yoghourt	5 fl oz
one 10 ml spoon	fresh lemon juice	1 dessertsp
	salt, pepper, nutmeg	
50 g	bacon or ham	2 oz

Wash the spinach, remove the stalks, and cook it with no additional liquid with a little salt for about ten minutes. Drain and chop it. Line a 20.5-cm (8-inch) flan ring with the pastry. Refrigerate it until it is chilled, then brush it with one of the egg whites, lightly beaten.

Preheat the oven to 200°C (400°F, mark 6).

Beat the two whole eggs and the remaining yolk until they are light and fluffy. Mix in the yoghourt, lemon juice, a little salt, pepper, and nutmeg, and stir in the spinach. Lay strips of cooked bacon or ham on the bottom of the flan, and carefully pour the spinach mixture on top. Bake the flan for 20 minutes, then reduce the heat to 160°C (325°F, mark 3) and cook it for a further ten minutes. Serve it warm or cold.

Chef's note: spring greens can be used instead of spinach.

Devilled mackerel fillets

Lower Brook House,
Blockley,
Gloucestershire
Chef/proprietors:
Robert & Gill
Greenstock

four	fresh mackerel fillets	four
one 15 ml spoon	cooking oil	1 tablesp
two 5 ml spoons	dry mustard	2 teasp
one 5 ml spoon	curry powder	1 teasp
one 5 ml spoon	caster sugar	1 teasp
two 15 ml spoons	H.P. sauce	2 tablesp
one	clove of garlic, crushed	one

For garnishing

	lemon	
	parsley	

Wipe the mackerel fillets with a damp cloth, and remove any stray bones. Mix together the remaining ingredients to form a smooth paste. Spread it thickly over the fillets and lay them on a buttered grill tray. Grill until they are cooked (about ten minutes). Garnish with lemon wedges or sprigs of parsley, and serve with crusty bread.

Editor's note: experiment with other piquant sauces, whether commercial or home-made, for example, mushroom ketchup, or chutney.

Braised breast of lamb with onion puree and tomato sauce

Plough, Fadmoor, North Yorkshire Chef/proprietor: Kathlyn Brown			
	one–two	breasts of lamb	one–two
	25 g	dripping	1 oz
	one	onion	one
	two	carrots	two
	500 ml	beef stock (page 207)	1 pint
	six	black peppercorns	six
	one 15 ml spoon	tomato puree or	1 tablesp
	125 ml	tinned tomatoes	5 fl oz
	one 5 ml spoon	dried mixed herbs	1 teasp
		salt	
For the topping	four	slices of white bread	four
	one 15 ml spoon	flour	1 tablesp
	50 g	grated Cheddar	2 oz
	six	onions	six
	25 g	butter	1 oz
		salt, pepper	
For the sauce		tomato ketchup	

Brown the breasts in the dripping in a large braising-tin. Remove them, and in the fat gently fry the sliced onion and quartered or sliced carrots until they are slightly coloured. Replace the meat on top of the vegetables, add the stock to a depth of about 1 cm ($\frac{1}{2}$ inch), the peppercorns, tomato puree (or tinned tomatoes), herbs and a little salt. Bring to simmering point, cover, and cook in a moderate oven (180°C, 350°F, mark 4) for 1–1$\frac{1}{2}$ hours, until the meat is tender enough for the bones to be easily removed. Leave in a cool place until the next day. Discard the congealed fat on top of the casserole. Remove the bones as neatly as possible.

In the liquidiser, crumb the crustless bread with the flour. Mix with the cheese and set aside. Slice the remaining six onions finely and fry them gently in the butter. Season lightly with salt and pepper, and liquidise. Set aside.

Put the braising liquid and vegetables (removing the peppercorns) in the liquidiser, and blend till smooth.

Rinse the braising-tin with hot water and put the meat back. Cover it with the onion puree, and gently press the breadcrumb mixture on top. Moisten with a little of the braising liquid. Cook, uncovered, in a moderately hot oven (190°C, 375°F, mark 5) for 30 minutes, until golden brown.

For the tomato sauce, heat up the braising liquid and any remaining cooking juices, thin it if necessary to sauce consistency, and add a dash of tomato ketchup to sharpen it. Serve the sauce over the sliced meat.

Chef's note: the use of the liquidiser for three of the steps in this recipe makes it less complicated than it might sound at first reading. Done in this order, there is no need to wash the liquidiser until the end.

Editor's note: if you prefer, cut the meat into serving-sized pieces before coating it with the onion puree and crumbs.

Banana cake (8)

Hathaways,
London, S.W.11
Chef/proprietor:
Kathie Scheiding

two	ripe bananas	two
three 15 ml spoons	plain yoghourt	3 tablesp
375 g	self-raising flour	12 oz
¾ of 5 ml spoon	bicarbonate of soda	¾ teasp
half 5 ml spoon	salt	½ teasp
125 g	butter	4 oz
275 g	caster sugar	10 oz
two	eggs	two
one 5 ml spoon	vanilla essence	1 teasp

For the filling

2–3	bananas	2–3
250 ml	double cream	10 fl oz

Preheat the oven to 180°C (350°F, mark 4). Grease three sandwich tins and line the bases with grease-proof paper. Butter the paper lightly.

Mash the ripe bananas and stir in the yoghourt. In a separate bowl, sift together the flour, bicarbonate of soda and salt.

In a mixing-bowl, cream together the softened butter and sugar till light and fluffy. Add the beaten eggs and beat until thoroughly mixed. (If the mixture shows any sign of curdling, beat in a spoonful of the sifted flour.) Add alternate spoonsful of the yoghourt mixture and flour mixture, beating after each addition. Add the vanilla essence.

Pour the batter into the sandwich tins and bake for about 35 minutes, when the cakes should be coming away from the sides of the tins. Allow them to cool slightly before turning out onto wire racks to cool completely. Fill the layers with the sliced bananas and whipped cream.

Chef's note: the cake keeps well (unfilled) wrapped in foil, and becomes even moister.

Editor's note: for a smaller cake, use slightly less than half quantities in one tin, and split it.

Syrup flan

Lake Vyrnwy Hotel,
Llanwddyn, Powys
Chef/proprietor:
Mrs Moir

175 g	rich shortcrust pastry (page 203)	6 oz
175 g	golden syrup	6 oz
half	lemon	half
25 g	fresh white breadcrumbs	1 oz
one 15 ml spoon	boiling water	1 tablesp
	cream (optional)	

Line a 15–18 cm (6–7 inch) flan ring with the pastry. Reserve the trimmings. Refrigerate until it is chilled.

Mix the syrup, grated lemon rind, breadcrumbs and boiling water together, and put the mixture in the pastry case. Decorate the top with a trellis made from the pastry trimmings. Bake the tart in a moderate oven (180°C, 350°F, mark 4) for 15–20 minutes. Serve the tart warm, with cream if you wish.

Spicy tomato soup
or
Consommé en gelée au citron

Sauté de boeuf Mirabelle, creamed potatoes *or* noodles, braised endive *or* fennel

Coffee meringues with Tia Maria or chocolate sauce
or
Lemon posset

When spring is far behind, and your recipe file dog-eared with use, turn to this menu, which breathes new life into some standard favourites. It is an appropriate meal to serve to friends who number both conservative and adventurous eaters among them, or to guests whose tastes you do not know very well. You have to pay, of course, for such apparent simplicity—in cash, for the beef fillet, and in concentrated effort before the party. However, although the beef requires last-minute cooking, the other courses can be treated as a 'part work' and fitted in round other activities.

First course

The jellied consommé, with its unexpectedly lemony tang, *must* be made ahead of time; the tomato soup, with its unnerving amount of mixed spice, comes to no harm if reheated. (Be sure you use a standard tablespoon rather than a family heirloom to measure.) It is worth making beef stock whenever your butcher has some nice-looking marrow bones, and freezing it for recipes like the consommé. Home-made scones (page 205) would go well with either soup. Salade périgourdine (page 46) or turnip soup (page 4) are other possible first courses.

Main course

The Mirabelle's sauté de boeuf with its deliciously tender meat in a rich sauce which begs for good 'blotting-paper' is a much more sophisticated dish than boeuf Stroganoff. If you have all the ingredients ready, measured and sliced, with the onions fried and the green pepper blanched, the final cooking takes very little time. The dish *can* be prepared just before dinner, and kept hot in the warming-oven, but it is even better if served directly. Since the sauce is colourful, we suggest one of the lovely pale vegetables which make up in flavour what they lack in colour-contrast potential: endive is pleasingly bitter, and fennel has aniseed overtones.

Sweet course

Most people like meringues, and these coffee ones are an interesting variation. Only a real sweet tooth will want a lot of chocolate sauce, but Tia

154

Maria makes an appealing alternative. Vanilla ice-cream could be substituted for the whipped cream, and with the chocolate sauce on hand, you can easily make poires Belle Hélène (see note on page 158). Lemon posset is an old dish rather than a new one, but for those who find syllabub rather heavily creamy while enjoying the tart lemon flavour, this will be a refreshing and slightly lighter sweet. (Do not duplicate lemon flavours by serving the consommé and the posset in the same meal.)

Wine suggestions

The rich sauté of beef calls for a red wine with plenty of body, either a mature claret or burgundy if it's a subsidised party, or as good a Rhône wine, Barolo or Rioja as you can afford. And if you have shot your cheque-book on the fillet, turn to a Chilean Cabernet, or your wine merchant's 'full red wine' as an acceptable alternative.

Main course   Full red wine

Spicy tomato soup

Home Farm Hotel, Wilmington, Devon Chef: Susan Rowatt

two	large onions	two
50 g	butter	2 oz
250 g	fresh tomatoes	8 oz
250 g	tinned tomatoes	8 oz
one 15 ml spoon	tomato puree	1 tablesp
one	clove of garlic	one
one 15 ml spoon	mixed spice	1 tablesp
one 5 ml spoon	sugar	1 teasp
	salt, pepper	
	mixed herbs	
1 litre	chicken stock (page 207)	2 pints

Fry the diced onions in the butter until they are tender and translucent but not brown. Skin and de-seed the fresh tomatoes. Add the chopped tomatoes (fresh and tinned) and the puree to the pan. Add the crushed garlic, spice, sugar, seasoning, herbs and stock and simmer the soup for 10–15 minutes. Serve the soup very hot.

Editor's note: garnish the soup, if you wish, with croûtons or chopped parsley. It may also be liquidised if you prefer a smooth soup.

Consommé en gelée au citron

La Frégate, St Peter
Port, Guernsey,
Channel Islands
Chef: Konrad Holleis

1 litre	strong beef stock (page 207)	2 pints
150 g	shin of beef	6 oz
one	carrot	one
one	stick of celery	one
one	bay leaf	one
one	pinch of mace	one
one	pinch of allspice	one
six	peppercorns	six
two	egg whites	two
100 ml	water	4 fl oz
	salt	
two	lemons	two
three 15 ml spoons	dry sherry	3 tablesp

For garnishing

	sliced, peeled lemon	
	chopped chives	

Chill the beef stock overnight. Separately, chill the coarsely-minced shin of beef, the chopped vegetables, the seasonings, the lightly-beaten egg whites and the water.

Next day, combine the two mixtures, bring slowly to the boil, stirring occasionally to prevent the egg white sticking, and simmer very gently for about three hours. Strain the consommé, season it with salt, the juice of the lemons and the sherry, and chill it until it is set. Serve it garnished with slices of peeled lemon and chopped chives.

Editor's note: use gelatinous bones (such as marrow) when making the stock (or add a calf's foot) to encourage it to set. With such long simmering, it is safest to make unsalted stock and season it at the end.

Sauté de boeuf Mirabelle

Mirabelle, West
Runton, Norfolk
Chef/proprietor:
Manfred Hollwöger

750 g	tail end of fillet of beef	1½ lb
one	green pepper	one
one	medium-sized onion	one
15 g	butter	½ oz
	flour	
one 5 ml spoon	tomato puree	1 teasp
one	clove of garlic	one
	salt, pepper	
125 g	mushrooms	4 oz
75 ml	red wine	3 fl oz
100 ml	brandy	4 fl oz
50 ml	double cream	2 fl oz

If you cannot find tail end, use fillet. Remove all skin and fat from the meat and slice it thinly. Quarter and slice the green pepper and blanch it for a few minutes in boiling water. Rinse it in cold water and drain thoroughly.

In a heavy sauté pan or frying-pan, cook the finely-chopped onion in the butter until it is transparent. Dust the beef slices lightly with flour and brown them briefly in the same pan. Add the tomato puree, crushed garlic, salt, pepper, green pepper, sliced mushrooms, wine and brandy to the pan and bring the mixture quickly to the boil. Add the cream, bring the sauce back to the boil, and serve promptly on very hot plates. (Do not over-cook the beef, or it will toughen.)

Coffee meringues

Gibson's, Cardiff,
South Glamorgan
Chef/proprietor:
Irene Canning

four	egg whites	four
one	pinch of salt	one
250 g	caster sugar	8 oz
two 15 ml spoons	instant coffee	2 tablesp
	cooking oil	
	whipped cream	
	Tia Maria *or*	
	chocolate sauce (page 158)	

Whisk the egg whites with the salt until very stiff. Whisk in half of the sugar, a spoonful at a time, along with a spoonful of the coffee. Whisk the mixture after each addition until very stiff. Carefully fold in the rest of the sugar.

Line a baking-tray with foil and oil it very lightly with a tasteless oil, wiping it with kitchen paper to leave only a very thin film. Pipe or spoon the mixture in whatever size you like and bake the meringues in a cool oven (120°C, 250°F, mark ½) for about four hours. They are cooked when they lift easily from the foil. Allow them to cool and store in an air-tight container.

Serve them sandwiched with whipped cream and with Tia Maria or chocolate sauce.

Chef's note: for a dinner party a big bowl of little meringues looks particularly nice.

Chocolate sauce

Gibson's, Cardiff,
South Glamorgan
Chef/proprietor:
Irene Canning

100 g	dark chocolate	4 oz
100 g	sugar	4 oz
one	vanilla pod	one
two 5 ml spoons	cocoa	2 teasp
one 5 ml spoon	instant coffee	1 teasp
250 ml	water	10 fl oz

Put all the ingredients in a large heavy pan and bring them to the boil, stirring continuously. Continue to boil until everything has dissolved (it will boil up like jam) and then simmer the mixture until it is syrupy and has the consistency of single cream. Retrieve the vanilla pod for further use and serve the sauce with the coffee meringues.

Chef's note: if you overcook the sauce it will become fudge-like. To correct the consistency, add a few drops of boiling water. It will keep, covered, for up to a week in the refrigerator.

Editor's note: home-made vanilla ice-cream, a poached pear and chocolate sauce add up to poire Belle Hélène.

Lemon posset

Plough, Clanfield,
Oxfordshire
Chef/proprietor:
Jean Norton

250 ml	double cream	10 fl oz
one	lemon	one
65 g	caster sugar	2½ oz
65 ml	dry white wine	2½ fl oz
two	egg whites	two

For decoration

	a few grapes *or* julienne of lemon peel	

Whip the cream until thick. Gradually add the finely-grated rind and juice of the lemon, the sugar and the white wine to the cream, beating the mixture continuously until it holds its shape. Fold in the stiffly-beaten egg whites. Spoon the posset into individual glasses and decorate with halved and pipped grapes or a julienne of lemon peel. Refrigerate until chilled.

Editor's note: the posset may be refrigerated for two or three hours. It separates out when kept for much longer (although it can be 'whipped back into shape' if that happens).

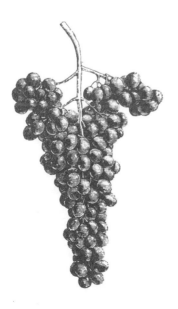

Prawn butter
or
Mussels and garlic stuffing

Elizabethan pork, noodles *or* rice, carrots, spinach

Pears with butter sauce
or
Lemon chiffon flan

If short days leave you short-tempered and the desire to hibernate is strong, perhaps what you need is a comfortable evening with family or close friends, and a menu which will neither work you into the ground nor break the bank balance. It is equally suitable for occasions when your attention must be committed somewhere other than the kitchen for several hours before the meal, whether on work, a fall of snow, a bridge class, or a wine-tasting. Almost everything can be prepared ahead, and last-minute fussing is at a minimum. It could even provide solace after an unsuccessful day at the January sales . . .

First course

Prawn butter is a Victorian delicacy worthy of revival. It is extremely rich (note that our quantities will serve several bridge tables) and achieves the miracle of 'extending' the prawns without dissipating their taste. Otherwise—and certainly if you plan to be carried away at the sales—choose the mussels and garlic stuffing, which take a little longer to prepare, but are inexpensive, very garlicky and delicious. They can be prepared ahead of time and finished at the last minute. If you prefer a non-fishy starter, consider the Stilton soup (page 110) or creamy baked tomatoes (page 72).

Main course

Many medieval recipes combined meat and dried fruit; this one is a little more unusual in its use of fresh fruit as well. The result is only slightly sweet but intriguingly complex. You may want to tinker with the recipe at repeat performances (perhaps dried apricots instead of dates, a pinch of cinnamon, cider instead of red wine, a few chunks of good pork sausage . . .) The gravy deserves well-cooked noodles or rice, and simple winter vegetables.

Sweet course

After all that richness, a fresh-fruit dessert seems appropriate, and the pears with butter sauce combine good winter fruit with a buttery sauce, flavoured with rum or not, as you wish. The lemon chiffon flan is pleasantly tangy, and can be easily portion-controlled. Of course, any of the sorbets in the book would be better for the waistline and digestion.

160

Wine suggestions

Even lovers of bone-dry wines often prefer something a little fuller in winter, so consider a fruity white wine with the first course, perhaps a Riesling or Gewürztraminer. The pork, with its own sweetness, also demands something light and fruity—a Tricastin from the Rhône, say, or a Provencal Bandol, or a good merchant's red house wine.

First course   Fruity white wine

Main course   Light and fruity red wine

Prawn butter (12–16)

**Vineyard,
Northampton,
Northamptonshire
Chef: Mrs Jo Clamp**

375 g	small prawns (shelled weight)	12 oz
375 g	halibut, cod or haddock	12 oz
375 g	melted butter	12 oz
half 5 ml spoon	anchovy essence	$\frac{1}{2}$ teasp
	salt, pepper, mace	
	cayenne pepper	
	cochineal	
	lemon, parsley *or* watercress	

If using fresh prawns, cook them in a little water, shell them, and boil up the shells in about 250 ml (10 fl oz) water for ten minutes. In this stock, cook the fish until just tender. If you are using frozen, shelled prawns, cook the fish in a little lightly salted water. Allow the fish to cool, flake it and remove any skin and bones. Put the prawns, fish, butter and seasonings in the liquidiser and blend till smooth. The mixture is stiff and should be blended in several small instalments. If the blades stick, add a little more melted butter to ease them. (Victorian cooks would have pounded it all in a mortar, and you may prefer this method yourself.)

Check the colour and add a little cochineal if the pink is at all 'muddy' from the anchovy essence. Put the prawn butter in one large, or several individual, white china dishes, and refrigerate till set. If it is not to be served within an hour or so, cover the top with clarified butter (page 213). Garnish with lemon, parsley or watercress, and serve with wholemeal toast.

Editor's note: some early recipes call for equal quantities of fish and butter, so don't think that you might spoil the proportions if you have to add more butter than the recipe suggests.

Mussels and garlic stuffing

Doyle's Seafood Bar,
Dingle, Co Kerry
Chef/proprietor:
Stella Doyle

3–4 litres	mussels	3–4 quarts
100 ml	dry white wine	4 fl oz
150 g	butter	5 oz
three	large cloves of garlic	three
four 15 ml spoons	chopped parsley	4 tablesp
100 g	fresh white breadcrumbs	4 oz

Keep the mussels alive in water until it is time to prepare them. Scrub each one thoroughly under cold running water, scrape off any barnacles, and pull off the 'beard'. Make sure all the sand is cleaned off, and discard any mussels already open or whose shells are loose. Put them in a large saucepan with the wine, cover, and shake over high heat until they have opened. (Discard any which do not open.)

Divide the shelled mussels among four oven-proof dishes or ramekins. Melt the butter, add the crushed garlic and chopped parsley, and allow the mixture to sit for ten minutes to blend the flavours. Stir the breadcrumbs into the butter, spread them over the top of the mussels and put the dishes under the grill or into a very hot oven for a few minutes until the crumbs are golden brown and crisp.

Editor's note: the mussels can be prepared ahead of time, and grilled at the last minute.

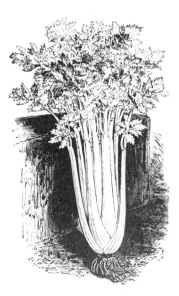

Elizabethan pork

The Refectory,
Richmond, Surrey
Chef/proprietor:
Mary Kingsley

750 g	boned shoulder, leg, *or* spare rib of pork	1½ lbs
	cooking oil, butter	
one	onion	one
one 15 ml spoon	flour	1 tablesp
half	lemon	half
half	orange	half
two	cooking apples	two
half	head of celery	half
50 g	dates	2 oz
50 g	raisins	2 oz
50 g	walnuts	2 oz
	fresh sweet herbs (optional)	
half 5 ml spoon	mace	½ teasp
half 5 ml spoon	curry powder	½ teasp
	salt, pepper	
one 15 ml spoon	honey	1 tablesp
	red wine	

In a heavy flame-proof casserole, fry the cubed meat quickly in a little cooking oil and butter. Remove the meat from the pan, and fry the sliced onion until it is golden. Replace the meat and sprinkle the flour over the meat and onion. Add the grated lemon and orange rind to the pan. Peel and add the orange and lemon segments. Then add the peeled and sliced apples, the chopped celery, the dates, raisins, nuts, chopped fresh herbs, spices, seasonings and honey, and mix well. Add enough wine just to cover all the ingredients, put the lid on the casserole, and cook in a slow oven (150°C, 300°F, mark 2) for three hours. Serve the pork with rice, noodles, or bread.

Pears with butter sauce

Lower Brook House,
Blockley,
Gloucestershire
Chef/proprietor:
Gill Greenstock

six	ripe pears	six
100 g	butter	4 oz
75 g	caster sugar	3 oz
one 15 ml spoon	flour	1 tablesp
two 15 ml spoons	double cream	2 tablesp

Peel and core the pears and place the halves in a serving dish. (If the pears are hard, poach them gently in a stock syrup [page 48] until they are tender.)

Melt the butter in a small saucepan and stir in the sugar until it is dissolved. Add the flour and cream and bring the mixture rapidly to the boil, stirring all the time. Simmer the sauce for about ten minutes.

Pour the sauce over the pears, and serve warm.

Chef's note: a small glass of rum added to the sauce makes it especially good.

Lemon chiffon flan (8)

La Belle Epoque,
Knutsford, Cheshire
Chefs: Yvonne
Shelmerdine & Mary
Horne

250 g	crushed digestive biscuits	8 oz
150 g	unsalted butter	5 oz
one	pinch of cinnamon	one
225 g	sugar	7 oz
two	lemons	two
125 g	butter	4 oz
three	eggs	three
125 ml	double cream	5 fl oz

For decoration

	double cream (optional)	

To make the base, mix together thoroughly the crushed biscuits, melted butter and cinnamon. Line a greased 23-cm (9-inch) flan ring with the biscuit mixture and leave it to set.

For the filling, heat the sugar, the juice and rind of the lemons, and the butter in a double boiler and stir until the sugar has dissolved. Add the thoroughly-beaten eggs and continue to stir until the mixture thickens, taking care not to let it boil. Allow it to cool. Fold in the whipped cream and pour the mixture into the flan case. Leave the flan to set in a cool place and decorate it with whipped cream, if you wish.

Aillade toulousaine
or
Légumes à l'aïoli

Duck with garlic and fresh ginger, mange-tout peas, carrots in orange and coriander

Crème brûlée
or
Peach yoghourt ice-cream

It is hard to take a balanced view of garlic. Most people love it or loathe it: this dinner is for those who love it a lot, indeed love a lot of it, and who grow impatient if a recipe suggests traces lurking in bowls, or even rubbing bowls with a quarter-clove. Obviously no one would want to make garlic their staple diet, but an orgy once in a while seems forgivable—even if you don't believe, along with the ancients, that it will give you supernatural powers or clear your lungs. But remember that your breath will clear your path through a room or tube train for about 24 hours, so find out first whether your like-minded guests have an important engagement on the morrow.

Frequently, when dining out, we have found ourselves enjoying snails with garlic butter or a hearty Provencal terrine, only to reach the main course with such impaired taste-buds that its delicate flavour—and especially that of the accompanying wine—was quite wasted. The obvious solution seems to be a garlic feast, where the raw-garlic flavours of the first course sauces are succeeded by the rather subtler garlic-and-ginger nuances of the duck. True devotees may then demand, 'Where's the garlic pudding?', but we suggest a gentler ending to the meal.

First course

Aillade toulousaine combines a delightful walnut and garlic mayonnaise with crisply-fried skewers of fish and bacon. The same sauce is a worthy partner to crudités or cold meat should you baulk at last-minute deep-frying. The *al dente* vegetables with aïoli is an equally beguiling first course, useful for a large party since it can be prepared ahead and extended easily to include extra guests. (In season you can use young broad beans, haricots verts, raw mushrooms, asparagus and fennel with the same sauce.) Provide plenty of crusty bread for extra dipping. In the unlikely event of any sauce being left over, use it up on baked potatoes or as dressing for steaks, fish or vegetables. Other first courses strong on garlic are gambas al ajillo (page 57), mussels and garlic stuffing (page 162) and mushrooms in garlic butter (page 9).

Main course

Edward Moss's duck does all that you could expect of a duck, and more. The skin is crisp; the subcutaneous fat is drained off; the flesh is tender and beautifully flavoured with the combined garlic and ginger, which are in perfect balance and not at all oppressive. We prefer it with a salad or a crisp green vegetable like mange-tout peas, but if you decide to make a sauce, continue the vaguely oriental theme with rice and carrots in orange and coriander (page 195). Other main courses for garlic-lovers are chicken with tremalki sauce (page 69), limande Monte Carlo (page 20) and chicken cocotte with garlic and fines herbes (page 52).

Sweet course

Something cooling or soothing seems needed to quench those fires. Crème brûlée is decadently rich and creamy, whether in the French or English versions. It can be made several hours ahead without the crisp topping softening, and the base can even be made the day before. The peach yoghourt ice-cream should not be made too far in advance, since it changes texture if kept for long, but it brings a lovely taste of summer to a winter meal. Any of the other fruit or ice-cream recipes in the book would be equally suitable.

Wine suggestions

Since this meal is not one for a fine wine, you might like to serve a good bottle of wine as an aperitif, before relaxing into your favourite ordinaire: anything interesting, unusual, or just plain good would be an appropriate talking point. It is always intriguing to taste a dry wine from an area or house better known for sweet (Ch. Doisy-Daëne in Barsac, for example), or a white wine from a château famous for its reds (Ch. Laville-Haut-Brion is the stable mate of Ch. La Mission-Haut-Brion, and the very best of the dry white Graves). Garlic makes you thirsty, and a large bottle of something red and quaffable would be best with both first and main courses, unless you are serving the fish with aillade toulousaine, when you will need some white wine as well as red.

Aperitif

Good white wine

First and main courses   Ordinaire

Aillade toulousaine

Horn of Plenty,
Gulworthy, Devon
Chef/proprietor:
Sonia Stevenson

75 g	unskinned walnuts	3 oz
6–8	small cloves of garlic	6–8
half 5 ml spoon	salt	$\frac{1}{2}$ teasp
one 10 ml spoon	tarragon vinegar	1 dessertsp
100–125 ml	olive oil	4–5 fl oz
500 g	fish and shellfish (see below)	1 lb
four	rashers of streaky bacon	four
one	egg	one
	fresh, white breadcrumbs	
	oil for deep-frying	

To make the sauce, put the broken walnuts, crushed garlic, salt and vinegar in the liquidiser, turn on the motor, and add enough olive oil to enable the blades to turn.

Choose a selection of white fish (monk-fish or cod, for example), raw prawns and scallops, and thread pieces on four skewers, interspersed with the bacon. Dip the skewers first in beaten egg, then breadcrumbs, and fry them in hot oil until they are cooked and golden (about three minutes).

Serve the skewers of fish with the garlic sauce.

Editor's note: the same sauce is delicious with raw vegetable strips, hard-boiled eggs or cold tongue.

Légumes à l'aïoli

Chez Nico,
London, S.E.22
Chef/proprietor:
Nico Ladenis

150 ml	olive oil	6 fl oz
50 ml	vinegar	2 fl oz
50 ml	white wine	2 fl oz
four	peppercorns	four
half 5 ml spoon	fresh thyme	½ teasp
one	bay leaf	one
one 5 ml spoon	sugar	1 teasp
one 5 ml spoon	salt	1 teasp
	pepper	
one	clove of garlic, crushed	one
one	small cauliflower	one
125 g	carrots	4 oz
500 g	mixed red and green peppers	1 lb
375 g	courgettes	12 oz
half	cucumber	half

For the aïoli

two	egg yolks	two
three	cloves of garlic	three
one 5 ml spoon	mustard	1 teasp
	salt, pepper	
250 ml	olive oil	10 fl oz
	sugar	
one 15 ml spoon	tarragon vinegar	1 tablesp
one 5 ml spoon	lemon juice	1 teasp

To make the vinaigrette, combine the oil, vinegar, wine and seasonings and bring them to the boil. Simmer for a few minutes to allow the flavours to amalgamate. Poach the cauliflower broken into florets and the thinly-sliced carrots in the vinaigrette for no more than five minutes. Remove them and next poach the diced pepper and the sliced courgettes and cucumber for three minutes at most. Put all the vegetables in a large bowl and cover them with the vinaigrette. Refrigerate when cool.

To make the aïoli, follow the method for mayonnaise (page 211), combining the crushed garlic and mustard with the beaten egg yolks before adding the oil.

To serve, arrange the vegetables decoratively on a flat platter round a heap of aïoli.

Chef's notes: be careful not to overcook the vegetables.

To make the aïoli really thick, warm the olive oil gently for one minute.

168

Duck with garlic and fresh ginger

Le Provençal,
Salisbury, Wiltshire
Chef/proprietor:
Edward Moss

one 2.25 kg	duck, dressed weight	one 5 lb
50 g	fresh ginger	2 oz
six	large cloves of garlic	six
one	handful of chopped parsley	one
three 15 ml spoons	olive oil	3 tablesp
	salt, pepper	

Wipe the duck inside and out, prick the skin all over with a sharp fork or skewer. Liquidise all the remaining ingredients to a coarse paste. (Use a little wine–or additional oil–if the blades stick.) Rub the paste into the skin of the duck, and put it, breast side up, on a rack in a roasting pan in a moderately hot oven (190°C, 375°F, mark 5). After 30 minutes, turn the duck over and roast it for a further hour, breast side down. Turn it again for the last 30 minutes.

Chef's note: if you wish to serve gravy, degrease the pan juices, flavour them with white wine, stock and a little stem or green ginger, and thicken slightly.

Crème brûlée (6–8)

Les Amoureux,
London, S.W.19
Chef/proprietor:
Nigel Thomson

For the brûlée

five	egg yolks	five
50 g	caster sugar	2 oz
500 ml	double cream	1 pint
40 ml	Grand Marnier	1½ fl oz

four 15 ml spoons	caster sugar	4 tablesp
one 15 ml spoon	water	1 tablesp

Combine the egg yolks, sugar, cream and Grand Marnier, and put the mixture in a shallow oven-proof dish or six ramekins. Cook the crème, uncovered, in a bain-marie (page 213) at 160°C (325°F, mark 3) for 45 minutes (about 30 minutes in individual dishes). Allow it to cool. For the brûlée, caramelise the sugar and water in a small, heavy pan, and pour it as evenly as possible over the crème. Cool, and serve when the caramel is crisp.

Editor's note: if you wish to try Cambridge burnt cream as a variation, use vanilla sugar in the cream, omit the liqueur, and chill the cream (uncovered) before covering with an even layer of caster sugar. Put it under a very hot grill and watch it carefully, turning it so that it caramelises as evenly as possible.

Peach yoghourt ice-cream (6–8)

Pool Court,
Pool-in-Wharfedale,
West Yorkshire
Pâtisserie chef:
Melvin Barry Jordan

250 ml	milk	10 fl oz
two	egg yolks	two
one	pinch of salt	one
55 g	caster sugar	2 oz
half 5 ml spoon	vanilla essence	$\frac{1}{2}$ teasp
250 ml	double cream	10 fl oz
375 ml	peach yoghourt	15 fl oz
125 ml	natural yoghourt	5 fl oz
half	lemon	half

Pre-set the refrigerator at its coldest setting.

To make the custard base, combine the milk, beaten egg yolks, salt and sugar. Cook the mixture slowly in a double boiler (page 213) until it thickens and coats a spoon. Allow it to cool and add the vanilla essence. Leave overnight.

The next day, make the ice-cream by mixing together the custard base, cream, and yoghourts in a deep bowl. Gradually add the lemon juice. Pour the mixture into an ice-cream container and put it in the freezer or freezing compartment, stirring sides to middle every 15 minutes for an hour. Then freeze the ice-cream until firm (1–3 hours depending on your freezer or refrigerator.)

Chef's note: the ice-cream changes texture if made too far in advance, so try to serve it soon after it is ready.

Editor's note: as an alternative, either serve this ice-cream with sliced fresh peaches in season, or use natural yoghourt and a puree of peaches instead of the peach yoghourt.

Sopa de pescadores Dulcinea
or
Sopa de Castilla la Vieja

Ternera Dulcinea, rice *or* potato pancakes,
spinach *or* green salad

Mousse au curaçao
or
Orange custard

They say that any competition for the best pot of tea and plateful of fish and chips would be won by a Spanish holiday resort, not a British one. With this meal we reverse the trend and serve some fine Spanish dishes—and others with Spanish overtones—to friends at home. Spain has exchanged ideas about cooking with France, Italy and Morocco, and the colourful and flavourful ingredients of this menu are also found in the Mediterranean one (page 92). But there are enough interesting variations to produce a distinctive meal. The soups, the sweets and the sauce for the veal can all be prepared ahead of time, leaving only the final frying of the escalopes and the cooking of the vegetables for the last minute. Embrace the spirit of it by serving tapas with the sherry: green olives bruised with garlic and herbs, toasted almonds, slices of spicy sausage on skewers, a few pickled prawns, dates rolled in ham, deep-fried squid rings if you are feeling ambitious—the list is endless, but even a couple of small dishes help to set the mood.

First course

The Dulcinea fish soup makes an intriguing contrast with the others in the book: it is a smooth puree rather than a chunky broth, and tastes vigorously 'Mediterranean' with its squid, olive oil and saffron. The almond soup is even more unusual and would make a light first course for delicate appetites. Other possibilities are simple gazpacho (page 56) and chick peas (garbanzos) provençale (page 196).

Main course

Señor Benavides' veal escalopes come in a fresh and tangy sauce which is not at all overwhelming but does require mopping up with rice or potato pancakes (page 189)—or crusty bread, if you prefer it. Spinach is a popular vegetable in Spain, but a green salad is customary.

Sweet course

Chocolate, oranges and eggs appear in several different combinations to make Spanish sweets, and all three of them are found in the mousse au curaçao, so it seems a legitimate borrowing for a Hispanic dinner. (Omit the almond decoration if you are serving the almond soup.) The orange custard is a popular dish in both Spain and Portugal, occasionally ousting the eternal *flan* from menus. Its texture is more spongy than a milk-based custard. If neither of these ideas appeals, oranges in brandy and Grand Marnier syrup (page 42) would be equally appropriate or bananes sautées jamaïque (page 190), if you attribute them to Cuba rather than Jamaica. If you can track down—or make—quince paste, it is a fine ending to a meal, served with a creamy cheese.

Wine suggestions

This is a good opportunity to explore some less well-known sherries, or their relatives. Manzanilla is a very dry, pale sherry, similar to fino, but with a salty tang to it. Montilla is unfortified (therefore cheaper than sherry) and it comes, like sherry, in various degrees of sweetness, labelled fino, amontillado and oloroso. If you prefer sherry itself, consider choosing an unusual one, perhaps Dos Cortados dry oloroso or Ynocente, from the only sherry vineyard named on a label. With the main course serve either a white Rioja (Marqués de Murrieta, say) or a red Rioja, Panadés or the lighter Valdepeña. And if you like to finish the evening with a glass of sweet wine, consider either Moscatel or Malaga.

Aperitif	Fino, Manzanilla or Montilla
Main course	White or red Rioja, Panadés or Valdepeñas
Sweet course	Moscatel or Malaga

Sopa de pescadores 'Dulcinea'

**Dulcinea,
Weybridge, Surrey
Chef/proprietor:
Longinos Benavides**

half	Spanish onion	half
four	cloves of garlic	four
100 ml	olive oil	4 fl oz
125 g	squid	4 oz
two	slices of green pepper	two
	salt, pepper	
	basil	
	parsley	
one	pinch of saffron (optional)	one
65 ml	white wine	$2\frac{1}{2}$ fl oz
two 15 ml spoons	tomato puree	2 tablesp
750–800 ml	water	$1\frac{1}{2}$ pints
125 g	monk-fish (or bones)	4 oz
25 g	cornflour	1 oz
50 ml	double cream	2 fl oz
	garlic croûtons	

In a large heavy pan fry the chopped onion and garlic in the oil until they are golden. Clean the squid, cut it into small pieces and add it to the pan with the sliced pepper, seasonings, wine, and tomato puree. Add enough water to cover the fish and bring the mixture to the boil. Add the monk-fish (cut into small pieces) or the bones and simmer the soup for ten minutes. Thicken the soup with the cornflour, cook for a further two minutes, and strain it through a very fine sieve. Add the cream and serve the soup garnished with garlic croûtons.

Sopa de Castilla la Vieja

**Dulcinea,
Weybridge, Surrey
Chef/proprietor:
Longinos Benavides**

25 ml	olive oil	1 fl oz
25 g	ground almonds	1 oz
1 litre	beef consommé	2 pints
	salt, pepper	
four	thin slices of French bread	four
75 g	Parmesan cheese	3 oz
50 g	toasted flaked almonds	2 oz

Mix the olive oil with the ground almonds and a little consommé, and pour the mixture into the remaining hot consommé. Bring the mixture to the boil, and check the seasoning. Pour the soup into individual dishes and top with

173

thin, lightly toasted slices of French bread, sprinkled with grated Parmesan. Place the bowls under the grill until the cheese is lightly browned and sprinkle the soup with flaked almonds.

Editor's note: consommé is clarified stock, made with meat as well as bones (page 207). (See also consommé en gelée au citron on page 156.)

Ternera Dulcinea

Dulcinea,
Weybridge, Surrey
Chef/proprietor:
Longinos Benavides

one	orange	one
one-quarter	lemon	one-quarter
125 ml	wine	5 fl oz
$\frac{1}{4}$ of a 5 ml spoon	tarragon	$\frac{1}{4}$ teasp
half 5 ml spoon	chopped parsley	$\frac{1}{2}$ teasp
	black peppercorns	
	salt, pepper	
four	tinned or cooked red cherries	four
125 ml	béchamel sauce (page 209)	5 fl oz
125 ml	cream	5 fl oz
one	pinch of paprika	one
one	pinch of ground cloves	one
one	pinch of nutmeg	one
one	bay leaf	one
25 ml	calvados	1 fl oz
four 125 g	veal escalopes	four 4 oz
25 g	flour	1 oz
two 15 ml spoons	oil	2 tablesp

For garnishing

four	red cherries	four

To make the sauce, combine the orange and lemon juice, wine, tarragon, parsley, peppercorns, salt, pepper, and cherries and reduce the liquor by half over high heat. Add the béchamel sauce, cream, paprika, ground cloves, nutmeg, and the bay leaf, and bring the mixture back to the boil. Add the calvados and check the seasoning. Sieve and reheat the sauce.

Meanwhile, coat the escalopes with flour and fry them in oil for about 2–3 minutes on each side, until the juices run yellow. Pour the sauce over the escalopes and garnish each one with a cherry.

Mousse au curaçao

Yew Tree, Odstock,
Wiltshire
Chef/proprietor:
Mrs Gould

150 g	plain cooking chocolate	6 oz
two	oranges	two
one 15 ml spoon	instant coffee	1 tablesp
four	leaves of gelatine *or*	four
15 g	powdered gelatine (approx)	$\frac{1}{2}$ oz
65 ml	orange curaçao	$2\frac{1}{2}$ fl oz
500 ml	double cream	1 pint
six	eggs	six
100 g	caster sugar	4 oz
	grilled almonds	

Slowly melt the chocolate in a thick-bottomed pan and stir in the zest of the oranges and the coffee. Dissolve the gelatine in the juice of one orange and stir it into the chocolate mixture with the liqueur. Allow it to cool.

Whip the cream until it holds its shape and fold it into the chocolate. Beat the eggs and sugar together in a bain-marie (page 213) until the mixture trebles in volume. Gradually add it to the chocolate mixture. Spoon the mousse into individual dishes and refrigerate overnight. Decorate with grilled almonds before serving. Make the mousse a day ahead to allow the flavours to ripen.

Editor's note: failing curaçao, use Cointreau or other orange liqueur.

Orange custard

three	eggs	three
150 g	caster sugar	5 oz
one	large orange	one
	orange segments	
	whipped cream (optional)	

Beat together the eggs, the sugar, and the grated rind and juice of the orange. Pour the mixture into a small greased soufflé dish (or other oven-proof dish), set it in a bain-marie (page 213), and cook it in a moderate oven (180°C, 350°F, mark 4) for about 50 minutes, until a toothpick inserted in the centre comes out clean. Turn the custard out, if you wish, and decorate it with orange segments and whipped cream. Alternatively, make it in four ramekins, cook it for about 40 minutes, and serve each one decorated with an orange segment or rosette of cream.

Filetto di sogliola marinato

Potted smoked mackerel

Pork and rabbit pie

Savoury braid

Creole jambalaya and salads

Grapefruit cheesecake

Iced chocolate cases with rum cream

Ice-cream and sauces

Some people achieve, apparently effortlessly, buffet displays like the gold-medal awards table at the *salon culinaire* of a catering exhibition. Others line up (neatly) a hundred matching sausage rolls and sink back exhausted. Most of us, however, fall somewhere between the two. The main thing to remember is that virtually an entire meal is going to be on display all at the same time rather than reaching the guests course by course. This makes it particularly important to consider contrast, in colour and texture as well as taste. No two dishes should look the same, taste the same, or have the same basic ingredients. For example, if a guest allergic to shellfish meets both prawn butter (page 161) and Creole jambalaya his choices have narrowed considerably.

The age and disposition of the guests, as well as the nature of the occasion, will dictate the sort of buffet you prepare. We have done no more than outline some ideas which seem attractive and fairly original; your own circumstances will help—or force—you to a decision as to what to serve. If it is a summer party, you may decide to have all the food cold; in winter it seems more sensible to have at least one hot dish. If the weather is particularly foul, soup makes a comforting beginning, served from a huge tureen or pot into bowls or mugs rather than flat plates, which are difficult to balance. (Remember that all recipes serve four unless otherwise specified.)

The marinated sole looks attractive, tastes interesting, and can be easily eaten with just a fork. The potted smoked mackerel is a cheap but tasty pâté, best served with French or wholewheat bread (page 205). Other attractive dishes to replace or supplement these are mushroom and walnut pâté (page 145), broccoli vinaigrette (page 128), légumes à l'aïoli (page 168) or Caroline's pizza (page 186). If you opt for soup, the chilled saffron one (page 15) would suit a summer party, and the cheese and vegetable chowder (page 145) a hearty winter one.

Some kind of pie always goes down well on a buffet. The pork and rabbit one is a satisfying dish, and if you decide on the savoury braid, you can make a variety of fillings. The braid has the additional advantage of being served either hot or cold. Other pies or flans to consider are tourtière québecoise (page 106), Stilton and spring onion wholemeal flan (page 78), or a quiche.

Creole jambalaya, a New World cousin of Spanish paella, is a decorative dish, ideal for a large party since it can be extended by increasing some of the ingredients—not necessarily the expensive prawns. If you have an electric hot plate, leave it on that. Otherwise, serve it from a very hot, rather deep casserole to retain as much heat as possible. A meat or fish casserole with barley or rice pilaff also works well as a buffet dish, since once again only a fork is needed. Serve a variety of salads, variously dressed, perhaps raw spinach and chick peas provençale (page 196), as well as a good simple green one. (Use Webb's, cos or iceberg lettuce which will not flop the moment they meet the salad dressing.)

If you have room for a second, smaller table, reserve that for the sweet course. If plates and cutlery are already set there, you can produce the various ice-creams and sauces quite quickly after the savoury dishes are finished. We suggest the lovely grapefruit cheesecake as a 'set piece', and several bowls of ice-cream (see the index for flavours), along with the Ballymaloe iced chocolate cases with rum cream, various sauces (the index lists butter, caramel, chocolate and raspberry) and perhaps some nuts or fresh or cooked fruit for decoration. Encourage people to make their own sundaes—and name them. (For an adult party, you might like to produce some liqueur bottles for even more inventive—or horrifying—concoctions.) Lemon biscuits (page 204) or meringues (coffee ones are on page 157) would provide a contrasting crunch.

Wine suggestions

If this is a summer celebration and expense is no object, serve something fizzy, at least to start with. If champagne is beyond your means, turn to sparkling Saumur or the lighter Crémant de la Loire. Otherwise, a rosé might be appealing, especially if the group is a young one, and after that you would probably feel most comfortable with modestly-priced wines, a red and a white, either a favourite brand, your wine merchant's own house wine, or a modest Chianti (for the red). In summer a fruit cup makes an attractive aperitif, but keep it simple: nothing is less appetising than a confusion of pulpy fruit and warring alcohols. A dessert wine would be wasted on either grapefruit or the ice-cream medley, but if a toast is to be drunk, Asti Spumante would come into its own after the meal.

Filetto di sogliola marinato

Don Pasquale,
Gloucester,
Gloucestershire
Chef: Philip Schettini

four	fillets of lemon sole	four
one 15 ml spoon	olive oil	1 tablesp
one	medium onion	one
40 g	seedless raisins	$1\frac{1}{2}$ oz
250 ml	white wine vinegar	10 fl oz
40 g	cashew nuts	$1\frac{1}{2}$ oz
	lettuce	

Skin the fillets and lightly fry them in the oil. Add the chopped onion, raisins and wine vinegar, and bring the mixture to the boil. Remove the pan from the heat, and leave the fish to marinate for 2–5 hours. About 30 minutes before serving, add the cashew nuts. Serve the cold sole on a bed of lettuce.

Potted smoked mackerel (12–15)

Refectory, Richmond,
Surrey
Chef/proprietor:
Mary Kingsley

two	smoked mackerel	two
125 g	cream cheese	4 oz
375 g	butter	12 oz
two	lemons	two
	pepper	
	lemon slices	
	watercress	

Skin and bone the fish and break it up into small pieces. Liquidise it with the cream cheese in two or more batches, gradually adding the melted butter and lemon juice. Season the paste with pepper and chill it until ready to serve, garnished with lemon slices and watercress.

Editor's note: if you wish to freeze the potted mackerel, cover it with clarified butter (page 213).

Pork and rabbit pie

Old Fire Engine
House, Ely,
Cambridgeshire
Chef/proprietor:
Ann Ford

one	rabbit	one
three 15 ml spoons	seasoned flour	3 tablesp
	butter for frying	
one	large onion *or* clove of garlic	one
	salt, pepper, mixed herbs	
one	bay leaf	one
half	lemon	half
500 ml	water	1 pint
65 ml	sherry	2½ fl oz
500 g	cooked pork *or* bacon	1 lb
175 g	shortcrust pastry (page 202)	6 oz
one	egg	one

Joint the rabbit into manageable pieces, coat them with seasoned flour, fry them in butter, and put them in an oven-proof casserole.

Fry the chopped onion or clove of garlic and add to the casserole along with a generous pinch of salt, pepper, herbs and the bay leaf. Add the lemon zest and juice, the water and the sherry to the frying juices in the pan and mix them well together. Pour the liquor over the rabbit and onions. Cook the casserole, covered, in a moderate oven (180°C, 350°F, mark 4) for 1½ hours.

Allow the meat to cool, then strip it from its bones and place it in a one-litre (two-pint) pie dish with the chopped pork or bacon. Add the cooking juices.

Pre-heat the oven to 230°C (450°F, mark 8).

Roll out the pastry 2.5 cm (one inch) larger than the pie dish. Cut off the surplus all round. Damp the edges of the dish, lay on the strip and brush with water. Put the pastry lid in position and press the edges firmly together. Trim away any surplus pastry, then flute the edges with the back of a knife or the fingers. Make a slit in the top to allow the steam to escape. Roll out any trimmings to make decorative leaves for the top; brush it all with the beaten egg. Put the pie in the oven, turn it down to 220°C (425°F, mark 7) and cook for a further 15–20 minutes.

Serve the pie hot.

Editor's note: with no fresh rabbit to hand, you could use the frozen, boned rabbit on sale in supermarkets.

Savoury braid (6)

White Moss House,
Grasmere, Cumbria
Chef/proprietor:
Jean Butterworth

500 g	sausage meat	1 lb
one	large stick of celery	one
one	medium-sized apple	one
one 5 ml spoon	chopped chives	1 teasp
	chopped parsley	
half 5 ml spoon	dry English mustard	$\frac{1}{2}$ teasp
	Worcestershire sauce	
	salt, pepper	
250 g	puff pastry (page 203)	8 oz
	milk, egg	

Fry the sausage meat lightly for about five minutes to extract some of the fat. Dice the celery and apple. Combine all the filling ingredients.

Roll out the pastry into a rectangle about 20 cm by 30 (8 inches by 12) and trim the edges. Put the filling in a long strip down the centre third of the pastry and slash the edges diagonally towards the centre. Brush them with water and fold each piece alternately over the filling to give the appearance of a plait. Brush the pastry with milk and beaten egg and cook it in a hot oven (230°C, 450°F, mark 8) for 7–10 minutes, until the pastry is risen and brown. Reduce the heat to 180°C (350°F, mark 4) and cook for a further 15 minutes.

Serve the braid hot or cold.

Chef's notes: shortcrust pastry may be used but does not look quite so attractive.

Try alternative fillings such as minced beef mixed with tomato and a little curry powder, or cooked fresh salmon in a flavoursome white sauce on a bed of diced cucumber, or cooked chicken or turkey in a sauce with chopped mixed herbs, and so on. If the filling is already cooked, 7–10 minutes will cook the pastry; if it is raw, cook for an extra 15–20 minutes (as in the recipe above).

The braid freezes well before being cooked.

Creole jambalaya (6–8)

David's Place,
Knutsford, Cheshire
Chef/proprietor:
David Molloy

375 g	cooked ham	12 oz
375 g	large prawns, shelled	12 oz
250 g	garlic ham *or* chorizo sausage	8 oz
four 15 ml spoons	olive oil	4 tablesp
two 15 ml spoons	melted butter	2 tablesp
two 15 ml spoons	lard	2 tablesp
one	Spanish onion	one
375 g	risotto rice	12 oz
one	stalk of celery	one
one	green pepper	one
six	tomatoes	six
one	small tin of tomato puree	one
one	bay leaf	one
half 5 ml spoon	oregano	½ teasp
one	pinch of thyme	one
one	pinch of ground cloves	one
two	cloves of garlic, crushed	two
	salt, pepper, cayenne	
1 litre	chicken stock (page 207)	2 pints
100 ml	dry white wine	4 fl oz
four 15 ml spoons	finely-chopped parsley *or* black olives	4 tablesp

Cut the ham into 2.5-cm (one-inch) squares, split the prawns if they are very large, and slice the sausage (use pork or garlic sausage if you cannot find chorizo). Heat the oil in a heavy frying-pan and sauté the ham and sausage until they are golden. Add the prawns for the last few minutes.

Heat the butter and the lard in a large flame-proof casserole or saucepan and sauté the finely-chopped onion until it is transparent. Stir in the rice and cook it over low heat, stirring gently, until it is golden. Add the ham mixture to the rice. Stir in the chopped celery and pepper, the peeled, seeded and chopped tomatoes, tomato puree and seasonings. (You will need very little salt.)

Bring the stock to the boil and add it to the casserole. Cover, and simmer over low heat for 25–30 minutes, until the rice is tender but still separate, adding a little more stock from time to time as necessary.

Just before serving, stir in the wine, correct the seasoning, and garnish the jambalaya with the parsley or a handful of pitted black olives.

Chef's note: if the casserole must be kept hot, put it in a very low oven.

Grapefruit cheesecake (6–8)

Food for Thought,
Cheltenham,
Gloucestershire
Chef/proprietors:
Joanna Jane Mahon &
Christopher Wickens

125–150 g	digestive biscuits	4–6 oz
25 g	caster sugar	1 oz
one	pinch of grated nutmeg	one
one	pinch of ground allspice	one
50 g	butter	2 oz
two	grapefruit	two
15 g	gelatine	$\frac{1}{2}$ oz
250 g	cream cheese	8 oz
125 ml	single cream	5 fl oz
two	eggs	two
125 g	caster sugar	4 oz
125 ml	double cream	5 fl oz

Crush the digestive biscuits into crumbs (either in the liquidiser, or in a plastic bag with a rolling-pin), and mix them with the sugar, nutmeg and allspice. Melt the butter and tip it into the crumbs. Mix them thoroughly, and scatter half the mixture on the bottom of a 20-cm (8-inch) loose-bottomed cake tin.

To make the filling, grate the rind and squeeze the juice of the grapefruit. Soak the gelatine in eight 15 ml (table) spoonsful of the juice for a few minutes. Heat it enough to dissolve the gelatine.

Beat the cream cheese and single cream together. Separate the eggs and whisk the yolks, sugar and grated rind together. Gradually beat in the grapefruit juice. Combine this mixture with the cream cheese mixture.

Whip the double cream until it begins to thicken and fold it into the cheese mixture along with the warmed juice and gelatine. When this has thickened somewhat, fold in the stiffly-beaten egg whites. Pour the mixture into the prepared tin, scatter the remaining crumbs on top, and refrigerate till set. Remove from the tin before serving.

Chef's note: for a mulberry cheesecake, cook 500 g (1 lb) mulberries with 125 g (4 oz) sugar until tender. Liquidise and sieve the puree, and gradually add the egg yolk and sugar mixture to it. Instead of the eight spoonsful of grapefruit juice in which the gelatine is dissolved, use a mixture of water and lemon juice.

Editor's note: if you wish to decorate the cheesecake, use segments of fresh grapefruit, neatly divested of all pith and membrane, or blanched julienne of peel in a cluster.

Iced chocolate cases with rum cream (6)

Ballymaloe House,
Shanagarry, Co. Cork
Chef/proprietor:
Myrtle Allen

250 g	plain chocolate (approx)	8 oz
2 dozen	paper cake cases	2 dozen
500 ml	chocolate ice-cream (approx)	1 pint
200 ml	whipping cream (approx)	8 fl oz
one 5 ml spoon	caster sugar	1 teasp
one 15 ml spoon	rum	1 tablesp

Melt the chocolate in a dish in a cool oven. Use the paper cases in pairs to give 12 of double thickness. Coat them inside with a thin layer of chocolate (a finger is a useful tool), and allow the cases to harden in a cool place. Fill the chocolate cases to the top with slightly softened chocolate ice-cream. Freeze till solid and pull off the paper cases. Top each one with a large rosette of whipped cream lightly sweetened and flavoured with rum.

Editor's note: other ice-cream and alcohol combinations are possible: try coffee ice-cream and Tia Maria, or gooseberry ice-cream (page 58) and kirsch.

Caroline's pizza

Cannelloni with haddock

Skinless sausages with apple sauce
Potato pancakes

Halstrad råbiff

Bananes sautées jamaïque

There are many advantages to giving a brunch party—none of which will necessarily occur to you as the first guests arrive. But if you have a large kitchen fit to be seen by other than close family, and if you have to entertain a dozen, say, with children involved as well as their parents, it makes good sense to put on a cheerfully casual meal, including some of the last-minute dishes which are delicious only when served straight from frying-pan to friend. It may make even better sense to have a second room—or in summer, the garden—set aside as a 'picnic area' for the very young.

People's metabolism varies so greatly that you have to consider what larks will enjoy and night-owls tolerate by way of noon refreshment. As larks ourselves, we are aware that our 'Pippa passes' mood can irritate those of our friends who get off to a slower start. Presumably the slowest starters will still be asleep anyway, but you could nevertheless be left with several guests who would prefer black coffee and the colour supplement to any amount of cheerful chat and creative cookery. Treat them gently: don't start the party before midday and serve food which is not too far removed from traditional country house breakfasts. The smells as you cook this meal will be the reassuring ones of eggs, ham, sausages, potatoes, smoked haddock . . .

It is not too early in the day to get your guests settled at the kitchen table with a drink in their hands: fresh fruit juice, Buck's Fizz (chilled fresh orange juice and champagne in roughly equal quantities) or its poor relation, a Mimosa (sparkling wine instead of the champagne), or a Normandy cocktail (a spoonful of calvados in chilled apple juice), or an Andaluzia (equal quantities of sherry and orange juice).

There are then several courses open to you. Either choose a few of the dishes suggested here and increase the quantities, so that you are serving, say, Caroline's pizza and bananes sautées jamaïque to everyone. Or, if you like to offer more variety to accommodate differing tastes, with at least a few dishes cooked ahead, offer rather smaller quantities of the lot.

The pizza uses puff pastry as a base (though you can substitute bread dough if you wish) and a savoury topping which is not overwhelmingly spicy. It can be served in small wedges while other things are being cooked, providing a literal stop-gap.

The cannelloni with smoked haddock has flavours reminiscent of that popular breakfast dish, kedgeree. It has the advantage of allowing preparation ahead of time and last-minute grilling, and it is also easy to serve and easy to eat. On the other hand, tagliatelle alla carbonara (page 39) is even more attuned to conventional breakfasts with its bacon-and-egg sauce.

Sausages, another familiar sight on the breakfast-room sideboard, are here transformed, first of all by being home-made and splendidly meaty, then by being dressed up with apples and calvados. We suggest serving them with potato pancakes, which, in the bacon version, would also make an ideal main course for this sort of meal. Enlist the aid of a friend so that you are not tied to the griddle and so that they are enjoyed at their crisp perfection.

If your friends are always fighting fit by Sunday lunchtime, you might try them on Halstrad råbiff, a Swedish version of boeuf tartare in which the beef patties are grilled briefly and served with a raw egg-yolk garnish. Not for the squeamish night-owl, this one. Serve bread—or the pancakes—and possibly a salad if this is your choice of main dish.

If you prefer the idea of several small tidbits to anything like a main course, consider several waves of fritters: crab (page 100), aubergine viennoise (page 144), Camembert (page 101), and bourekakia (page 94). This takes for granted that you have a good ventilation system or have warned everyone to come in old clothes. And if you enjoy showing off, a series of immaculate omelettes would go down well.

Bananes sautées jamaïque, though fiddly for a dinner party, are easy if everyone is in the kitchen, and they are delicious with their rum and coffee sauce. Serve conservatives fresh fruit, a fruit compote (page 48), dried fruit salad (page 147) or sorbets. On the other hand, for the smell of Christmas, hot mince pies (page 64) would round off your kitchen feast in style.

For drink, some people may prefer to stick to Buck's Fizz or whatever they started with, others might like to switch to a gentle white wine (German Riesling comes into its own on such an occasion, when the balance of fruit, sugar and acidity is balm to a surprised digestion). You could serve a spritzer (equal quantities of dry white wine and soda), or simply lots of good coffee. The decision is yours, but we would strongly advocate avoiding any extremes, whether sweet white or inky red.

Caroline's pizza

Timothy's, Cupar, Fife
Chef: Mrs Caroline
Laing

300 g	puff pastry (page 203)	10 oz
500 g	onions	1 lb
	olive oil	
two 15 ml spoons	chopped ham	2 tablesp
500 g	fresh tomatoes	1 lb
two 15 ml spoons	tomato puree	2 tablesp
two 5 ml spoons	dried herbs (see below)	2 teasp
	pepper	
250 g	Cheddar	8 oz
250 g	Gouda	8 oz

Preheat the oven to 200°C (400°F, mark 6).

Line a 23-cm (9-inch) oiled deep flan dish with the pastry, bringing it well up the sides to form a rim. Sauté the chopped onions in a little oil until they are translucent but not brown. Cool them and sprinkle them over the pastry. Put the ham on top and cover the onions and ham completely with the sliced tomatoes. Dot the tomatoes with the tomato puree to intensify their taste. Sprinkle on the herbs and the pepper. Cover the tomato layer with the grated Cheddar and, finally, the grated Gouda. Bake the pizza for 50 minutes until the cheese is melted and bubbling and beginning to turn brown. Serve it alone as a first course, or with a green salad as a main course.

Chef's note: the mixed dried herbs should contain at least thyme, basil and parsley.

Editor's notes: if you are making bread, use 250 g (8 oz) of the dough as a base for a more conventional pizza. Bake it in a hot oven (220°C, 425°F, mark 7) for about half an hour.

As a change from ham, try anchovies, capers, black olives . . .

Cannelloni with haddock

**Home Farm Hotel,
Wilmington, Devon
Chef: Susan Rowatt**

twelve	cannelloni tubes	twelve
one	pinch of salt	one
150 g	butter	6 oz
250 g	smoked haddock	8 oz
250 ml	milk	10 fl oz
one	bay leaf	one
125 ml	flavoured milk (page 209)	5 fl oz
50 g	flour	2 oz
	chopped parsley	
	salt, pepper	
50 g	grated cheese	2 oz

For garnishing

	lemon wedges	
	parsley	

Cook the cannelloni in salted boiling water with 25 g (1 oz) butter for 10–15 minutes. Rinse them in hot water and lay them on a tea towel to drain. Poach the haddock in 125 ml (5 fl oz) milk with 75 g (3 oz) butter and the bay leaf for ten minutes on top of the stove or 15 minutes in the oven (if it is already being used).

Combine the poaching milk and the flavoured milk and make a thick béchamel sauce (page 209) with the remaining 50 g (2 oz) butter and the flour. Add the flaked fish and chopped parsley to half of the sauce and season it with salt and pepper. (Be sparing with salt since the fish may already be salty.)

Split the cannelloni down the middle lengthways and fill them generously with the creamed haddock. Roll them up and put them, split side down, on a buttered oven-proof dish.

Thin down the rest of the béchamel sauce with the remaining 125 ml (5 fl oz) milk, season it with salt and pepper and pour it over the cannelloni. Sprinkle the top with grated cheese and grill the dish under moderately high heat for about ten minutes until the cheese is golden and bubbling.

Serve the cannelloni garnished with lemon wedges and sprigs of parsley.

Skinless sausages with apple sauce

Leith's, London, W.11
Chef: Max Markarian

125 g	raw boneless chicken *or* veal	4 oz
375 g	fatty pork (belly, for example)	12 oz
four	slices of white bread, crustless	four
three	leaves of sage *or*	three
one 5 ml spoon	powdered sage	1 teasp
one	egg	one
one	small onion (optional)	one
	salt, pepper	
	flour	
125 g	butter	4 oz
one	small onion	one
two 15 ml spoons	calvados	2 tablesp
125 ml	chicken or veal stock (page 207)	5 fl oz
	salt, pepper	
half 5 ml spoon	pale Dijon mustard	$\frac{1}{2}$ teasp
two	dessert apples	two
four 15 ml spoons	double cream	4 tablesp

To make the sausages, combine the finely-minced chicken or veal and pork, the bread made into crumbs, the chopped fresh or powdered sage, the egg, the finely-chopped onion and some salt and pepper. Lightly flour your hands and form the mixture into sausage shapes. (You will have about 16.) Roll each sausage in flour.

Melt 25 g (1 oz) butter in a heavy pan. Gently fry the sausages until they are brown all over, lift them out, and in the same fat fry the remaining onion, finely-sliced, very slowly until it is pale brown. Return the sausages to the pan, pour in the calvados and set it alight. Shake the pan around to burn off some of the fat. Pour off any remaining fat. Then add the stock and seasonings and simmer the sauce very gently for about 15 minutes, until the sausages are cooked through.

In a saucepan, melt the remaining butter and add the sliced apples to it. Cover the pan and simmer the apples very gently until they are soft but unbroken, and slightly brown underneath.

To serve, put the apples on top of the sausages in a serving dish. Add the cream to the juices in the frying-pan, and stir as you bring it to the boil. Reduce the sauce by rapid boiling if necessary.

Chef's note: instead of calvados, you may use sherry, which does not need to be flamed.

Potato pancakes

Horn of Plenty,
Gulworthy, Devon
Chef/proprietor:
Sonia Stevenson

500 g	cooked potatoes	1 lb
six 15 ml spoons	flour	6 tablesp
five	eggs	five
four 15 ml spoons	cream or milk	4 tablesp
	salt, pepper	
	streaky bacon or cheese (optional)	

Liquidise the potatoes, flour, eggs, cream and seasonings. If you wish, add fried and crumbled bacon or grated cheese to the batter. Cook it in small spoonsful like dropped scones on a greased griddle or in a heavy pan.

This quantity makes about 24 pancakes, sufficient for six as an accompaniment to a main course, four as the main feature of brunch.

Editor's note: if you must keep the pancakes hot in the warming-oven, you will find they lose a little crispness but do not toughen.

Halstrad råbiff

Anna's Place,
London, N.1
Chef: Eric Norrgren

750 g	minced beef fillet (see below)	1½ lb
250 g	cooked beetroot	8 oz
150 g	capers	6 oz
two	medium-sized onions	two
	salt, pepper	
	dry mustard	
two	eggs	two

For garnishing

	parsley or garlic butter or	
eight	onion rings and	eight
four	eggs	four

Choose fillet or other high-quality beef (rump or topside, for example). Ask your butcher to mince it finely. Combine it with the finely-chopped beetroot, capers and onions, mix them together thoroughly, add the seasonings, and bind the mixture with the two beaten eggs. Divide it into four square patties, cross-hatch them lightly with the back of a knife, and grill them for a few minutes, according to how rare you like beef.

189

Serve each helping garnished with either a pat of parsley or garlic butter or two onion rings and a raw egg yolk sitting in half its shell.

Chef's note: lovely when served rare, almost like steak tartare.

Editor's note: remember, when seasoning, that the capers may be fairly salty.

Bananes sautées jamaïque

La Frégate, St Peter Port, Guernsey, Channel Islands Chef: Konrad Holleis

six	medium-sized bananas	six
25 g	butter	1 oz
two 15 ml spoons	brown sugar	2 tablesp
two 15 ml spoons	rum	2 tablesp
two 15 ml spoons	Tia Maria	2 tablesp
	freshly-made black coffee (optional)	
one 5 ml spoon	finely-ground coffee	1 teasp
one	pinch of ground cinnamon	one
one	pinch of ground cloves	one

For serving

	vanilla ice-cream (page 118)	
	whipped cream	

Cut the bananas in half lengthways. Fry them gently in the melted butter and set them aside on a warm dish. Add the sugar to the pan and when it has dissolved add the rum, Tia Maria and a little freshly-made black coffee if more sauce is required. Add the bananas to the sauce, sprinkle them with the ground coffee, cinnamon and cloves and heat them through thoroughly.

Serve them with vanilla ice-cream and whipped cream, served separately.

Basic recipes, methods and definitions

Artichoke and potato puree

Kinchs, Chesterton, Oxfordshire Chef/proprietor: Christopher Greatorex		
1 kg	Jerusalem artichokes	2 lb
500 g	potatoes	1 lb
	salt, pepper	
50 g	butter	2 oz

For garnishing		
	chopped parsley	

Peel or scrub the artichokes and potatoes and boil them together in salted water. When they are cooked sieve or push them through a vegetable mill. Season the vegetables with salt and a generous amount of pepper and beat in the butter. Serve the puree sprinkled with the chopped parsley.

Chef's note: celeriac may be cooked with potatoes in the same way.

Editor's note: if you have any puree left over, dilute it with stock or milk for an easy lunchtime soup.

Stir-fried mushrooms

Le Provençal, Salisbury, Wiltshire Chef/proprietor: Edward Moss		
500 g	small button mushrooms	1 lb
four 15 ml spoons	olive oil	4 tablesp
one	large onion	one
four	cloves of garlic	four
two 15 ml spoons	soy sauce	2 tablesp
50 ml	white wine or water	2 fl oz
	salt, pepper	

For serving		
	parsley	
	bread croûtes	

Choose mushrooms which are small and unopened. Wipe and trim them as necessary. Heat the oil in a large, heavy frying-pan, and when it is smoking, add the finely chopped onion and crushed garlic. Stir them for about half a minute before adding the mushrooms. Stir vigorously and also shake the pan, until the mushrooms have absorbed most of the oil and started to brown. Add soy to taste: the mushrooms should develop a dark brown shiny coat. Add the white wine or water and adjust the seasoning (remember that soy sauce is salty). Serve the mushrooms very hot, dusted with chopped parsley, with croûtes of fried bread on the side.

Hot beetroot

Rosie's Place,
Ipswich, Suffolk
Chef/proprietor:
Rosemarie Farrell

500–750 g	small, cooked beetroot	1–1½ lb
one	large onion	one
15 g	butter	½ oz
375 ml	béchamel sauce (page 209)	15 fl oz
two 5 ml spoons	mixed sweet herbs	2 teasp
	salt, pepper	

Slice the beetroot. Slice the onion paper-thin and fry it in the butter. Put layers of beetroot and onion in a casserole and cover with the hot béchamel sauce, seasoned with the herbs and salt and pepper. Cook in a moderate oven (180°C, 350°F, mark 4) for 15 minutes, until it is warmed through.

Hassleback potatis

Anna's Place,
London, N.1
Chef: Eric Norrgren

four (10 cm×5)	baking potatoes	four (4 inches×2)
one 15 ml spoon	soft butter	1 tablesp
three 15 ml spoons	melted butter	3 tablesp
one 5 ml spoon	salt	1 teasp
two 15 ml spoons	dry breadcrumbs	2 tablesp

For garnishing

two 15 ml spoons	grated Parmesan (optional)	2 tablesp

Preheat the oven to 220°C (425°F, mark 7). Peel the potatoes and drop them into cold water. Place them, one at a time, on a large wooden spoon, and slice down crossways at 2.5-mm (⅛-inch) intervals, taking care not to go right through the potato. Drop each semi-sliced potato back into the cold water.

When ready to roast, drain the potatoes and pat them dry with a cloth or kitchen paper. Generously butter a baking dish with the softened butter, and arrange the potatoes side by side, cut side up. Baste them with half the melted butter, sprinkle them liberally with salt, and bake in the centre of the oven for 30 minutes. Sprinkle them with the breadcrumbs, baste with the remaining butter, and roast for another 15 minutes, or until they are golden brown. If you wish to use the cheese, sprinkle it on five minutes before the end of the cooking time.

Editor's notes: if you overcook these potatoes, they fall apart, so time them carefully. We like them best with the buttery crumbs alone, when they are an appropriate accompaniment to many main dishes.

Lemon-baked cabbage (4–6)

Food for Thought,
Cheltenham,
Gloucestershire
Chef/proprietors:
Joanna Jane Mahon &
Christopher Wickens

1 kg	spring cabbage	2 lb
one	large onion	one
one	lemon	one
	salt, pepper	
50 g	butter	2 oz

Trim, wash and chop the cabbage. In a greased oven-proof dish, layer the cabbage and sliced onion. Pour over the lemon juice and season with salt and pepper. Dot with butter, cover, and bake in a moderately hot oven (200°C, 400°F, mark 6) for about 30 minutes.

Puree of carrots with cheese

Annfield House,
Kingskettle, Fife
Chef/proprietor:
Dorothy Kelly

500 g	carrots	1 lb
	salt, pepper	
two 15 ml spoons	butter	2 tablesp
75 g	grated cheese	3 oz

Slice the carrots and cook them in a little boiling salted water until they are tender. Puree them with a little of the water and season with salt and a generous amount of pepper. Stir in the butter and grated cheese. If you are serving the puree at once, reheat it in the oven for five minutes after liquidising. If you wish to make it ahead, cover it with foil and keep it hot in a slow oven.

Carrots in orange and coriander

Ashburton House,
Stratford-upon-Avon,
Warwickshire
Chef/proprietor:
Mrs Kathleen Fraser

500 g	carrots	1 lb
	salt	
one	medium-sized orange	one
half 5 ml spoon	ground coriander	$\frac{1}{2}$ teasp
15 g	butter	$\frac{1}{2}$ oz

Peel (or scrape) and slice the carrots into small finger lengths (unless they are tiny, new ones). Cook them in salted water until they are just undercooked (this may take 10–30 minutes, depending on their age). Drain them, return them to the pan and add the juice of the orange, the ground coriander and the butter. Boil vigorously over high heat, shaking the pan frequently, until the juices are reduced by half, and the carrots glazed.

Editor's note: add chopped parsley at the last moment for additional colour. Since the orange and coriander add a delicate flavour to the carrots, serve them with a plain or bland main course which will not overwhelm them. With roast pork or duck, you might also like to experiment with a little of the grated orange rind.

Hot cucumber

Anna's Place,
London, N.1
Chef: Eric Norrgren

one	cucumber	one
	butter	
	chopped parsley	

Peel the cucumber, split it in half, and remove the seeds with a spoon. Cut it into 2.5-cm (one-inch) pieces, drop them into boiling salted water, and cook them till they are barely soft (about three minutes). Drain them well, toss them in a little melted butter, and sprinkle them with chopped parsley.

Chick peas provençale

Henderson's Salad
Table, Edinburgh
Chef: Catherine M.
Henderson

500 g	chick peas	1 lb
two	medium-sized onions	two
one	clove of garlic	one
four 15 ml spoons	olive oil	4 tablesp
two	green peppers	two
750 g	tomatoes (fresh or tinned)	1½ lb
	salt, pepper	
half 5 ml spoon	dried basil	½ teasp
two 15 ml spoons	tomato puree	2 tablesp

Soak the rinsed and washed chick peas for 12 hours in enough unsalted water to cover them by about two inches. Boil them in the water in which they have been soaking for about an hour until they are fairly soft.

Sauté the chopped onions and crushed garlic in the oil for about five minutes, then add the chopped peppers and cook for a further ten minutes. Add the skinned tomatoes, salt, pepper, basil and tomato puree, and if using fresh tomatoes also add about 75 ml (3 fl oz) of the chick pea liquid. When the chick peas are almost cooked, combine them with the sauce in an oven-proof casserole. Cook it, covered, in a moderate oven (180°C, 350°F, mark 4) for half an hour. Serve the casserole hot with a lettuce salad, or cold with a little vinaigrette (page 210).

Editor's note: for authentic Provencal variations, add anchovies, olives, or capers. If your oven is not otherwise needed, cook the casserole on top of the stove. Non-vegetarians would enjoy the chick peas with plainly-grilled or roast meat.

Stir-fried garden vegetables

Tullich Lodge,
Ballater,
Aberdeenshire
Chef/proprietor:
Neil Bannister

For garnishing

1 kg	mixed fresh vegetables	2 lb
two 15 ml spoons	virgin olive oil	2 tablesp
one	clove of garlic	one
half 5 ml spoon	curry paste (optional)	$\frac{1}{2}$ teasp
	salt, pepper	
	chopped fresh herbs	

Use as varied a selection of roots and greens as possible. (For example, turnips, carrots, celeriac, fennel, onions, cabbage, leeks, cauliflower, celery, beans. Do not use Jerusalem artichokes as they have too dominant a flavour.) Cut the roots into distinctive shapes, onions into eighths, cauliflower and broccoli into florets, cabbage and runner beans chopped into small pieces. Pod any peas and broad beans.

Heat the oil and add first the garlic and curry paste, then the root vegetables. Cover the pan and slowly increase the heat. After about five minutes, add the greens and other tender vegetables and salt and pepper. (If the root pieces are more than about $\frac{1}{4}$ inch thick, they may need cooking for slightly longer.) Continue to steam the vegetables for a further five minutes, stir them, and serve them sprinkled with chopped herbs.

Chef's note: this is also delicious in winter with Savoy cabbage and chopped bacon.

Fried courgettes

Limpets, Lymington,
Hampshire
Chef/proprietor:
Douglas Craig

six	small courgettes *or*	six
four	medium-sized ones	four
	salt	
125 ml	milk	5 fl oz
	flour	
	oil for deep frying	

Wash the courgettes (do not remove the skins), slice them thinly, sprinkle the slices with salt, and leave them for about 30 minutes to exude their bitter juices. Pat the slices dry, dip them in milk, toss them in flour, shake off the excess, and fry them in hot oil (200°C, 400°F) until crisp and brown (no more than two minutes). Drain them on absorbent paper and serve at once.

Chicche del nonno verdi

San Carlo,
London, N.6
Chef: Dino Valeri

For serving

500 g	potatoes (King Edward)	1 lb
250 g	spinach	8 oz
150 g	flour	6 oz
one	egg yolk	one
	butter, pepper	
	grated Parmesan	

Boil the potatoes, drain them well and mash them. Cook the spinach in a little boiling salted water, drain it thoroughly and chop it finely. In a large mixing-bowl, combine the flour, potatoes, spinach and egg yolk, and mix into a firm dough. Using small pieces, roll the dough into long sausage shapes with your hands on a lightly-floured board. Cut off 2.5-cm (one-inch) lengths and pinch each end (to make a 'humbug' shape). Sprinkle the chicche with flour and leave them to dry for 30 minutes or longer.

Cook them, not too many at a time, in a large pan of boiling salted water for about three minutes. They bob to the top when ready. Remove them with a slotted spoon, drain them on paper towelling, and keep them warm in a slow oven in a buttered oven-proof dish. Before serving, turn them in more butter and sprinkle some black pepper and grated Parmesan on top.

Chef's note: if you prefer, serve a sauce with the chicche—a fresh tomato one, for example.

Editor's note: the above quantity makes about sixty little dumplings ('Grandfather's green sweetmeats') a generous first course for four. If you are serving the chicche as an accompaniment to a main course, forty would be enough.

Indian salad

Hall Garth Hotel, Coatham Mundeville, Durham Chef/proprietor: Janice Crocker		
three	large onions	three
three	green peppers	three
three	large tomatoes	three
	salt	
	lemon juice	

Try to choose onions, peppers and tomatoes of roughly the same diameter. Peel the onions, cut them into thin rings, sprinkle them well with salt and rub it well into the rings. After 30 minutes, rinse off the brine, pat the onions dry and combine them with the thinly-sliced green peppers and tomatoes. Season the salad with a little lemon juice.

Mushroom salad

Chef's Kitchen, Halsetown, Cornwall Chef/proprietor: F. N. Tetley		
two 15 ml spoons	olive oil	2 tablesp
one 15 ml spoon	chopped onion	1 tablesp
one 15 ml spoon	chopped green or red pimento	1 tablesp
one 15 ml spoon	grated carrot	1 tablesp
one 15 ml spoon	tomato flesh	1 tablesp
one	clove of garlic	one
one 15 ml spoon	lemon juice	1 tablesp
	salt, pepper	
175–225 g	small button mushrooms	6–8 oz

Make a cooked vinaigrette by heating the olive oil over high heat in a heavy pan and adding to it the onion, pimento, carrot, tomato flesh and crushed garlic. Cook until the onion is translucent but not brown, add the lemon juice and remove the pan from the heat. Season with salt and pepper and allow the mixture to cool.

Wipe the mushrooms, slice them finely, and dress them with the vinaigrette at the last moment.

Salade aux lardons

Singing Chef,
Badwell Ash, Suffolk
Chef/proprietor:
Kenneth Toyé

one	crisp lettuce	one
50–100 g	streaky bacon	2–4 oz
	olive oil	
	lemon juice	
	salt, pepper	

Use very crisp lettuce (Webb's, cos, density). Tear it into small pieces and mix with the crisply-fried bacon (either cut into strips before cooking, or broken into small pieces afterwards). Toss with olive oil. Sprinkle with lemon juice to taste, and season with salt and pepper.

Editor's note: try this salad also with raw, young spinach instead of lettuce.

Lemon pickle

Carved Angel,
Dartmouth, Devon
Chef: Joyce Molyneux

1 kg	lemons	2 lb
500 g	onions	1 lb
50 g	fresh ginger	2 oz
25 g	fresh chillies	1 oz
7 g	cardamom pods	$\frac{1}{4}$ oz
7 g	coriander seeds	$\frac{1}{4}$ oz
15 g	whole allspice	$\frac{1}{2}$ oz
570 ml	vinegar	1 pint
750 g	granulated sugar	$1\frac{1}{2}$ lb

Squeeze the lemons and put the juice in a large bowl. Slice them thinly and remove the pips. Peel and slice the onions finely. Peel and grate the ginger on a coarse grater. Remove the seeds from the chillies before slicing them finely. Add all these to the lemon juice. Put the spices in a muslin bag and bury it in the mixture, add the vinegar, cover, and leave overnight.

The following day, bring the mixture slowly to the boil in a preserving pan or heavy-based saucepan, and cook gently for about $1\frac{1}{2}$ hours until the peel is really tender. Add the sugar and stir carefully to dissolve it. Boil the mixture briskly, stirring continuously, for 20 minutes. Pot in sterilised jars, cover, and leave to mature for at least a month.

Risotto

50 g	butter	2 oz
one	small onion	one
375 g	Italian rice	12 oz
100 ml	white wine	4 fl oz
1 litre	chicken stock (page 207)	2 pints
	or water	
	salt, pepper	
25 g	grated Parmesan	1 oz

Melt half the butter in a large heavy pan, and in it fry the chopped onion until it is pale golden. Add the washed rice and turn it until all the grains are glistening. Pour in the wine and let the rice cook over a moderate heat until the wine has been almost completely absorbed. Start adding the stock, a cupful at a time, and let the rice simmer, uncovered, stirring it occasionally with a fork. When almost all the first cupful has been absorbed, add another and continue in this way until almost all the stock has been incorporated. Test for tenderness—you may not need the last half-cupful of stock—and seasoning. The whole process should take no more than half an hour. Stir in the remaining butter and the cheese and serve at once.

Brown rice and wheat with onions

Refectory, Richmond, Surrey Chef/proprietor: Mary Kingsley

one 5 ml spoon	salt	1 teasp
150 g	wheat-grains	6 oz
150 g	brown rice	6 oz
two	onions	two
50 g	butter	2 oz
	soy sauce	
100 g	walnut pieces (optional)	4 oz

Bring a large saucepanful of salted water to the boil, and add the wheat-grains. Bring to the boil again and simmer, covered, for 25 minutes. Add the brown rice, bring back to the boil, and simmer for a further 30 minutes. Soften the chopped onions in the butter and a few drops of soy sauce. Drain the rice and grains, rinse in hot water, and mix with the onions. Check the seasoning; and add the walnuts before serving.

Chef's note: instead of onions, try 150 g (6 oz) sliced mushrooms fried for a few moments in 75 g (3 oz) of butter and some soy sauce over high heat.

Batter for pancakes / crêpes (285 ml / 10 fl oz)

100–125 g	flour	4 oz
half 5 ml spoon	salt	$\frac{1}{2}$ teasp
one	egg	one
285 ml	milk and water, mixed	10 fl oz
15 g	melted butter	$\frac{1}{2}$ oz

Sift the flour and salt into a basin. Put the egg in a well in the centre and start mixing in the milk and water a little at a time, until half has been added. Beat the batter very well at this stage until it is smooth. Add the melted butter and whisk in the rest of the liquid. Leave the batter to stand for up to two hours to allow the flour to absorb the liquid—this ensures a lighter pancake.

Shortcrust pastry / pâte brisée (175 g / 6 oz)

100 g	flour	4 oz
half 5 ml spoon	salt	$\frac{1}{2}$ teasp
50 g	butter	2 oz
two 15 ml spoons	cold water (approx)	2 tablesp

Sift the flour and salt into a bowl. Cut up the butter and crumble it into the flour with the fingertips or a wire pastry mixer. Mix in enough cold water with a knife to make a firm dough, and roll it into a ball. On a floured board, stretch out the pastry bit by bit with the heel of the palm, then gather it up again into a ball. Repeat this process, dust the pastry with a little flour and wrap it in buttered paper or foil. Refrigerate it for up to two hours to firm.

To line a flan case, roll out the pastry on a floured board to the thickness of 2.5–5 mm ($\frac{1}{8}$-$\frac{1}{4}$ inch) and about 5 cm (2 inches) bigger than the flan case. Grease the case and lay the pastry gently in it, pressing it down to fit the bottom and sides. Ease a little extra down the sides before cutting off the excess. Prick the bottom lightly. Leave it to rest in a cool place for 30 minutes, to prevent its shrinking during cooking.

If the pastry case is to be cooked empty or 'blind', line it with a piece of foil or grease-proof paper weighted with dry beans and bake it on a baking sheet for ten minutes at 200°C (400°F, mark 6). Remove the paper and put the case back in the oven for another 7–10 minutes until it is lightly browned. Remove the pastry shell from its tin and cool it on a rack. (Using a flan ring, rather than a case, makes this operation very simple.)

Rich shortcrust pastry (250 g / 8 oz approx)

100 g	flour	4 oz
half 5 ml spoon	salt	$\frac{1}{2}$ teasp
65 g	butter	$2\frac{1}{2}$ oz
one	egg yolk *or* small egg	one
two 15 ml spoons	cold water (approx)	2 tablesp

Make the pastry as described, but add the beaten egg to the flour before the water, and use just enough water to bind the ingredients together.

Sweet shortcrust pastry / pâte sucrée (250 g / 8 oz)

100 g	flour	4 oz
half 5 ml spoon	salt	$\frac{1}{2}$ teasp
50 g	sugar	2 oz
50 g	softened butter	2 oz
one	egg yolk	one

Sift the flour and salt into a bowl and make a well in the centre for the other ingredients. Mix them together with the fingertips and gradually draw the flour into them until it is all incorporated. Knead the pastry lightly until it is smooth, flour and wrap it, and put it in the refrigerator to chill for up to two hours.

Puff pastry / pâte feuilletée (500 g / 1 lb)

250 g	strong flour	8 oz
half 5 ml spoon	salt	$\frac{1}{2}$ teasp
250 g	unsalted butter	8 oz
one	squeeze of lemon	one

The coolest possible conditions, utensils and ingredients are essential when preparing this kind of pastry, which contains a high proportion of fat; on the other hand, it is then baked in a really hot oven so that the air trapped between the layers will quickly expand and puff it up.

Sift the flour and salt and rub in about 15 g ($\frac{1}{2}$ oz) of the butter. Make it into a fairly soft dough with about 100 ml (4 fl oz) of ice-cold water and a squeeze of lemon (the lemon strengthens the dough but too much liquid toughens it), and knead it well on a floured surface until it is smooth. Rest it for 15 minutes in the refrigerator.

Roll out the dough into an oblong roughly 30 cm by 10 (12 inches by 4). Flatten the remaining piece of butter—it should be slightly softened—into a rectangle about half the size, and place this on one half of the dough, or cut the butter in thin slices and place them evenly over half the surface of the dough. Fold the other half over and press the edges together with a rolling-pin or with the side of your hand. Turn the fold to one side and roll out the pastry again, with short, quick movements, into an oblong the size of the original one. Keep the pastry regular in shape with square corners and do not roll the pin over the edges or stretch the dough. Fold it into three and seal the edges to trap the air inside. Wrap the pastry in grease-proof paper and put it to rest in a really cool place or in the refrigerator for twenty minutes.

Repeat this turning, rolling, folding and resting operation five more times, always starting with the fold to the same side, and chilling between rollings.

To cover a pie: see page 179.

Puff pastry can be made in quantity and frozen—it freezes very well. Prepare it up to, but not including, the last rolling. Bought puff pastry is an acceptable alternative but should be rolled out to a thickness of 2.5 mm ($\frac{1}{8}$ inch) as it rises very well.

Lemon biscuits

Miller Howe,
Windermere, Cumbria
Chef/proprietor:
John Tovey

120 g	butter	4 oz
50 g	caster sugar	2 oz
140 g	self-raising flour	5 oz
one	lemon	one
	vanilla sugar (page 213)	

Either cream the butter and sugar together and add the sifted flour and finely-grated lemon rind to make a firm dough, or put the ingredients in the bowl of an electric mixer and blend them together with the K-beater. Break off small pieces of the dough and roll them into balls about one cm ($\frac{1}{2}$ inch) in diameter. Put them on a baking-sheet and flatten them lightly with the back of a damp fork. Bake for about ten minutes at 180°C (350°F, mark 4). As the biscuits cool, sprinkle them with vanilla sugar.

Wholewheat bread

Peacock Vane,
Bonchurch,
Isle of Wight
Chef/proprietor:
Rosalind Wolfenden

25 g	fresh yeast	1 oz
one 5 ml spoon	demerara sugar	1 teasp
375 ml	lukewarm water (approx)	15 fl oz
one 5 ml spoon	salt	1 teasp
20 g	melted butter	$\frac{3}{4}$ oz
650 g	stoneground wholewheat flour	$1\frac{1}{2}$ lb

Cream the yeast and sugar together in a small basin and add enough of the warm water to cover it—about three 15 ml (table) spoonsful. Leave it in a warm place for about 15 minutes until the mixture is frothy.

Add the salt and butter to the remaining water. Stir the yeast into a well in the centre of the flour and gradually add the water and butter mixture. Mix the ingredients together thoroughly until there is no remaining dry flour. Leave the dough in a greased and floured bowl in a warm place for at least $1\frac{1}{2}$ hours, covered with a tea towel.

Knead the dough on a floured board until it has a springy texture, and divide it into two round loaves. Bake the bread on greased and floured baking sheets in a hot oven (200°C, 400°F, mark 6) for 45–50 minutes, turning it over for the last five minutes of cooking. Allow the bread to cool for a while before serving.

If you wish to make rolls, these ingredients make about twenty and bake at the same temperature for 15–20 minutes.

White scones

Doyle's Seafood Bar,
Dingle, Co Kerry
Chef/proprietor:
Stella Doyle

375 g	self-raising flour	12 oz
one 5 ml spoon	baking powder	1 teasp
one 5 ml spoon	salt	1 teasp
50 g	butter *or* margarine	2 oz
one	egg	one
250 ml	milk	10 fl oz

Sift the flour, baking powder and salt together, and rub in the butter. Beat the egg and milk together and add, little by little, to the dry ingredients until you have a soft dough. Knead it lightly, roll or pat it out on a floured board and cut it into rectangles, wedges or circles (12–15 scones). Bake them on a floured tray in a hot oven (220°C, 425°F, mark 7) for 10–15 minutes.

Thickening agents and methods

Roux

A blend of roughly equal weights of butter and flour, first cooked together before the liquid is incorporated for a sauce. A roux can be described as white (for a béchamel), light brown, or brown (for a demi-glace).

Melt the butter gently in a saucepan, blend in the flour and stir over heat for a minute or two to cook the flour. If a light brown roux is required cook until it starts to turn a golden colour. For a brown roux, continue until it is nut-brown. (This can be done very easily by putting the pan in a hot oven for about ten minutes.)

Beurre manié

This is an uncooked mixture of butter and flour kneaded together and added to the liquid at the end of cooking.

Mix to a paste equal quantities of softened butter and flour, then add it to the liquid in pieces the size of a sugar lump. Stir in each one off the heat until it has dissolved, and return the pan to the stove to allow the liquid to thicken.

Cornflour and arrowroot

Thickening agents which can be used when you do not want more fat in a sauce (or for a last-minute thickening of a well-flavoured stock).

One 15 ml (table) spoonful of cornflour thickens 285 ml (10 fl oz) of liquid. Mix it with two 15 ml (table) spoonsful of cold water before stirring it into the hot liquid. Bring it to the boil and simmer the sauce until it thickens. Continue to simmer for a few minutes to cook the cornflour. (Potato flour and rice flour are the French equivalents.) Two 5 ml (tea) spoonsful of arrowroot thickens 285 ml (10 fl oz) of liquid. Mix as above but do not simmer once it has thickened, or the sauce will go thin again. Arrowroot gives a very clear, shiny sauce.

Egg yolk and cream

This mixture (a 'liaison') is used for both thickening and enriching sauces and soups at the end of the cooking.

Beat the egg yolk and cream together and blend into them a little of the hot liquid. Pour this mixture slowly back into the rest of the liquid and reheat gently. Do not allow the sauce or soup to boil or it will curdle. If the sauce must be kept hot, use a bain-marie (page 213).

Reduction

A sauce, stock or soup, can be thickened by boiling it steadily (uncovered) until the quantity of liquid is reduced through evaporation.

Chilling

Any sauce or soup will become thicker when chilled, if it already has a thickening agent in it.

Brown beef stock

1 kg	beef or veal bones *or* part meat, part bones	2 lb
one	large carrot	one
one	onion	one
one	bouquet garni (page 213) with celery leaves	one
six	peppercorns	six

Brown the pieces of meat, bones and sliced vegetables for 30 minutes in a roasting-tin in a hot oven (220°C, 425°F, mark 7). Put them with the herbs and peppercorns into a large saucepan with enough cold water to cover them by at least 2.5 cm (one inch)—about two litres ($3\frac{1}{2}$ pints). Bring slowly to the boil, skim, and simmer very gently with the lid partly off for 4–5 hours. Skim off any scum as it rises. Strain the stock and leave it to stand to allow the fat to rise to the surface. Remove this with a spoon or absorbent paper, or leave the stock to get cold when the congealed fat can be easily removed. If strongly-flavoured stock is required, reduce it by boiling, before adding the seasoning.

Stock can be deep-frozen and kept for several weeks, otherwise it must be re-boiled every day, or every few days if it is stored in the refrigerator.

Chicken stock

one	boiling fowl with giblets (*or* portion, *or* carcase with trimmings plus 500 g [1 lb] giblets)	one
one	piece of chopped veal bone (optional)	one
	vegetables and herbs as for beef stock	

Prepare as for beef stock but without the preliminary browning. Simmer for only 2–3 hours. Chill the stock and remove the fat before use. If a whole fowl is being used, remove it from the stock after the first hour, carve off the breasts and use these for any dish calling for cooked chicken. Stock made from cooked meat only, such as the remains of a roast chicken, does not taste at all the same and might impart its distinctive flavour to a delicate dish.

Fish stock

500–750 g	fish, fish bones *and/or* trimmings	1–1½ lb
one	onion	one
six	parsley stems	six
half	lemon	half
half 5 ml spoon	salt	½ teasp
eight	white peppercorns	eight
570 ml	water *or* water and dry white wine, mixed	1 pint

This can be used as the basis of a fish velouté sauce. Use less fish for a lighter stock for poaching fish or as the base for a fish soup.

Wash the fish and trimmings thoroughly in cold water. Break them into pieces and put them with the sliced onion, the parsley stems, the juice and rind of the half-lemon, the salt, pepper and water (or wine and water) in a large saucepan. Bring slowly to the boil, skim, reduce the heat, and simmer the stock slowly, partly covered, for 30 minutes. Strain it, and either use it at once or refrigerate it.

This stock has a delicate flavour. For a heartier stock add a bouquet garni (page 213) or thyme alone, diced carrot or turnip, celery or mushroom trimmings.

Fish fumet is well-reduced and flavoured fish stock. Strain the stock before reducing it.

Béchamel sauce (425 ml / 15 fl oz)

425 ml	milk	15 fl oz
one	small onion	one
four	peppercorns	four
	salt, nutmeg	
25 g	butter	1 oz
25 g	flour	1 oz

(Although this white sauce can be made without flavouring the milk first, this does improve the taste.) Bring the milk, with the onion and seasonings, to simmering point and leave it, off the heat, for 5–10 minutes, so that the flavours can be absorbed.

Make a white roux (page 206) and blend in the milk through a strainer, a little at a time. Reheat the sauce, stirring continuously while it thickens and comes to the boil. Leave it to simmer for 5–10 minutes to ensure that the flour is properly cooked. Check the seasoning.

If the sauce is to stand and be reheated later, spread a piece of buttered grease-proof paper with a hole in the middle over the surface. When you lift off the paper, the skin will come with it. Allow 70–145 ml (2½–5 fl oz) of sauce per person.

Sauce espagnole or brown sauce

25 g	butter	1 oz
25 g	flour	1 oz
570 ml	beef stock (page 207)	1 pint
one	slice of unsmoked bacon	one
one	medium-sized onion	one
one	carrot	one
one	stick of celery	one
one–two	mushrooms	one–two
one 15 ml spoon	tomato puree	1 tablesp
	a few peppercorns	
one	bouquet garni (page 213)	one
	salt, pepper	

A 'grande sauce de base' which is the basis of a demi-glace (page 210), and, among others, sauce madère, sauce périgueux and sauce bordelaise.

Make a brown roux (page 206) with the butter and flour and blend into it three-quarters of the stock. Bring this to the boil, stirring it continuously, and let it simmer gently. Chop the bacon and vegetables and fry them until they are brown. Add them to the sauce with the tomato puree, the peppercorns and the bouquet garni, and continue to simmer it, partially covered, for at least two hours so that it reduces. From time to time skim off the fat which rises by adding a little of the remaining cold stock, bringing the sauce back to the boil and skimming the surface. When the sauce is reduced by at least half, rub it through a sieve into a clean pan and add some seasoning. This quantity yields about 285 ml (10 fl oz) of sauce.

Demi-glace sauce

285 ml	sauce espagnole (page 209)	10 fl oz
two 15 ml spoons	meat jelly *or*	2 tablesp
145 ml	brown stock (page 207)	5 fl oz
	salt, pepper	

A brown sauce, or sauce espagnole, enriched with strong brown stock or meat jelly, and sometimes also with madeira. This is a simplified version.

Make the sauce as described on page 209. Add the meat jelly. (If this is not available, reduce 145 ml [5 fl oz] of beef stock to two 15 ml [table] spoonsful by rapid boiling.) Heat the sauce, check the seasoning, and add a little madeira if you wish.

Vinaigrette or French dressing

This is an oil and vinegar dressing, seasoned with salt and pepper, in the proportions of one part of vinegar (or lemon juice) to every three of oil. You may safely increase the proportion of oil, but not that of vinegar. If a good olive oil and a good wine vinegar are used, it is unnecessary to add further flavourings but this is largely a matter of individual taste. Many people like a pinch of sugar, especially with tomato salad.

If you wish to add other seasoning such as dry mustard, garlic, or any fresh herb (chopped parsley, chervil, tarragon or basil), mix them first with the vinegar. Those who find the flavour of olive oil too strong may prefer to use half quantity, diluted with vegetable oil. Walnut oil may be used instead of the olive oil (see salade périgourdine on page 46).

Mayonnaise

two	egg yolks	two
half 5 ml spoon	salt	$\frac{1}{2}$ teasp
	white pepper	
285 ml	olive oil	10 fl oz
	lemon juice *or* white wine vinegar	

The eggs and the oil should be at room temperature. Beat the yolks with a wooden spoon until they are thick before adding the salt and a little pepper.

Start dripping in the oil, a little at a time, beating continuously. When the mayonnaise has thickened slightly, the oil can be added rather more quickly, but it is essential to start drop by drop. When half the oil has been beaten in and the mayonnaise has become very thick, whisk in some lemon juice or vinegar to thin it a little. Continue beating in the rest of the oil. Taste, and add more lemon juice or seasoning if required.

If the oil is added too quickly at the beginning, or if the eggs or oil are too cold, the mayonnaise may curdle. To rescue it, start in another bowl with another egg yolk and add to it the curdled mayonnaise, spoonful by spoonful, beating continuously as before. Half a 5 ml (tea) spoonful of dry mustard beaten into the egg yolks initially helps stabilise the mixture.

If the mayonnaise is to be kept for some time, or if you need to thin it for coating, whisk in two spoonsful of boiling water at the end. Refrigerate.

Tartare sauce

two	hard-boiled egg yolks	two
one 5 ml spoon	made mustard	1 teasp
	salt, pepper	
285 ml	olive oil	10 fl oz
	wine vinegar *or* lemon juice	
	chopped chives *or* spring onion	
	tarragon, parsley, capers, gherkins	

Mash the yolks in a basin and mix into them the mustard and a little salt and pepper. Start adding the oil, drop by drop, and beating it in as for mayonnaise (page 211). At the end, stir in the chopped herbs. The classic French recipe for this sauce specifies chopped chives only, but other chopped herbs and pickles are frequently added.

The same herbs and pickles can be used with mayonnaise, but this gives a rather solid sauce tartare, whereas the rémoulade (with the hard-boiled egg yolks) is lighter and creamier.

Equivalent temperatures

Celsius	Fahrenheit	Gas mark
110°	225°	$\frac{1}{4}$
120°	250°	$\frac{1}{2}$
140°	275°	1
150°	300°	2
160°	325°	3
180°	350°	4
190°	375°	5
200°	400°	6
220°	425°	7
230°	450°	8
240°	475°	9
260°	500°	–
270°	525°	–

Basic definitions

Bain-marie

A shallow pan or dish half-filled with water near simmering point, in which are placed smaller dishes or pans containing pâté, for example, or eggs, or a sauce. The bain-marie can be used on top of the stove or in the oven either to keep the contents hot or to cook them by indirect heat without danger of curdling or burning. An adaptation of the bain-marie is the double boiler where the inner container is suspended *over* the simmering water.

Bouquet garni

A bundle of aromatic herbs used to add flavour to stocks, sauces or stews. It is composed of one or two parsley stalks, a bay leaf and a sprig of thyme. When other herbs or vegetables are required (such as celery leaves), these are usually specified.

Tie the herbs together with a long piece of cotton or string so that they can easily be removed at the end of the cooking. If dried herbs are being used, put them in a square of muslin and tie the ends together.

Clarified butter

Butter which has been heated to separate from it the buttermilk, salt, water and any sediment it contains. These cause butter to burn when it is heated to a high temperature, as in frying. Clarified butter also keeps better and can be used for sealing the tops of pâtés.

Heat the butter gently in a heavy saucepan. When it starts to foam, skim off the top. Spoon or pour the clear butter carefully into a container, leaving the milky sediment in the bottom of the pan.

Court-bouillon

A light, quickly-cooked vegetable broth, slightly acidulated, in which fish or vegetables are poached. (Use fish stock recipe on page 208; omit the fish.)

Duxelles

A preparation of minced mushroom and shallot or onion, cooked until it is dry, used for flavouring stuffings.

Chop 125 g (4 oz) mushrooms very finely and wring them out in a cloth to dry them as much as possible. Fry them in a very little butter with two chopped shallots or half an onion until all the liquid has evaporated and the mixture is cooked. Season. The duxelles can be made in bulk, packed into a sealed container and kept in the refrigerator, or frozen.

Vanilla sugar

Sugar which has absorbed the flavour of a vanilla pod, used in the making of sweet pastry, custard and fruit dishes.

Put one or two pieces of vanilla pod into a tightly-stoppered jar of caster sugar. After a few days the sugar will have become flavoured. The pieces of vanilla can be left in the jar which can be topped up with fresh sugar as required; the flavour will continue to be imparted for years.

Index